Peter Bogdanovich: Interviews

Conversations with Filmmakers Series
Gerald Peary, General Editor

Peter Bogdanovich
INTERVIEWS

Edited by Peter Tonguette

University Press of Mississippi / Jackson

www.upress.state.ms.us

The University Press of Mississippi is a member of the Association of American University Presses.

Copyright © 2015 by University Press of Mississippi
All rights reserved
Manufactured in the United States of America

First printing 2015

∞

Library of Congress Cataloging-in-Publication Data

Bogdanovich, Peter, 1939–
  Peter Bogdanovich : interviews / edited by Peter Tonguette.
    pages cm. — (Conversations with filmmakers series)
  Includes index and filmography.
  ISBN 978-1-62846-184-8 (cloth : alk. paper) — ISBN 978-1-62846-187-9 1. Bogdanovich, Peter, 1939– —Interviews. 2. Motion picture producers and directors—United States—Interviews. 3. Actors—United States—Interviews. I. Tonguette, Peter Prescott, 1983– editor. II. Title.
  PN1998.3.B64A3 2015
  791.4302'33092—dc23
                        2014031698

British Library Cataloging-in-Publication Data available

Contents

Introduction vii

Chronology xv

Filmography xviii

Peter Bogdanovich 3
    Eric Sherman and Martin Rubin / 1968

Without a Dinosaur 17
    Gordon Gow / 1972

An Interview with Peter Bogdanovich 27
    Martin Rubin / 1974

Dialogue on Film: Peter Bogdanovich 41
    American Film Institute / 1978

Peter Bogdanovich Interview 63
    Stephen Myers and Larry Estes / 1979

Peter Bogdanovich: "What Is the Point of Making Pictures?" 84
    Michael Ventura / 1982

Dialogue on Film: Peter Bogdanovich 92
    American Film Institute / 1986

Peter Bogdanovich Interview 98
    Thomas J. Harris / 1988

Between Action and Cut: Peter Bogdanovich 107
    John Gallagher / 1997

Interview with Peter Bogdanovich 132
    Gerald Peary / 2002

Peter Bogdanovich's Year of the Cat 142
    Alex Simon / 2002

Peter Bogdanovich 160
    Stephen Lemons / 2002

Peter Bogdanovich 164
    Peter Tonguette / 2005

Additional Resources 173

Index 175

Introduction

Near the beginning of his collection of interviews with directors, *Who the Devil Made It*, Peter Bogdanovich recalls a vivid exchange he had with John Ford in 1969.

"Oh, for Chrissake, Bogdanovich! Can't you do anything but ask *questions?!*" Ford thundered. "I mean, Jesus Christ, haven't you even *heard* of the declarative sentence?"[1] Since the director of *Stagecoach, The Quiet Man,* and *The Searchers* was frequently on the receiving end of Bogdanovich's questioning—having been the subject of lengthy interviews both in print (in Bogdanovich's book *John Ford*) and on film (in Bogdanovich's documentary *Directed by John Ford*)—it is not hard to understand his good-humored mock outrage at his unremitting interlocutor.

As if to prove Ford's point, the quote appears in the context of an introduction to a book made up of nothing but questions asked by Bogdanovich—about casting and acting, camera angles and cutting rooms—and the answers proffered by Alfred Hitchcock, George Cukor, Edgar G. Ulmer, and Howard Hawks, along with about a dozen others. In fact, Ford once shared his bewilderment with Hawks ("Howard, does he ask *you* all those goddam questions, too?"),[2] as though Bogdanovich's interrogations represented a kind of secret handshake among directors of a certain age.

As amusing as these two anecdotes are, however, in some ways they are misleading. Bogdanovich was not a fresh-faced fan, who happened to have a microphone at the ready, but—in time—a peer who was talking shop. Although a number of the interviews gathered in *Who the Devil Made It* were conducted before Bogdanovich (who arrived in California as a film journalist) broke into moviemaking, many others took place *after* he began directing in 1968, the year his debut film, *Targets*, was released. In other words, when Bogdanovich spoke with Cukor in 1969 or Ulmer in 1970 or Hawks in 1972, he was doing so as a colleague.

By then, other interviewers—proto-Bogdanoviches, perhaps—began seeking Bogdanovich himself out to ask questions of their own, to which he gladly, often at great length, and always intelligently replied.

To put it another way, for nearly as long as he has been asking questions, he has been answering them. It is not for nothing that he writes, in his collection of memories of movie stars, *Who the Hell's In It*, that one of his big regrets about a youthful stint in summer stock is that he was too talkative, even though one of his co-stars was legendary actress Sylvia Sidney: "I wish now that I had talked less and asked more questions."[3] Reviewing that book for the *New York Times*, critic Stephanie Zacharek picked up on this. "Reading these profiles," she wrote, "you get the sense that Bogdanovich is a talker who learned to be a listener."[4]

So, to reply to Ford's joshing query: Bogdanovich has heard of the declarative sentence, thank you very much, and he was never shy about using it, either.

Assembled in *Peter Bogdanovich: Interviews* are thirteen interviews with Bogdanovich, conducted between 1968 and 2005, and even the earliest among them offers ample evidence of Bogdanovich's precocious verbosity. In 1968, Eric Sherman and Martin Rubin paired Bogdanovich with Budd Boetticher, Samuel Fuller, Arthur Penn, and Abraham Polonsky for their interview book, *The Director's Event*. Which of these is not like the other? Boetticher, Fuller, and Polonsky were widely admired veterans of Old Hollywood, while Penn was an already prolific participant in the American New Wave. On the other hand, Bogdanovich had not yet even started production on *The Last Picture Show*. The future classic comes up, but only as one of several potential projects he has idling on the back burner. The truth of the matter is that when Sherman and Rubin spoke to him—as Thomas J. Harris (author of the critical study *Bogdanovich's Picture Shows*, and of a fine interview included here) put it—"by contrast to the other filmmakers included, he had produced only one feature to date."[5] Yes, Bogdanovich had just one lonely film of his own to talk about—but talk about it he did.

In a new introduction written expressly for this book, Rubin refers to Bogdanovich as a peer—"like a hip upperclassman or older sibling"—which is understandable since they were in the same age group and were, at least some of the time, engaged in the same activity: interviewing directors. Yet the way Sherman and Rubin framed their interview suggests that they already sensed that their friendly, accessible contemporary was destined for great things. At the start of the interview, Bogdanovich went on for several pages about, among other things, his abortive career as a theater director (though his off-Broadway staging of *The Big Knife* was, he said, "a successful production critically"); his fate-altering encounter with Roger Corman ("Roger called me a couple of days later and said, 'You're a writer. Wouldn't you like to write for pictures?'"); and what his favorite films were at age ten (*Red River* and *She Wore a Yellow Ribbon*). There is chutzpah in the way Bogdanovich assumed that someone, someday, will care about this highly detailed backstory, and prescience in his interviewers' tolerance for it. Subsequent conversations—especially those with critic Gerald Peary and filmmaker-writer John Gallagher—delved even more deeply into his early days, but here he was talking to Sherman and Rubin *about* them while he was still *in* them.

Sherman and Rubin were also the first, but far from the last, to ask Bogdanovich about his purported "homages" to other directors, when they bring up several allusions to Hitchcock in *Targets*. This was, Bogdanovich told Peary more than three decades later, "the standard Bogdanovich review." As he explained, "So, *The Last Picture Show* was my homage to Orson, *Targets* was my homage to Hitchcock, and *Daisy Miller* was my homage to Cukor, and so on. It was all a lot of crap." To Sherman and Rubin, Bogdanovich admitted "stealing" a shot here or a sequence there (albeit unconsciously), but even with one film under his belt, he clarified his position articulately. Far from pilfering Hitchcock just for the hell of it, he saw his work—modest as it was in 1968—as part of a thread that reached back to the roots of the medium. "I don't think it's possible for anyone who's starting to make films today not to be influenced by what's gone before," he said. "Ford, Hawks, Dwan, and these other directors have already done everything, and *they* were all influenced by Griffith."

Maybe it was a little early in the day for Bogdanovich to answer questions by referring back to the creator of *The Birth of a Nation*. But his comments in *The Director's Event* disprove the notion that he was more at home asking questions than answering them.

Everything about Bogdanovich's station had changed when Gordon Gow interviewed him for *Films and Filming* in 1972. Given the success of *The Last Picture Show*—a film beloved by audiences, critics (one famously likened it to *Citizen Kane*), and Oscar voters (two wins out of eight nominations)—Gow could begin his article with a knockout of an opening line. "In the American cinema," Gow wrote of Bogdanovich, "he is the man of the hour."

If anything, this turned out to be an understatement, since Gow was speaking with Bogdanovich as the director was absorbed in making his next film—*What's Up, Doc?*, a screwball comedy tailor-made for Ryan O'Neal and Barbra Streisand that was as big a success as *The Last Picture Show*, just in different ways: the reviews weren't quite as ebullient, and the awards less plentiful, but it grossed more than any other film released in 1972, save *The Godfather* and *The Poseidon Adventure*. A year later, *Paper Moon* sealed the deal: more praise, more box office, another Oscar.

Then things changed. "Peter was *so* famous that his fall was equally notorious," said Quentin Tarantino, his friend, admirer, and soon-to-be producer of his upcoming film *Wait for Me*. "Even as a little kid, I knew that he'd had three flops in a row."[6] Yet the failure of *Daisy Miller*, *At Long Last Love*, and *Nickelodeon* did not make a wallflower of Bogdanovich—far from it. Three of the lengthiest and most in-depth interviews in this book—those conducted by Martin Rubin in 1974; at the American Film Institute in 1978; and by Stephen Myers and Larry Estes in 1979—date from this period. What may have seemed like hauteur then sounds like foresight now, since he anticipated the appreciative attention all three of his "flops" would, in time, receive; in fact, recently released director's cuts of *At Long Last Love* and *Nickelodeon* have significantly improved their reputations (in some interviews, Bogdanovich refers to wanting to change aspects of these films—as well as the later *Mask*—and, happily, now he has). "In any event, I think in ten years you'll like *Daisy Miller* better," Bogdanovich told the AFI back then. "It's amazing how pictures change. I've seen movies I adored ten years ago and now find lousy, and others I hated ten years ago I now think are masterpieces."

To put it another way, while many critics regard his post–*Paper Moon* career as a kind of ill-considered epilogue, Bogdanovich never did. He was as eloquent arguing for the irrelevance of *Daisy Miller*'s eponymous heroine's much-gossiped-about innocence to Martin Rubin ("It's like making a movie against capital punishment, and the man who's going to be executed is innocent") as he was extolling the benefits of being able to shoot *The Last Picture Show* in black-and-white to Gordon Gow ("You wouldn't say to a painter, 'No, no, you can't paint that with charcoal, you must do it in oils'")—no matter that *Daisy Miller* was thought of as a washout and *The Last Picture Show* a classic.

For this reason, in going over potential interviews to include in this book, I gravitated towards those presented in question-and-answer format: twelve out of the final thirteen are Q&As. Since few critics grasped Bogdanovich's work as perceptively as he did, why not give him the floor? Fortunately, he had smart interviewers on his tail who allowed him to do just that. In 1979, Stephen Myers (a future film and television editor then working as a journalist) and Larry Estes focused their interview on *Saint Jack*, which was Bogdanovich's most interesting film since *The Last Picture Show*—a Singapore-set tale starring Ben Gazzara as a pimp with unlikely moral fiber—but not half as well-known.

In 1982, critic Michael Ventura took the occasion of the release of *They All Laughed*—the director's favorite film for its romantic view of affairs and near-affairs, played by an inspired cast including Gazzara, Audrey Hepburn, John Ritter, and Dorothy Stratten—to ask him about the decline in production values in American films. Ventura saw in Bogdanovich the same thing Bogdanovich saw in *himself* all those years ago when, to Sherman and Rubin, he invoked D. W. Griffith in explaining the paternity of his work. "I went to Bogdanovich because he's the conscious inheritor of everything that's been best in American movies," Ventura wrote. Meaning, in part, classically directed films that partook in audience-friendly genres, like the coming-of-age drama (*The Last Picture Show*) and the screwball (*What's Up, Doc?*) or romantic (*They All Laughed*) comedy.

In 1988, writer Thomas J. Harris introduced his interview by taking the contrarian position that Bogdanovich's work had become "more and more personal" even as it was becoming "less and less successful, both critically and commercially," while, explaining the background of his 2002 conversation with the director, Gerald Peary writes admiringly of such underappreciated works as *Texasville* and *The Thing Called Love*. So, the virtues some critics missed, many of Bogdanovich's interviewers recognized, and the interviews are the better for it.

"What do you call well directed?" Michael Ventura asked.

"So you don't see the seams, you know? So you can't tell it was directed," Peter Bogdanovich replied—although, of course, he does make the seams visible in many of the conversations included here. He discusses his distaste for conventional film scores ("I can name you any number of movies that had the most brilliant scores, from *Citizen Kane* through the Hitchcock movies, but I'm embarrassed to have a movie scored," he told Gow); his fondness for location shooting ("It becomes a kind of marvelous boys and girls camp, or a reasonably peaceful army of occupation," he told the AFI in 1978); his theories about rehearsing actors ahead of production ("You never let them really get it perfect," he told the AFI in 1986); and his conviction that directors should have the editing of a scene in mind before they go to the set ("Now, when people say a person spends millions of dollars to make a movie, I say he doesn't know what he's cutting," he told Ventura). He is also, as writer Patrick McGilligan observed in a 1975 *Boston Globe* profile, "a great raconteur"[7]—referring to his gift for impressions of, and stories about, Hollywood legends. But insider tips and firsthand anecdotes—while both extremely valuable—are not, finally, what make these interviews lasting.

It is the candor they contain that makes them stand out—and, on this count, I speak from experience. I have been interviewing Bogdanovich, on and off, for over a decade. I first spoke to him in 2003, when I was writing an article focusing on several films of his that I especially admired, such as *Daisy Miller* and *They All Laughed*, and I kept up the habit in the years that followed. Most of our conversations ended up being included in the book I am writing about his career, soon to be published by the University Press of Kentucky. (One exception—a 2005 interview focusing exclusively on his relationship with Orson Welles and his experience acting in Welles's unfinished film, *The Other Side of the Wind*—is included here.) Setting aside our friendly relationship—not to mention my admiration for his films—I do not think I would have interviewed him for so many years were it not for his *honesty*—a characteristic specifically highlighted by Peary, but present in every one of these interviews.

Bogdanovich is unafraid to call a spade a spade. To Myers and Estes, he confessed that he had a poor working relationship with Timothy Bottoms on *The Last Picture Show*: "He hasn't gotten along with anybody, before or after. Nobody seems to get along with Tim." But he doesn't cut himself slack either. To Ventura, he criticized the scenes in *Nickelodeon* that were shot on the backlot: "The best parts of *Nickelodeon* were made on location, the rest of the stuff had that studio feeling I hate." To Harris, he admitted that post-production dithering damaged *At Long Last Love*: "And I agreed with the critics when it came out. I didn't like it either." He acknowledges his missteps as surely as he recognizes his successes, and he seldom conforms to his image as an apologist for the Golden Age of Hollywood. While he savors the artistry of his predecessors, he harbors few illusions about the business, as he succinctly expressed to Myers and Estes: "We all write about the wonderful days of Hollywood, but it was always shitty. People were always going through hell. And they're always going to when you have an art that is essentially ruled by money."

He is also upfront about the joys and tragedies of his personal life, including his divorce from his first wife, production and costume designer Polly Platt; his relationship with one of the stars of *The Last Picture Show*, Cybill Shepherd; and the ten months that Dorothy Stratten—the beautiful, gifted model and actress (featured in *They All Laughed*) who was murdered by her estranged husband—was in his life. Few of these interviews touch on these subjects directly, but when they do, Bogdanovich is expansive.

After Stratten's murder, he told Ventura, his view of moviemaking changed. "But when something *happens*, and it's real, and there's no way to change it, no way to rewrite it, no way to re-cut it or re-shoot it, you suddenly say, 'What *is* the point of making pictures? What is the point of doing anything? Because *this* is *real*.'" Twenty years later, in 2002, journalist Stephen Lemons asked him for his views on the afterlife, picking up both on his reference to Orson Welles's posthumous presence in his life, but also, perhaps, the way in which Stratten continues to guide him (look no further than the themes—both obvious and not-so-obvious—in his latest film, *She's Funny That Way*). "Kind of a personal question," he said to Lemons—but he answered it anyway, as he always does, in my experience with him. "I don't think the spirit dies," he continued. "I think the spirit is imperishable, that it remains, and is around or not, depending on different things."

Towards the end of his interview with Peary, Bogdanovich returned to John Ford. "He was crusty, surly, didn't want to talk about intellectual things, didn't want to be thought of as an intellectual, or an artist, or a poet, or any of that stuff," he said, adding that Ford, of course, had some of those qualities underneath.

For his part, Bogdanovich never bothered with the mask—instead he is more than willing to go into his themes, preferences, aversions, and innermost thoughts to anyone intelligent enough to ask, as you will find in these pages.

Above all, I am grateful to Peter Bogdanovich for his endorsement of this book, as well as his cooperation and assistance as it came together. When I told Peter that the project was a go, he immediately emailed me a list of interviews he thought highly of—several of which ended up making the final cut. I am also grateful for the support and patience of the University Press of Mississippi, including director Leila Salisbury, managing editor Anne Stascavage, editorial associate Valerie Jones, and series editor Gerald Peary. My brother, Patrick Tonguette, expertly transcribed interviews that existed only in print form. For their friendship and advice, I thank Nick Dawson, Dave Kehr, Bill Krohn, Vincent LoBrutto, Joseph McBride, Patrick McGilligan, and Matt Zoller Seitz.

PT

Notes

1. Peter Bogdanovich, *Who the Devil Made It* (New York: Alfred A. Knopf, 1997), 4.
2. Ibid., 5.
3. Peter Bogdanovich, *Who the Hell's In It* (New York: Alfred A. Knopf, 2004), 9.
4. Stephanie Zacharek, "Breathless," *New York Times*, March 20, 2005.
5. Thomas J. Harris, *Bogdanovich's Picture Shows* (Metuchen, NJ: Scarecrow), 1990, 7.
6. Tad Friend, "The Moviegoer," *The New Yorker*, April 8, 2002.
7. Patrick McGilligan, "At Long Last, Bogdanovich," *Boston Globe*, March 30, 1975.

Chronology

1939   Born July 30, in Kingston, New York, to Borislav and Herma (Robinson) Bogdanovich.

1952   Sister, Anna Thea, born. Starts keeping card file documenting every film seen. Cast in title role in musical *Finian's Rainbow* in a Collegiate School production.

1954   Takes acting classes at the American Academy of Dramatic Arts. Stars in the leading role in Owen Davis's *The Ninth Guest* in a Collegiate School production.

1955   Begins studying acting with Stella Adler. Apprentice and actor at the Cherry County Playhouse in Traverse City, Michigan.

1956   Apprentice and bit player at Stratford Shakespeare Festival in Stratford, Connecticut.

1957   Apprentice and bit player at New York Shakespeare Festival.

1958   Plays ten roles in ten plays in summer stock in Falmouth, Massachusetts.

1959   Directs off-Broadway production of Clifford Odets's *The Big Knife*.

1961   Makes first voyage to Los Angeles, where he makes many introductions and takes notes for first major Hollywood article. As artistic director at Phoenicia Playhouse in Phoenicia, New York, directs productions of *Camino Real*, *Once in a Lifetime*, *Ten Little Indians*, and *Rocket to the Moon*. Meets costume designer Polly Platt. Monograph *The Cinema of Orson Welles* published.

1962   Begins writing for *Esquire*. Marries Polly Platt. Monograph *The Cinema of Howard Hawks* published.

1963   Monograph *The Cinema of Alfred Hitchcock* published.

1964   Directs off-Broadway production of Moss Hart and George S. Kaufman's *Once in a Lifetime*, the failure of which spurs Bogdanovich and Platt to move to California.

1965   Meets producer Roger Corman, who assigns him to write first screenplay, *The Criminals*.

1966   Gains filmmaking experience on Roger Corman's *The Wild Angels*, as assistant to Corman and second-unit director; he also completely rewrites the screenplay. The same year narrates and directs ten minutes of *Voyage to the Planet of Prehistoric Women*.

1967 Daughter, Antonia, born. Directs first feature, *Targets*, in Los Angeles. *John Ford* published.

1968 *Targets* released.

1969 *Fritz Lang in America* published. Hired to direct Sergio Leone's *Duck, You Sucker* (*A Fistful of Dynamite*), but quits prior to completion of screenplay.

1970 Daughter, Alexandra, born. Directs *The Last Picture Show* in Texas. Begins affair with Cybill Shepherd. Cast by Orson Welles in *The Other Side of the Wind* (first in one role, then another).

1971 *The Last Picture Show* released. *Directed by John Ford* first shown. *Allan Dwan: The Last Pioneer* published. Directs *What's Up, Doc?* in San Francisco and at Warner Bros. Studios.

1972 Nominated for Oscars for Best Director and Best Adapted Screenplay for *The Last Picture Show*. Nominated for Golden Globe for Best Director for *The Last Picture Show*. Wins Best Adapted Screenplay from the New York Film Critics Circle for *The Last Picture Show*. *What's Up, Doc?* released. With Francis Ford Coppola and William Friedkin, one-third of the Directors Company, a production unit at Paramount. Directs *Paper Moon* in Kansas and Missouri. Divorces Polly Platt.

1973 *Paper Moon* released. *Pieces of Time* published. Directs *Daisy Miller* in Vevey, Switzerland, and Rome.

1974 Nominated for Golden Globe for Best Director for *Paper Moon*. *Daisy Miller* released. Directs *At Long Last Love* in Los Angeles.

1975 *At Long Last Love* released. Directs *Nickelodeon* in Modesto, California, and Los Angeles.

1976 *Nickelodeon* released.

1978 Directs *Saint Jack* in Singapore. Cybill Shepherd affair ends. Briefly meets Dorothy Stratten.

1979 *Saint Jack* released. *Saint Jack* wins Pasinetti Award at Venice Film Festival.

1980 Begins relationship with Dorothy Stratten. Directs *They All Laughed* in Manhattan. Dorothy Stratten murdered by her estranged husband.

1981 *They All Laughed* released.

1984 *The Killing of the Unicorn: Dorothy Stratten 1960–1980* published. Directs *Mask* in Los Angeles.

1985 *Mask* released.

CHRONOLOGY xvii

1987	Directs *Illegally Yours* in St. Augustine, Florida.
1988	*Illegally Yours* released. Marries Louise Stratten (sister of Dorothy Stratten).
1989	Directs *Texasville* in Texas.
1990	*Texasville* released.
1991	Directs *Noises Off* in Los Angeles. *A Year and a Day Engagement Calendar* (edited by PB from 1991 to 1998; later titled *The White Goddess Engagement Diary*) first published.
1992	*Noises Off* released. *This Is Orson Welles* published. Directs *The Thing Called Love* in Nashville and Los Angeles.
1993	*The Thing Called Love* released.
1994	"Song of Songs," episode of series *Picture Windows*, airs on Showtime.
1995	"A Dime a Dance," episode of series *Fallen Angels*, airs on Showtime. Directs Yoko Ono music video "Never Say Goodbye." *A Moment with Miss Gish* published.
1996	*To Sir, with Love II* airs on CBS.
1997	*The Price of Heaven* airs on CBS. *Rescuers: Stories of Courage: Two Women* airs on Showtime. *Who the Devil Made It: Conversations with Legendary Film Directors* published.
1998	*Naked City: A Killer Christmas* airs on Showtime.
1999	*A Saintly Switch* airs on ABC. *Peter Bogdanovich's Movie of the Week* published.
2000	Begins making regular appearances over the next six years as Dr. Elliot Kupferberg on *The Sopranos*. Directs *The Cat's Meow* in Berlin and Greece.
2001	*The Cat's Meow* released. Divorces Louise Stratten.
2004	*The Mystery of Natalie Wood* airs on ABC. *Hustle* airs on ESPN. "Sentimental Education," episode of *The Sopranos*, airs on HBO. *Who the Hell's In It: Portraits and Conversations* published.
2007	*Runnin' Down a Dream: Tom Petty and the Heartbreakers* released.
2009	Wins Grammy for Best Long Form Music Video for *Runnin' Down a Dream: Tom Petty and the Heartbreakers*.
2013	Directs *She's Funny That Way* in Manhattan.
2014	*She's Funny That Way* premieres at Venice Film Festival.

Filmography

TARGETS (1968)
Saticoy Productions–Paramount Pictures
Director: **Peter Bogdanovich**
Producer: **Peter Bogdanovich**
Screenplay: **Peter Bogdanovich**
Story: Polly Platt and **Peter Bogdanovich**
Cinematography: Laszlo Kovacs
Editing: **Peter Bogdanovich**
Production Design: Polly Platt
Cast: Tim O'Kelly (Bobby Thompson), Boris Karloff (Byron Orlok), Arthur Peterson (Ed Loughlin), Monty Landis (Marshall Smith), Nancy Hsueh (Jenny), **Peter Bogdanovich** (Sammy Michaels)

THE LAST PICTURE SHOW (1971)
BBS Productions-Columbia Pictures
Director: **Peter Bogdanovich**
Producer: Stephen J. Friedman
Executive Producer: Bert Schneider
Screenplay: Larry McMurtry and **Peter Bogdanovich** (based on the novel by Larry McMurtry)
Cinematography: Robert Surtees
Editing: Donn Cambern
Production Design: Polly Platt
Cast: Timothy Bottoms (Sonny Crawford), Jeff Bridges (Duane Jackson), Cybill Shepherd (Jacy Farrow), Ben Johnson (Sam the Lion), Cloris Leachman (Ruth Popper), Ellen Burstyn (Lois Farrow), Eileen Brennan (Genevieve), Clu Gulager (Abilene), Sam Bottoms (Billy), Sharon Taggart (Charlene Duggs), Randy Quaid (Lester Marlow)

DIRECTED BY JOHN FORD (1971)
American Film Institute-California Arts Commission
Director: **Peter Bogdanovich**

Producers: James R. Silke and George Stevens, Jr.
Screenplay: **Peter Bogdanovich**
Cinematography: Laszlo Kovacs, Brick Marquard, Gregory Sandor, and Eric Sherman
Editing: Richard Patterson
Cast: Henry Fonda, John Ford, James Stewart, John Wayne, Orson Welles (Narrator)

WHAT'S UP, DOC? (1972)
Saticoy Productions-Warner Bros. Pictures
Director: **Peter Bogdanovich**
Producer: **Peter Bogdanovich**
Screenplay: Buck Henry and David Newman & Robert Benton
Story: **Peter Bogdanovich**
Cinematography: Laszlo Kovacs
Editing: Verna Fields
Production Design: Polly Platt
Cast: Barbra Streisand (Judy Maxwell), Ryan O'Neal (Howard Bannister), Madeline Kahn (Eunice Burns), Kenneth Mars (Hugh Simon), Austin Pendleton (Frederick Larrabee), Michael Murphy (Mr. Smith)

PAPER MOON (1973)
The Directors Company-Saticoy Productions-Paramount Pictures
Director: **Peter Bogdanovich**
Producer: **Peter Bogdanovich**
Screenplay: Alvin Sargent (based on the novel *Addie Pray* by Joe David Brown)
Cinematography: Laszlo Kovacs
Editing: Verna Fields
Production Design: Polly Platt
Cast: Ryan O'Neal (Moses Pray), Tatum O'Neal (Addie Loggins), Madeline Kahn (Trixie Delight), John Hillerman (Deputy Hardin / Jess Hardin), P. J. Johnson (Imogene)

DAISY MILLER (1974)
The Directors Company-Copa de Oro-Paramount Pictures
Director: **Peter Bogdanovich**
Producer: **Peter Bogdanovich**
Screenplay: Frederic Raphael (based on the short novel by Henry James)
Cinematography: Alberto Spagnoli

Editing: Verna Fields
Production Design: Ferdinando Scarfiotti
Cast: Cybill Shepherd (Annie P. "Daisy" Miller), Barry Brown (Frederick Winterbourne), Cloris Leachman (Mrs. Ezra Miller), Mildred Natwick (Mrs. Costello), Eileen Brennan (Mrs. Walker), Duilio Del Prete (Mr. Giovanelli), James McMurtry (Randolph C. Miller)

AT LONG LAST LOVE (1975)
Copa de Oro-20th Century Fox
Director: **Peter Bogdanovich**
Producers: **Peter Bogdanovich** and Frank Marshall
Screenplay: **Peter Bogdanovich**
Cinematography: Laszlo Kovacs
Editing: Douglas Robertson
Production Design: Gene Allen
Cast: Burt Reynolds (Michael Oliver Pritchard III), Cybill Shepherd (Brooke Carter), Madeline Kahn (Kitty O'Kelly), Duilio Del Prete (Johnny Spanish), Eileen Brennan (Elizabeth), John Hillerman (Rodney James), Mildred Natwick (Mabel Pritchard)

NICKELODEON (1976)
EMI Films-British Lion-Columbia Pictures
Director: **Peter Bogdanovich**
Producers: Robert Chartoff, Frank Marshall, and Irwin Winkler
Screenplay: **Peter Bogdanovich** and W. D. Richter
Cinematography: Laszlo Kovacs
Editing: William C. Carruth
Art Direction: Richard Berger
Cast: Ryan O'Neal (Leo Harrigan), Burt Reynolds (Buck Greenway), Tatum O'Neal (Alice Forsyte), Jane Hitchcock (Kathleen Cooke), Brian Keith (H. H. Cobb), Stella Stevens (Marty Reeves), John Ritter (Franklin Frank)

SAINT JACK (1979)
Copa de Oro-Playboy Productions-Shoals Creek-New World Pictures
Director: **Peter Bogdanovich**
Producers: Roger Corman and George Morfogen
Executive Producers: Hugh M. Hefner and Edward L. Rissien
Screenplay: Howard Sackler, Paul Theroux, and **Peter Bogdanovich** (based on the novel by Paul Theroux)

Cinematography: Robby Muller
Editing: William C. Carruth
Art Direction: David Ng
Cast: Ben Gazzara (Jack Flowers), Denholm Elliott (William Leigh), James Villiers (Frogget), Joss Ackland (Yardley), Rodney Bewes (Smale), Mark Kingston (Yates), Lisa Lu (Mrs. Yates), Monika Subramaniam (Monika), Judy Lim (Judy), George Lazenby (Senator), **Peter Bogdanovich** (Eddie Schuman)

THEY ALL LAUGHED (1981)
Moon Pictures-Time-Life Films
Director: **Peter Bogdanovich**
Producers: George Morfogen and Blaine Novak
Screenplay: **Peter Bogdanovich**
Cinematography: Robby Muller
Editing: William C. Carruth and Scott Vickrey
Art Direction: Kert Lundell
Cast: Audrey Hepburn (Angela Niotes), Ben Gazzara (John Russo), John Ritter (Charles Rutledge), Dorothy Stratten (Dolores Martin), Colleen Camp (Christy Miller), Blaine Novak (Arthur Brodsky), Patti Hansen (Sam), Linda MacEwen (Amy Lester), George Morfogen (Leon Leondopolous), Sean H. Ferrer (Jose)

MASK (1985)
Universal Pictures
Director: **Peter Bogdanovich**
Producer: Martin Starger
Executive Producer: C. J. Kettler
Screenplay: Anna Hamilton Phelan
Cinematography: Laszlo Kovacs
Editing: Eva Gardos and Barbara Ford
Art Direction: Norman Newberry
Cast: Cher (Florence "Rusty" Dennis), Sam Elliott (Gar), Eric Stoltz (Roy L. "Rocky" Dennis), Estelle Getty (Evelyn), Richard Dysart (Abe), Laura Dern (Diana Adams), Micole Mercurio (Babe), Harry Carey, Jr. (Red), Dennis Burkley (Dozer), Lawrence Monoson (Ben)

ILLEGALLY YOURS (1988)
De Laurentiis Entertainment Group-Crescent Moon-United Artists
Director: **Peter Bogdanovich**

Producers: **Peter Bogdanovich** and Dino De Laurentiis
Executive Producers: William Peiffer and Peggy Robertson
Screenplay: Max Dickens and M. A. Stewart
Cinematography: Dante Spinotti
Editing: Richard Fields and Ronald Krehel
Production Design: Jane Musky
Cast: Rob Lowe (Richard Dice), Colleen Camp (Molly Gilbert), Kenneth Mars (Hal B. Keeler), Kim Myers (Suzanne Keeler), Marshall Colt (Donald Cleary), Harry Carey, Jr. (Wally Finnegan), George Morfogen (Judge Norman Meckel), Linda MacEwen (Ruth Harrison), Louise Stratten (Sharon Woolrich)

TEXASVILLE (1990)
Nelson Entertainment-Cine-Source-Columbia Pictures
Director: **Peter Bogdanovich**
Producers: **Peter Bogdanovich** and Barry Spikings
Executive Producers: Jake Eberts and William Peiffer
Screenplay: **Peter Bogdanovich** (based on the novel by Larry McMurtry)
Cinematography: Nicholas von Sternberg
Editing: Richard Fields and Ronald David Krehel
Production Design: Phedon Papamichael
Cast: Jeff Bridges (Duane Jackson), Timothy Bottoms (Sonny Crawford), Cybill Shepherd (Jacy Farrow), Cloris Leachman (Ruth Popper), Randy Quaid (Lester Marlow), Annie Potts (Karla Jackson), William McNamara (Dickie Jackson), Eileen Brennan (Genevieve Morgan)

NOISES OFF (1992)
Amblin-Touchstone Pictures-Buena Vista
Director: **Peter Bogdanovich**
Producer: Frank Marshall
Executive Producers: **Peter Bogdanovich** and Kathleen Kennedy
Screenplay: Marty Kaplan (based on the play by Michael Frayn)
Cinematography: Tim Suhrstedt
Editing: Lisa Day
Production Design: Norman Newberry
Cast: Michael Caine (Lloyd Fellowes), Carol Burnett (Dotty Otley / Mrs. Clackett), Denholm Elliott (Selsdon Mowbray / The Burglar), John Ritter (Garry Lejeune / Roger Tramplemain), Christopher Reeve (Frederick Dallas / Philip Brent), Nicollette Sheridan (Brooke Ashton / Vicki),

Marilu Henner (Belinda Blair / Flavia Brent), Julie Hagerty (Poppy Taylor), Mark Linn-Baker (Tim Allgood), Louise Stratten (Broadway Stagehand)

THE THING CALLED LOVE (1993)
Davis Entertainment-Paramount Pictures
Director: **Peter Bogdanovich**
Producer: John Davis
Executive Producer: George Folsey, Jr.
Screenplay: Carol Heikkinen
Cinematography: Peter James
Editing: Terry Stokes
Production Design: Michael Seymour
Cast: River Phoenix (James Wright), Samantha Mathis (Miranda Presley), Dermot Mulroney (Kyle Davidson), Sandra Bullock (Linda Lue Linden), K. T. Oslin (Lucy), Anthony Clark (Billy), Webb Wilder (Ned), Earl Poole Ball (Floyd)

"SONG OF SONGS" (episode of Showtime series PICTURE WINDOWS) (1994)
Director: **Peter Bogdanovich**
Producers: Jeff Freilich, Scott J. T. Frank, Daniel Halperin, and David Wachs
Executive Producers: Norman Jewison and S. Howard Rosen
Screenplay: Harry Mark Petrakis and John Petrakis (based on the story by Harry Mark Petrakis)
Cinematography: Paul Sarossy
Editing: David Hicks
Production Design: Franco De Cotiis
Cast: George Segal (Ted), Brooke Adams (Angie), Sally Kirkland (Blossom), **Peter Bogdanovich** (Lucca), Louise Stratten (Sally)

"NEVER SAY GOODBYE" (music video) (1995)
Director: **Peter Bogdanovich**
Producer: Marc Kolbe
Executive Producer: Yoko Ono
Editing: Marc Kolbe
Song: Yoko Ono
Cast: Eric Stoltz, Tate Donovan, Yoko Ono, Louise Stratten

"A DIME A DANCE" (episode of Showtime series FALLEN ANGELS) (1995)
Director: **Peter Bogdanovich**
Producers: Stuart Cornfeld and William Horberg
Executive Producers: Sydney Pollack and Lindsay Doran
Screenplay: Allan Scott (based on the story "The Dancing Detective" by Cornell Woolrich)
Cinematography: Robert Brinkmann
Editing: David Siegel
Production Design: Rick Heinrichs
Cast: Eric Stoltz (Nick Ballestier), Jennifer Grey (Ginger Allen), Richard Portnow (Jack Malkov), Wayne Grace (Pat Marino), Douglas Roberts (Jack Chieseman), Estelle Harris (Mom Henderson), Louise Stratten (Julie)

TO SIR, WITH LOVE II (1996)
Adelson-Baumgarten Productions-TriStar Television-Verdon-Cedric Productions-CBS
Director: **Peter Bogdanovich**
Producer: Richard Stenta
Screenplay: Philip Rosenberg (based on characters by E. R. Braithwaite)
Cinematography: William Birch
Editing: Dianne Ryder-Rennolds
Production Design: Gary Baugh
Cast: Sidney Poitier (Mark Thackeray), Christian Payton (Wilsie Carrouthers), Dana Eskelson (Evie Hillis), Fernando Lopez (Danny Laredo), Casey Lluberes (Rebecca Torrado), Michael Gilio (Frankie Davanon)

THE PRICE OF HEAVEN (1997)
Konigsberg Productions-CBS
Director: **Peter Bogdanovich**
Producer: Jack Clements
Executive Producers: Joyce Eliason and Frank Konigsberg
Screenplay: Joyce Eliason (based on the short novel by Allan Gurganus)
Cinematography: Ronn Schmidt
Editing: David Siegel
Production Design: Norm Baron
Cast: Grant Show (Jerry Shand), Cicely Tyson (Vesta Lotte Battle), Lori Loughlin (Leslie), George Wendt (Sam), Cari Shayne (Claire Gundry), Louise Stratten (Sandy)

RESCUERS: STORIES OF COURAGE: TWO WOMEN (1997)
Barwood Films-Paramount-Showtime
Director: **Peter Bogdanovich**
Producer: Jeff Freilich
Executive Producers: Cis Corman and Barbra Streisand
Screenplay: Ernest Kinoy and Susan Nanus (based on the book by Gay Block and Malka Drucker)
Cinematography: Miroslaw Baszak
Editing: Dianne Ryder-Rennolds
Production Design: Franco De Cotiis
Cast of story "Mamusha": Elizabeth Perkins (Gertruda Babilinska), Nicky Guadagni (Lydia Stolowitsky), Michael Cameron (Young Mickey), Fraser McGregor (Older Mickey), Mark Humphrey (Tomas Kolchak), George Morfogen (Narrator)
Cast of story "Woman on a Bicycle": Sela Ward (Marie-Rose Gineste), Fritz Weaver (Father Theas), Michael Landes (Rene Klein), Theresa Tova (The Abbess), Louise Stratten (Annette)

NAKED CITY: A KILLER CHRISTMAS (1998)
Magnum Productions-Paramount Network Television-Showtime
Director: **Peter Bogdanovich**
Producer: Jeff Freilich
Executive Producers: Andrew W. Garroni and Walter Gernert
Screenplay: Jeff Freilich and Christopher Trumbo (based on characters by Malvin Wald)
Cinematography: James Gardner
Editing: David Baxter
Production Design: Franco De Cotiis
Cast: Scott Glenn (Sgt. Daniel Muldoon), Courtney B. Vance (Officer James Halloran), Laura Leighton (Gerry Millar), Barbara Williams (Eva), Nigel Bennett (Joseph Soloff), Lisa Vidal (Lori Halloran), Al Waxman (Burt), Jason Blicker (Officer Alonzo) Louise Stratten (Officer Wendy)

A SAINTLY SWITCH (1999)
Pacific Motion Pictures Corporation-Walt Disney Television-ABC
Director: **Peter Bogdanovich**
Producers: Sally Hampton and Iain Paterson
Screenplay: Sally Hampton and Haris Orkin
Cinematography: James Gardner
Editing: David Baxter

Production Design: Susan Longmire
Cast: Vivica A. Fox (Sara Anderson), David Alan Grier (Dan Anderson), Rue McClanahan (Aunt Fanny), Al Waxman (Coach Beasily), Scott Owen Cumberbatch (Clarke), Louise Stratten (Kimberly)

THE CAT'S MEOW (2001)
CP Medien-Dan Films-Lions Gate
Director: **Peter Bogdanovich**
Producers: Julie Baines, Kim Bieber, Carol Lewis, and Dieter Meyer
Executive Producers: Michael Paseornek and Wieland Schulz-Keil
Screenplay: Steven Peros (based on his play)
Cinematography: Bruno Delbonnel
Editing: Edward Norris
Production Design: Jean-Vincent Puzos
Cast: Kirsten Dunst (Marion Davies), Edward Herrmann (William Randolph Hearst), Eddie Izzard (Charlie Chaplin), Cary Elwes (Thomas Ince), Joanna Lumley (Elinor Glyn), Jennifer Tilly (Louella Parsons), Claudia Harrison (Margaret Livingston)

THE MYSTERY OF NATALIE WOOD (2004)
Cypress Point Productions-Von Zerneck/Sertner Films-ABC
Director: **Peter Bogdanovich**
Producers: Richard Fischoff and Randy Sutter
Executive Producers: Gerald W. Abrams, Suzanne Finstad, Robert Sertner, and Frank von Zerneck
Screenplay: Elizabeth Egloff (based on the books by Suzanne Finstad and Warren G. Harris)
Cinematography: John Stokes
Editing: Scott Vickrey
Art Direction: Scott Bird
Cast: Justine Waddell (Natalie Wood), Michael Weatherly (Robert Wagner), Matthew Settle (Warren Beatty), Elizabeth Rice (Teenage Natalie Wood), Grace Fulton (Young Natalie Wood), Alice Krige (Maria Gurdin)

HUSTLE (2004)
Orly Adelson Productions-ESPN
Director: **Peter Bogdanovich**
Producer: Terry Gould
Executive Producers: Orly Adelson and Mark Shapiro
Screenplay: Christian Darren

Cinematography: James Gardner
Editing: Bernadette Kelly
Production Design: David Davis
Cast: Tom Sizemore (Pete Rose), Dash Mihok (Paul Janszen), George DiCenzo (Bartlett Giamatti), Melissa DiMarco (Carol Rose)

"SENTIMENTAL EDUCATION" (episode of HBO series THE SOPRANOS) (2004)
Director: **Peter Bogdanovich**
Producer: Martin Bruestle
Creator: David Chase
Executive Producers: Mitchell Burgess, David Chase, Robin Green, Brad Grey, Ilene S. Landress, and Terence Winter
Screenplay: Matthew Weiner
Cinematography: Phil Abraham
Editing: Sidney Wolinsky
Production Design: Bob Shaw
Cast: James Gandolfini (Tony Soprano), Lorraine Bracco (Dr. Jennifer Melfi), Edie Falco (Carmela Soprano), Michael Imperioli (Christopher Moltisanti), Steve Buscemi (Tony Blundetto), David Strathairn (Robert Wegler)

DIRECTED BY JOHN FORD—REVISED VERSION (2006)
Turner Classic Movies-Warner Home Video-AFI
Director: **Peter Bogdanovich**
Producer: Frank Marshall
Executive Producer: Tom Brown
Screenplay: **Peter Bogdanovich**
Cinematography: Laszlo Kovacs, Brick Marquard, David Sammons, Gregory Sandor, Patrick Stewart, and Eric Sherman
Editing: Mark Fitzgerald and Richard Patterson
Cast: **Peter Bogdanovich**, Harry Carey, Jr., Clint Eastwood, Henry Fonda, John Ford, Walter Hill, Martin Scorsese, Steven Spielberg, James Stewart, John Wayne, Orson Welles (Narrator)

RUNNIN' DOWN A DREAM: TOM PETTY AND THE HEARTBREAKERS (2007)
Penn/Bright Entertainment-Warner Bros. Records
Director: **Peter Bogdanovich**
Producers: Skot Bright and George Drakoulias

Executive Producers: John Berg, Tony Dimitriades, and Diarmuid Quinn
Cinematography: Ted Hayash, David Sammons, and Patrick Alexander Stewart
Editing: Bill Berg-Hillinger, Jeffrey Doe, John Gutierrez, and Mary Ann McClure
Cast: Tom Petty and the Heartbreakers, Jackson Browne, Johnny Depp, Bob Dylan, George Harrison, Stevie Nicks, Rick Rubin, Eddie Vedder

SHE'S FUNNY THAT WAY (2014)
Lagniappe Films-Venture Forth
Director: **Peter Bogdanovich**
Producers: Holly Wiersma, Logan Levy, George Drakoulias, Louise Stratten
Executive Producers: Wes Anderson, Noah Baumbach, Cassian Elwes, et al.
Screenplay: Louise Stratten and **Peter Bogdanovich**
Cinematography: Yaron Orbach
Editing: Pax Wassermann and Nick Moore
Production Design: Jane Musky
Cast: Owen Wilson (Arnold Albertson), Imogen Poots (Isabella Patterson), Jennifer Aniston (Jane Claremont), Will Forte (Joshua Fleet), Kathryn Hahn (Delta Simmons), Rhys Ifans (Seth Gilbert), Austin Pendleton (Judge Pendergast), George Morfogen (Harold Fleet), Cybill Shepherd (Nettie), Richard Lewis (Al), Illeana Douglas (Interviewer), Joanna Lumley (Vivian Claremont)

Peter Bogdanovich: Interviews

Peter Bogdanovich

Eric Sherman and Martin Rubin / 1968

From *The Director's Event: Interviews with Five American Film-makers* (New York: Signet, 1972 [1969]). Reprinted by permission of the authors.

Eric Sherman and I interviewed Peter Bogdanovich at his home in Van Nuys, California, in November 1968, three months after the release of his first film *Targets*. Although we had never met him before, Peter was uncommonly generous, not only with his own time, but also with helping us to arrange interviews with other directors (Budd Boetticher, Samuel Fuller, Abraham Polonsky) that were included in our book *The Director's Event*.

Those other directors were equally gracious toward us, but there was a difference with Peter. He was more of a peer, like a hip upperclassman or older sibling. Peter was much closer to us in age, his house was the kind of cluttered, family-friendly suburban domicile that we had grown up in, and, most important, he was an early adherent of the heady wave of 1960s auteurist cinephilia that had also captivated Eric and me. His MoMA monographs on Hawks and Hitchcock and his *Esquire* articles on such figures as John Ford and Jerry Lewis had been part of our education, and we eagerly solicited tips from Peter on films by lesser-known auteurs such as Joseph H. Lewis and André de Toth. He had seemingly seen everything, which in those pre-cable, pre-homevid days could be accomplished only by watching a lot of late-night commercial television and putting in time at New York's museums and revival/repertory houses.

Peter was a wonderful storyteller, both in print and in conversation—articulate, humorous, with an encyclopedic memory of old movie dialogue and an ability to do spot-on imitations of everyone from Cary Grant to Orson Welles to Walter Brennan. *Targets* marked his first full-fledged opportunity to extend that storytelling flair to filmmaking and to combine it with the sophisticated sense of film history that he had already demonstrated as a critic and journalist.
—*Martin Rubin*

Peter Bogdanovich: I always considered myself a director who was making a living writing about pictures, not the other way around. In other words, I had always wanted to direct films, even when I didn't know it. The writing was something I never really cared much about.

I was on the stage first. We've all sinned! I directed plays in New York. The first thing I did was *The Big Knife* by Clifford Odets. I directed and co-produced it off-Broadway in 1959–60. It was a successful production critically, but it didn't last too long—a couple of months. I had never directed anything before that except a scene from *The Big Knife* for one of Stella Adler's acting classes. From the time I was fifteen, I studied acting with Stella. I had also done some acting with the American and the New York Shakespeare Festivals.

Then I directed a season of summer theater in Phoenicia, New York, in 1961. I did four plays, among them Agatha Christie's *Ten Little Indians*, which was the best thing I ever did. I did *Ten Little Indians* a la Hawks or Welles—it was the fastest production you've ever seen. Every line overlapped with another. You know Agatha Christie—it was all exposition, dull as hell. The first act was forty-six pages, and it played in twenty-six minutes. The whole thing was just a set-up for a murder. I tried for a great effect in the last act. I killed every light in the theater, including the exit lights. It was absolutely black. The audience started to get screaming mad. Suddenly you heard this rustling noise on the stage, then a gunshot. Bang! You saw the actors for just one second, like a one-frame cut. It was very exciting.

In those years, I began to write a lot about movies. I wrote monographs for the Museum of Modern Art on Orson Welles in 1961, on Howard Hawks in 1962, and on Alfred Hitchcock in 1963. I was asked to do these because I had written some program notes for the New Yorker Theater [a New York movie house]. I helped Dan Talbot, the owner, program some films in the theater's early months. That's where I got to know who Hawks was. We booked a lot of pictures just so I could see them. In 1962, I started to write for *Esquire*. I did pieces on Jerry Lewis, Jimmy Stewart, John Ford, Humphrey Bogart, and others.

Q: Your film criticism is really different from most of that being written in this country. How did you develop your ideas? Was it through seeing films, or were there outside influences like *Cahiers du Cinema* and Andrew Sarris? Did you start out, like most of us, in the art-house cycle of Bergman, Fellini, Kurosawa?

A: The main influences were Andrew Sarris and Eugene Archer. Archer was the four-string critic for the *New York Times*, and he was brilliant. He influenced a lot of Sarris's opinions. He and Sarris opened my eyes to film. They got me to see films like *Land of the Pharaohs* [Howard Hawks, 1955] and *Fort Apache* [John Ford, 1948]. I was stupid about certain things, I didn't like *Psycho* at the time. I thought it was brilliant but immoral, or something idiotic like that. I remember sitting over coffee one night, and they explained to me why *Psycho* was a great film. They had a big influence on me for about two years, opening things up. But I was ready for that, because I had already gone through my art-film cycle. I was past all that.

Truthfully, my best days as a film-goer were around the time I was ten. My taste was purest then. My favorite films were *Red River* [Hawks, 1948] and *She Wore a Yellow Ribbon* [Ford, 1949]. I saw the first about five times and the second about ten times. Then, as I grew older, I was influenced by critics, as we all are, and my taste went bad. I used to sit in the Thalia [a New York art-house] and look at all those boring foreign films. My taste was really formed when I booked all those films at the New Yorker. We had a series called "The Forgotten Film," and in the first two weeks we had about ten Hawks pictures. That was a revelation to me. You see, I really always loved Hawks. When *Rio Bravo* came out, I loved it, but I didn't know about Hawks. Then I said, "Wait a minute! He did *Red River*!" I put it all together. I had liked all his films, but I hadn't known who he was.

I think too many critics write about a movie as though it exists alone in time. This is crazy. You have to take every movie not only in the perspective of the other films of that director, but also in the whole context of film history—which isn't very long, so I don't know why it isn't done. The worst thing we have in film writing is a lack of film scholarship and the fact that the first thirty years are virtually lost.

A whole school of critics think they like movies, but they don't. They think it's all very nice to like films—within limits. You can't have a passion for them, because after all, it's still a bit juvenile to sit in a movie theater for six hours. Something's not quite right about it. However, people who read books for hours are eggheads, geniuses. It's really a kind of Victorian anti-movie theory.

After my off-Broadway production of *Once in a Lifetime* flopped in 1964, Frank Tashlin [the film director] came to see us. I was depressed. He said, "What are you going to do now?" I said, "I don't know." He said, "What do you want to do?" I said, "I want to make pictures." He said, "Then what are you doing in New York? If you want to make pictures, come to the West Coast. That's where they're made."

He planted the idea in my head. Three months later my wife, Polly, and I moved out here with the expressed purpose of continuing to write and hopefully to make a movie. It never occurred to me that I'd be directing a film in less than two years. To sum up, I always wanted to direct, but I must say that being a critic led me into it. My first job on any picture was a direct result of my having written, and that was with Roger Corman.

In 1965, I went to a screening of *Bay of Angels*. Sitting behind me were Roger Corman and a mutual acquaintance. He introduced me to Roger, who had heard of me through my *Esquire* articles. Roger called me a couple of days later and said, "You're a writer. Wouldn't you like to write for pictures?" "Sure, I'd love to." He said, "I'm looking for something along the lines of *Lawrence of Arabia* or *Bridge on the River Kwai*." I said, "Oh! Well, that's not too difficult!" So Polly and I started to work on a story about World War II.

In January 1966 Roger called me again and said, "I'm going to start a picture called *The Wild Angels*. Would you like to work on it?" I said, "Sure. What do you want me to do?" He said, "I don't know. Just be around." I asked him how long it would take. He said six weeks. So I went to work for Roger. *The Wild Angels* was quite an odyssey, it stretched out to twenty-two weeks.

First I had to find locations for the picture. Then, about ten days before the start of shooting, believe it or not, the script came in. I read it, and it was terrible. It had all these ridiculous sequences like: horse's point of view, cut to frog, motorcycles, cut to frog's point of view as the motorcycles go by. I said to Roger, "This is a Disney picture!" Roger said, "I know. What am I going to do?" I said, "Why don't you rewrite it?" He said, "Oh, no. I don't have time." Jumping in, opportunistic bastard that I am, I said, "I'll do some work on it." He said, "Well . . . O.K."

I rewrote about 80 per cent of the script, although a lot of the dialogue was changed on the set. The actors wouldn't pay any attention to it. They each added about forty "man"s to every line. In a way that helped, because the actors had spent some time with the Hell's Angels and knew their dialect. Afterwards, somebody called me up and said, "Didn't you work on the script for that picture?" I said, "Yes. How did you know?" You see, I didn't receive any official credit for the screenplay. He said, "Well, it has a line that's right out of *Rio Bravo!*" When Peter Fonda and the others go into a garage to get back The Loser's stolen bike, he says, "One of you guys here stole a bike." The other guy says, "Nobody here stole nothin'." Fonda says, "I'll *remember* you said that." He didn't say it quite as well as John Wayne did.

Anyway, we started to shoot. We fell behind schedule very quickly, because the motorcycles gave us problems. Roger kept throwing sequences out and saying, "I can't do this. The second unit will do it." I said, "There *is* no second unit." He said, "I know, I know!" I said, "Well, I'd love to do it." So I shot all the second-unit stuff: backgrounds for the main title, all the sequences of Fonda riding through L.A. I also shot the entire chase on the mountain between Loser and the cop. I was trying to do the chase in *High Sierra* [Raoul Walsh, 1941], and I failed. I tried to repeat that chase in *Targets*, when the cop is chasing the boy.

I shot another scene that I thought was very funny. It's at night, when Peter Fonda comes back to his house. He sees the police are there. Depressed, he goes back to his motorcycle and starts it up. Roger had said, "We don't have any scenes where we show Fonda's attachment to his motorcycle." This came about because one of the real Angels said to Roger, "You don't show how we dig our bikes, man." So Roger said, "Let's have a scene where he's loving his bike." Being very literal, I said, "Let's show him screwing it!" So we did. Later, the editor said, "We don't have any music for this scene." I said, "Why don't you put in the sound of a couple of cats screwing?" I was just joking. He said, "That's a good idea!" They got a couple of cats, and I don't know what they did to them, but they got the sound.

After I shot for two or three weeks with different units, I got to cut the footage, because the editor was tired and had so much else to do. Some kid showed me the mechanics, and then I did most of it myself with a Moviola in my living room. I never had so much fun. I never enjoyed anything so much as physically cutting the film, which I also did on *Targets*.

The Wild Angels was eventually finished. My voice is in it, and I even run through it. If you look carefully, you can see me getting beat up by the Hell's Angels, who were used as extras. You see, I was always with Roger, and they hated Roger, so they hated me, too. During the final fight scene, we needed more extras, so Roger said to me, "Run in there!" Well, they just tried to kill me—they really did. I fell to the ground, and they murdered me.

Anyway, when the picture was finished, I had received, in twenty-two weeks, a paid course on just about everything you could do in a picture: scouting locations, writing script, directing, getting laundry, acting, cutting, doing sound work. I learned a hell of a lot. That was 1966.

The picture turned out to be a big hit. Roger called me and said, "Thank you, but rather than thanking you, I'd like to ask you if you would want to direct a picture." I said, "Of course. What do you want me to do?" He said, "Look, Boris Karloff made a picture with me called *The Terror* and part of the deal is he still owes me two days. Here's what I want you to do: Shoot with Karloff for two days. Get about twenty minutes of footage. Then take about twenty minutes of Karloff out of *The Terror*. Then shoot another forty minutes with some other actors, put it all together, and I'll have a new Karloff picture!"

I'm skipping one thing that was also part of the deal. Roger had bought a Russian picture called *Storm Clouds of Venus* or something like that. Unbelievably bad film. Roger said, "I've got a deal with AIP [American International Pictures]. They'll buy this picture, but they want some girls in it. Just shoot for five days, and stick some girls in. Then you can do the Karloff picture. It'll all be one package deal." Well, putting those women in that goddamned picture dragged on for months. It was the worst thing I've ever had to do.

Finally, I thought of a way of putting girls in: they'd be "gill-women" on Venus. Mamie Van Doren was the lead girl. The picture is now called *Voyage to the Planet of Prehistoric Women*, but I made it as *Gill-Women of Venus*: you see how art is corrupted. The idea was that these guys come to Venus. Since the original actors were Russian, we couldn't intermingle the two parts. I got the idea of showing the women looking at the men, but the men never see *them*. It was a damn good idea.

In the Russian picture, the men kill a pterodactyl. So I made it the god of the gill-women. They worship a statue of a pterodactyl. Since the men killed one, the women now want to kill the men. There was a rain sequence in the original. So the women call upon the god, and the rains fall—they try to drown the men. The original had a volcano sequence. So I have the women try to kill the men with the volcano. It doesn't kill them, but it makes them leave the planet.

In the Russian picture, the men have this big, wonderful robot who can do everything. In the volcano sequence, the only thing that gets hurt is the robot. It floats away in the lava. So I wrote in that the girls find the robot encrusted with lava. For $300, we faked a robot and encrusted it with lava. My ending was that when the men fly away, the girls realize that these guys were stronger than their god. So they knock down the pterodactyl and put up the robot. That's their new god. The sad thing is that these guys could have banged the beautiful gill-women if they had only stuck around.

It was so exhausting, much more than anything on *Targets*. Almost killed me. It went on and on. Finally, I wrote this narration which is told by one of the guys on the Russian ship. At the end of the film, the

Russians find this little stone which has a sculpture of one of the women on it. But it's too late, and they blast off anyway. The narration comes on: "I know she's here. Maybe someday I'll find her. Maybe I'll die trying." Which is a switch on the last line of *The Lady from Shanghai* [Orson Welles, 1948]!

Anyway, it was an awful picture with nothing to commend it except some inside jokes and some nice shots. If I had to do it again today, I'd have the women fighting each other, ripping each other's cockleshells off (they wore shells over their breasts). I'd make it sexy. But now, as you can tell, it's just lyrical and simply awful. This took up so much time that I couldn't get to the Karloff picture. I had worked on *Gill-Women* until October 1966.

The evolution of *Targets* is quite interesting, because we started out by having Karloff as a heavy, a strangler. Then, I had an idea for a joke. The only fairly good sequence in *The Terror* was the flood. It lasted twenty minutes. I was going to cut it down to two minutes and open the picture with it. "The End" comes on the screen. We cut to the inside of a projection room. Lights come on. Sitting in the front row is Boris Karloff. Next to him is Roger Corman. Boris turns to him and says, "Well, Roger, it's really frightful, isn't it?" From that came an idea. I said, "Hey, wait a minute. Karloff is an actor! Then the footage is of him as an actor, and I don't have to use it as the story." Believe it or not, that little thing made all the difference in the world. Then I could pawn off the *Terror* footage; I didn't have to take credit for it.

So, first Karloff was the heavy. Now he's an actor. He's been playing horror-monster parts all his life, and he hates it. What he really wants to do is to be Cary Grant. So he goes into his room in the daytime (I like murder in the daytime), he pushes a secret button, and there's his dressing room. He puts on a handsome mask, and he goes out and strangles women in supermarkets. I wanted that, because the floor of the supermarket is great for dollying. You know, you have this shot of a murder, and you pan up, and a sign says, "PEAS REDUCED THIS WEEK." This shows you the kinds of ideas you can have when you're desperate.

But we were still working under the theory that Karloff would be the heavy. Finally, Polly and I decided that was a stupid idea. What were we going to do? Make another picture like *The Gill-Women*? Or would we do something good? Polly said that we should have a modern killer. We both decided that the most modern, terrifying murderer—*modern horror*—was the sniper in Texas.

We started to develop a story about Karloff as an actor and a boy like that sniper. Originally, the two met early in the picture, and they knew each other. As the script developed, we thought more and more that they shouldn't meet. I took the treatment to Sam Fuller and asked him for his views on it. Sam had some great ideas and helped us a lot with the construction of the story. I wrote the script based on that treatment. Roger liked it, and we cast it. Roger paid for the whole picture. It's all his money. $130,000.

Q: What about this "Why Gun Control?" angle that was used in the film's publicity and was tacked on to the film as a prologue? How socially conscious did you intend the film to be?
A: I didn't at all. The gun control pitch came about because Senator Kennedy was shot after Paramount bought the film. As you know, everybody felt weird about censorship and violence. Paramount thought the gun control notion would be a respectable way of selling the picture. I felt that it wouldn't be good for the picture financially, because message pictures are usually box-office poison. But frankly, if they hadn't put that on, I don't think the picture would have been released this year. Everybody was scared.

The gun control angle helped us with some critics. It also hurt us with several critics who started to look for a message or a statement about Why He Did It. We didn't tell why he did it. We never wanted to. The ad said, "This Picture Sheds a Little Light on a Dark Topic." I don't think we shed much light on it. I wasn't trying to shed light on it. I just wanted to *show* the thing. In fact, the most horrifying thing about these murders is that there doesn't seem to be any reason commensurate with the size of the crime. So I didn't have any socially conscious motivations at all. By the way, that prologue has now been taken off the picture.

Q: Were you satisfied with the narrative structure of *Targets*—telling two stories at once?
A: It was very tough to do. While we were making it the nagging worry was: would it work to tell the two stories so independently of each other? I always thought it would because audiences have seen enough movies so that they would just *know* the two of them would meet. Just because he's Boris Karloff and the boy is the other star of picture. Whether they knew it or not, they would feel it. It's a sort of unspoken quality of suspense.

But it's not easy to tell a story like that. On the one hand, you're worried about whether the audience can jump from one thing to another. On the other hand, that's good, because if a scene gets dull, you can cut away to the other story without an excuse. I tried very much not to cut on moves or subject matter the way Brooks did in *In Cold Blood*. I did it once, when I panned from Karloff to a table and then cut to an identical pan to the boy. If I had to do it again, I'd cut the pan. It's too self-conscious.

Q: Although you would like to avoid self-consciousness, there seem to be many rather obvious "quotes" in the film. For example, when the boy is arranging the bodies of his family, it reminded me of Anthony Perkins cleaning up after the murder of Janet Leigh in *Psycho*. Also, when the boy drops his guns and is reaching for them, that reminded me of Robert Walker going after the lighter in *Strangers on a Train*.
A: The *Psycho* one wasn't conscious. Although the cleanliness idea was the same, it's not really done in the same way. Perkins is much more thorough than my boy. The sequence in *Psycho* is phenomenally brilliant, and I don't particularly like the scene in *Targets*. It came out of something that the Whitman boy really did in Texas. He put his wife and mother to bed after he killed them. I thought it was a chilling touch, so I used it in the film. He buried them, so to speak. The cleaning-up was just carrying that out. If I had thought of *Psycho*, the sequence might have been a little better.

The *Strangers* reference wasn't conscious either. When I saw the footage, I realized what I had done, but not while I was shooting. The most fascinating thing is that it was all subconscious. Of course, *all* of that drive-in sequence is *Strangers*: timing, dusk, music. I didn't know that at the time. About three months later, I saw *Strangers* again and said, "Jesus Christ! Look at this!" However, I made some references consciously. For example, there's a shot from the top of the tank as the boy runs away—I pan from the stuff he left behind over to him running. That's from *North by Northwest*, when Cary Grant runs out of the U.N.—a shot I've always loved.

Q: What do you think the relevance of these cinematic quotes is? Do you think they're a valid form of self-expression?
A: Just as much as in any other art. Novelists will quote and even imitate other writers for a definite purpose. I think most novelists begin by consciously imitating others to get a certain effect, not as parody or homage, but because the other writers "do it good," and you know it'll be good if you do it their way.

Sometimes you're criticized for stealing. On the contrary, I think it's admirable, because nothing's original anymore. It's all been done. They were doing it in the silent days—all this split-screen junk and fast cutting. I just interviewed Allan Dwan, and he said that he had done it way back when he was making films in the 1920s. He said, "That's the kind of stuff we threw away when we grew up."

One of my pleasures in making films is sometimes to reproduce shots that I've seen and loved. For example, I love one of the corniest shots ever done. You see it in any Johnny Mack Brown Western: the guy rides by, and you pan back to see the people who are chasing him. I just love that shot, so I used it in the chase in *Targets*. It's a good piece of grammar, a good sentence. It says, "Here he goes; now let's see how far back they are." It's a continuous movement, and the audience knows that nothing's been manipulated, that it's real. I don't think it's possible for anyone who's starting to make films today not to be influenced by what's gone before. Ford, Hawks, Dwan, and these other directors have already done everything, and *they* were all influenced by Griffith. Unless you're some sort of primitive talent, you have to know the history of what came before to be any good.

Also, I think that in my film, there's a criticism of other films. When I make a picture, I'm criticizing other pictures by doing something that is opposed to the way others are doing it. Sternberg once said that *The Salvation Hunters* was a criticism of other pictures. They said, "What do you mean?" He said, "All the others were fast, and mine was slow." Well, *Targets* is a criticism of other pictures in a way, too, because I don't split the screen, I don't have any arty cutting or arty shots, and I don't move the camera for no reason at all. It's a very Jesuit film—self-denying. I didn't indulge myself at all. I was telling a thriller, and I didn't want to indulge in any ego shots. So the film is a criticism of a self-conscious style.

To give you an example, there's a shot in *Targets* of the boy going toward the tanks. He opens a chain-link gate, and the camera dollies with him, with the fence in the foreground. Behind him are all kinds of religious floats that were kept in storage and brought out during Christmas and Easter. Of course, the temptation was very great to shoot from the other side. You'd see crosses in the foreground—sort of an Aldrich shot, or Aldrich doing Welles. I love Welles, but I didn't want to do that, because everybody's doing it. I purposely said, "No. Keep it in the background. Don't get fancy." I didn't want everybody to nudge one another and say, "Oh! He's making a religious point." I just wanted to show the boy going to the tanks.

I try to avoid as much of that as possible. Whenever I'm tempted, I try not to. I've been thinking of doing an absolutely insane baroque movie next, but I probably won't, because I prefer the simplicity of Hawks, Walsh, Ford, and even Hitchcock. Hitchcock doesn't have any arty shots. They may be odd, but they're always done for an emotional, not an artistic, effect—like the cut to the high angle in *The Man Who Knew Too Much* when Stewart hears that his son has been kidnapped. It's got to hit you in an emotional way.

Q: One critic said that *Targets* was the logical movie for a film critic to make. He was referring to your cinematic quotes. But he expressed bitterness and resentment.
A: Yes, most American film critics resent any sense of passion for movies. For example one critic commented on the various color patterns in *Targets* and the sterility of the boy's house. He said that he doubted I had intended it. Well, this is the biggest insult of all. That was all planned in the film. It's patronizing. It's like saying, "A movie director can't think those big thoughts."

I wrote a piece for *New York* magazine about these forty educators in Santa Barbara who saw *Targets*. They attacked me for making a commercial picture, a sell-out. Sell-out! Hah! I'd hate to tell you what I got paid for *Targets*. It's funny, because I'm usually defending other directors who are accused of selling out, like Siegel, Ford, Walsh. The accusers are the same kind of people who say, "Yes, Hitchcock's really talented. It's a pity he doesn't make anything good. Those awful stories—why doesn't he make something important?" These are the people who listen to films; they don't watch them. They're concerned with the literary content and nothing beyond it.

Q: The visual style of *Targets* struck me as being very planar, almost two-dimensional. It seemed to create a flat sense of space around the characters.
A: We wanted a contrast between Karloff's world and the boy's world, so we were careful with the color control. The Karloff sequences were all brown, gold, yellow—warm colors. The boy's sequences were green, blue, white—cold colors. I wanted to make the boy's home, as much as possible, like the homes here in the San Fernando Valley. The houses really are that way—blank walls. We made it even more bare. We wanted a kind of sterility. What Norman Mailer calls "The Plastic Society." I was very much influenced by Mailer's essays on architecture, particularly *Cannibals and Christians*, in the whole concept of the boy's life. Rather than give a reason for the murders, I just wanted to convey that the boy

is an outgrowth of this kind of society. In fact, at one point I wanted to shoot the film during Christmas out here, because the street decorations in L.A. are not to be believed. The plastic angels on Van Nuys Boulevard are just marvelous. Someday, I will shoot a horror story during Christmas in L.A.

Q: What about this two-dimensional aspect?
A: It comes from not wanting to be decorative. I wanted a kind of simplicity. I tried to get more shadows and depth into the Karloff scenes, but I don't think it worked that well. I think the boy's scenes are much more successful. If I could reshoot the film I'd do many things differently.

Q: I think a tension between sophistication and your desire for simplicity is very apparent in *Targets*. It gives the film an unusual sense of depth at certain points—for example, in the scene where Karloff comes toward the boy at the foot of the movie screen, and the boy shoots first at Karloff's image on the screen and then at the real Karloff. In one sense, this scene has sophisticated connotations: illusion and reality, schizophrenia, and all that. In another sense, though, it's the simplest and most innocent story in the world: the old story of the cowboy in the early 1900s who shot at the villain on the screen when he saw a movie for the first time.
A: You're right. I was more worried about that scene than anything else in the picture. I thought that we stood the chance of getting laughed out of the theater. The idea was Sam Fuller's. Sam has a simpler, more basic approach to a story than I do. At first, I found the scene hard to believe in. Then I embraced it as a marvelous kind of melodramatic thing.

Of course, the whole drive-in scene is illusion-reality. The boy shooting through the screen is like reality breaking through illusion. Originally I wanted to have a shot of the whole drive-in from above the candy stand. Slowly the camera would start moving in toward the screen. It goes all the way in, and then you see the gun poking through the screen. We couldn't do it, because it was too complicated. What you saw was a compromise; it was done with a cut. But the idea was the same: looking at an illusion and out of it comes this harsh reality.

I think that what you saw is that I tried to intellectualize the moment for myself. I had to say, "Now, what am I doing here?" I thought it was hokey and melodramatic, but also very theatrical and effective. So, all through the picture, with the plot, I tried to prepare for that moment. For that reason, I think it works.

One critic made an interesting point. He said that he thought the ending was not meant to be realistic. He thought that it was my way of saying that art would triumph over reality. Although I really didn't have that in mind, I thought it was a very nice way of reading the ending. I think Karloff wins in the picture because I wanted him to.

Q: Yes, but do you have any particular feelings about this tension?
A: Well, I think that's something you've spotted in me. I have an intellectual background. My father is an artist. On the other hand, I'm attracted to the less intellectual aspects of things. I try to fight against that. I respond emotionally—and I suppose intellectually, too—to Hawks, Walsh, Hitchcock. I have that duality, that tension in me. If it comes through in the picture, that's good, because it's part of me.

You see, a Walsh picture like *High Sierra* has much more than most people see. It's intuitive—*intelligent* rather than intellectual. I like to see that intuitive intelligence at work. With the exception of Welles, who is, I think, more consciously intellectual, I like the intuitive directors better—Ford, Walsh, Hawks. I know I work better when I do things intuitively. For instance, I thought some of the best stuff in *Targets* was the boy's characterization. I don't know how he behaved in real life, but I followed my emotions. It's been successful; audiences are chilled by that.

Also, I must say I'm attracted to the kind of action film that I would like to make and am *going* to make. I think sequences in *Targets* work on an action level. However, I don't think I could make a pure action film, unfortunately. I probably don't have the purity to do it.

So, I'm fighting against the intellectual part of my own nature, I guess. For example, I think the Karloff sequences, which are intellectual, are the weakest things in the picture. The best sequences are the drive-in, the freeway shooting, and the chase. I get the biggest kick out of seeing them with an audience and feeling the silence when they're really gripped. I watched the film with my agent in a projection room, and after it was over, I heard him let go of his breath. That was the biggest kick I got—the kind of emotional involvement I want.

That's why I think Hitchcock is so good. He has that ability to really manipulate an audience. It's just like making people laugh. But I get more satisfaction out of suspense, because it's harder to do. People will laugh at a lot of things: look at all the TV shows. To make somebody really nervous is very difficult.

People say, "Oh, Hitchcock. The Master of Suspense. Big deal." Well, wait a minute. That's not so easy to do. Film is the most emotional medium in the world. That's why this whole literary approach, publishing scripts and so on, is so ridiculous. Film affects you. It has nothing to do with anything else. If you're able to stop and think about a movie, which you can't do if it's done well, then it's after all "just a movie." Something has to happen; it must come into your eyes and affect you.

Q: What are your future projects?
A: One film I want to do very much is based on a book called *The Looters*. Hopefully, I'll produce and direct it for Cinema Center. It's a kind of gangster picture, a thriller. It's the story of a bank robbery and its effect on a small town, the Mafia, and the FBI. I'm going to try to make a movie that never lets up. No build-up, start right out with a fifteen-minute bank robbery, then no let-up. It has a lot of coincidence, but I'm beginning not to mind coincidence in movies. Someone once said to Chaplin, "This is a lousy scene. Don't you think it's too much of a coincidence?" Chaplin said, "Do you think it's convenient?" The guy said, "No." Chaplin said, "Well, then it's all right. I don't mind coincidence. Life is coincidence." This would be a bigger production than *Targets*. About a million dollars. It'll be a regular picture. You know: a *movie*. For people. For a movie company. The executive producer might want to make an expose of the Mafia. All right, but I'm more interested in making an exciting picture. By the way, they originally wanted Don Siegel to direct but couldn't get him, so he recommended me, which was a great compliment. It'll have a Siegel quality.

I'm anxious to do a few other things. *Death on the Sixth Day* would be a great suspense story involving a cross-country chase. It's from a book by the man who wrote *What Ever Happened to Baby Jane?* Another possible project is *The Last Picture Show* based on a novel by Larry McMurtry. It takes place in a small Texas town during the early 1950s and you'd see the decline of a small town symbolized by the gradual degeneration of its movie house. The soundtrack would be all songs from that period—"The Hit Parade," etc. What I'm most excited about, though, is a project on Hollywood from 1909 to the present. It's about a Dwan-Griffith-like figure: great instinctive genius done to death by the system, self-consciousness. . . .

Also, Hawks has indicated he might produce some pictures that I'd direct. You know, Hawks said a wonderful thing about some of the action scenes in *Targets*. He said, "That stuff's good, and that stuff's hard to do." That to me was the ultimate compliment.

Without a Dinosaur

Gordon Gow / 1972

From *films and filming*, June 1972.

In the American cinema, he is the man of the hour. Peter Bogdanovich has made it in the financial as well as the artistic areas of appreciation. Made it with *The Last Picture Show*, beyond question. Although there are some of us—quite a number, probably—who would have said that in terms of cinema art and concomitant sociology he had already done handsomely in his first, less famous effort, *Targets*: a skilled juxtaposition of two stories, one about a young gun-crazy killer, sniping away madly in contemporary Los Angeles, and the other about an elderly horror star (Boris Karloff), still at home in his period chillers but quite disorientated by the seemingly motiveless violence in the real world around him.

There is a choice little scene in *Targets* where Bogdanovich, in a bit part as a young and eager director of second-rate movies, calls to see Karloff at his home and looks compulsively at the old movie unreeling on the television set. "It's *The Criminal Code*," he cries, "Howard Hawks directed this picture." And Karloff, who is in it, replies with a quiet, "I know."

The newest Bogdanovich film, *What's Up, Doc?*, while taking its title from the well-known Bugs Bunny question, is basically inspired by quite a different work by Hawks, his 1938 comedy with Katharine Hepburn and Cary Grant and a leopard and a dinosaur and a dog, *Bringing Up Baby*. That is the motivating thing. Barbra Streisand and Ryan O'Neal are in it, and Bogdanovich calls it "a kind of combination of a Feydeau farce, with much running in and out of rooms and slamming of doors, and a kind of screwball comedy, such as *Bringing Up Baby* was—the sort of comedy Hollywood made in the 1930s and the early 1940s. It plays awfully fast—it's ninety-three minutes. And there's a twelve-minute chase in it, which cost a great deal of money to make. It took us four weeks just to do the chase, with four cars and a grocery cart, all through San Francisco—all real, no process. It's a Buster Keaton kind of chase."

Cinematic references come frequently into a conversation with Bogdanovich, whose predilection is firmly for American films of the past, including many that were made before he was of filmgoing age. "It was my idea to have a Howard Hawks season at the Museum of Modern Art in New York, and I arranged it in 1962. And the real reason I did that was so that I could see the Hawks films I hadn't seen. Out of the twenty-seven or twenty-eight films that we ran in that season, I'd only seen eleven or twelve and the rest were all new to me." He used also to be a constant viewer of old movies on TV, rather like the young enthusiast he portrayed in *Targets*. "It was a weekly ritual to go through the TV listings, and see what was on and who directed what." Therefore he follows the trend, at the age of thirty-one, of looking back rather than forward: a sizable trend, this—and one that Bogdanovich acknowledges.

"Perhaps people have discovered something that I've suspected for a while, which is that the future's rather bleak and the present is not terribly pleasant. So where else can we look but to the past? It interests me. I think one learns from the past. It inspires me. The main reason I wanted to do *The Last Picture Show* was because the novel is set back in the 1950s. The book was rather more amorphous than the movie is: it wasn't specifically 1951 and 1952 in the book, and when we started to do the movie we fixed that specific period rather than just the fifties as a whole."

His personal affection for the American cinema of the era is discernible in the emphasis placed on the two films we see being screened at the decaying picture show: Vincente Minnelli's *Father of the Bride* (1950) and more especially *Red River* (1948), which was directed by Howard Hawks. His enthusiasm for directors of the Hawks and John Ford vintage would seem to imply less enchantment with contemporary American filmmakers.

"Most of the directors that I like have gotten older and have either ceased to make pictures or make them very infrequently, so that there isn't much for me to go and see. To see and love, that is—there's quite a bit to see and admire; but none of the younger directors have filled the same needs as the older ones for me. This is a very personal opinion. I don't want to be a critic on this point and say that movies are not as good as they used to be—though indeed I feel that way. I'm just talking now about the American film. The European film is in a healthier condition than the American. I mean, in France I can say that there's Truffaut and Chabrol, whom I admire a great deal; and I used to admire Godard until he got so political and so obscure. There's Bertolucci in Italy. I'm not so familiar with the British cinema. Now there are young American directors I admire, like Cassavetes and Bob Rafelson. And there are others. But looking at the situation generally, it seems to me that the artists of every country should really remain faithful to their own origins. Perhaps I don't mean that they *should*, but it seems to me that they're at their best when they do. And when they become overly influenced by another culture, they tend to become muddied, I think. Some American directors have become so influenced by Antonioni and Fellini and Bergman and Godard that they've lost their American identity, and have not replaced it with anything really substantial. And it seems to me that the great vigor of the American cinema has always been its Americanism."

One notices, too, in *The Last Picture Show*, a return of stylistic effects that have tended to evaporate over the years. The slow dissolve is employed once or twice, most notably at the end when the two-shot of Cloris Leachman and Timothy Bottoms is superimposed for quite a long time over the final image of the town. "It just seemed like a nice technique to revive for this particular story, since it was meant to be slow moving, and we were covering a period of a year. There's a long slow dissolve at the end of *Targets* too, though. It's a very nice technique, the dissolve, which sort of went out of favor for a few years. I don't see any reason not to use it when it's right. It had become rather over-used, just at any point; and I think when the French stopped using it, and then everybody picked that up, it was nice to get away from the dissolve for a while so that we could re-evaluate its use. We were just using it for time lapses, conventionally, all the time, which is unnecessary because you can just cut from one place to another. But when you want to indicate something else, to give a different mood, it's nice to use it. But for *The Last Picture Show* I wasn't using it just because it was a technique directors used in the 1950s. I really wasn't consciously trying to recreate a fifties film. It never occurred to me. I was just telling the story as simply as possible, because I like telling stories simply, and I don't think that picture warranted any fancy camera work. There are a lot of things in it that I don't think you would see in an average fifties film: in fact, I doubt that it could have been made in the fifties, because of the sex and the language and so on."

The somewhat rebellious employment of monochrome camerawork, at a time when virtually all feature films in the English language are being shot in color, gives *The Last Picture Show* a certain apartness. It looks unusual. It looks right; but, as distinct from that rightness to its time and place and its pervasive mood, it seems to be making a stand for another neglected technique, black-and-white photography.

"I used it because I didn't want the film to look pretty. I didn't want it to be a nostalgia piece like *Summer of '42*, which I hadn't seen at the time—but anyway, that was what I was trying to avoid. Color always had a tendency to prettify, and I didn't want that. Orson Welles encouraged me. In fact, he suggested I do it in black-and-white, at one time when we were talking about how to achieve depth of field and sharpness of image in a certain way, he said 'You can't do it in color—you'll have to do it in black-and-white.' Well, several months before that, the writer Larry McMurtry had also suggested that we shoot it in black-and-white. And I said, 'Of course it should be in black-and-white but I don't think that anybody's going to let me do it'—and I just sort of let it go. I realized, being a fellow with a memory about movies, that if I were making this film even fifteen years ago, this is the kind of film that would have been shot in black-and-white. And since those days were better in terms of filmmaking, and nobody was put under the restriction of being told they had to shoot in color because of television, the great directors who used both color and black-and-white made the right choices. Ford would shoot *Wagonmaster* in black-and-white and then he'd shoot *The Quiet Man* in color, then go back and shoot in black-and-white for *The Sun Shines Bright* and shoot *Mogambo* in color. You alternated, you know, depending on the story and not on any kind of economic consideration. However, I didn't think I'd be allowed to make that kind of choice for *The Last Picture Show*. But then when Orson suggested it—rather forcefully—I said I thought he was right and that I'd ask the producer, Bert Schneider. He knew Bert himself, because I'd introduced them, and he said, 'I think Bert will go along with it.' So I went and talked to Bert, and indeed Orson was right. Bert was rather sanguine about it."

Whether this will prove influential remains to be seen. A return to the kind of flexibility Bogdanovich indicated in respect of Ford's work could be of decided benefit to current English-language cinema. "*The Last Picture Show* is a tremendous success in the States, and nobody has ever said, 'Gee, it's too bad it wasn't in color.' In fact, almost unanimously, everybody has said what a relief it is to see a picture in black-and-white. Also in black-and-white, it's much easier to maintain print quality. And it's much cheaper. So I hope the picture brings back that freedom for the director to shoot in whatever medium he chooses for the story. I don't think by any means we should have all black-and-white. Color is a wonderful medium. I've just used it on *What's Up, Doc?* But if a director feels a story is right for black-and-white, he should be allowed to do it, as any visual artist would be allowed to work with the tools at his disposal. You wouldn't say to a painter, 'No, no, you can't paint that with charcoal, you must do it in oils.' That's silly."

Thinking back to *Targets*, effectively photographed in color, I wondered if he had decided immediately in that case to choose the accepted norm. "I didn't originally. When I started work on it, I would have hoped to make it in black-and-white. But Roger Corman, who financed it, persuaded me that color was more commercial. And, as it turned out, I'm very glad I shot it in color, because part of the effectiveness of that picture, at least to me, is in its plastic surfaces: that very American plastic blue and all that, which is I'm afraid very much a part of a certain culture in the States. I never would have achieved that look in black-and-white. We really controlled the color as much as we possibly could, and worked rather hard on that—on what everybody would wear, for example. All the Karloff sequences were in warm colors: brown and gold and yellow. Consciously, you know. The boy's colors were very cold: blue, green, white. That was very carefully done—as much as we could when we were out on the streets. Sometimes we'd get some wrong color working its way in. But we even got very lucky up to the drive-in movie, where the two stories meet. The drive-in was just luckily painted blue and yellow."

Both *Targets* and *The Last Picture Show*, in their respective settings of California and Texas, show a sterile social background, driving the young to extremes and even to neurosis, more evident in *Targets* with the instinctive violence of the boy. There is a contrast between this sterility and the comfortable middle-class American background depicted in Minnelli's *Father of the Bride*, with comic family tensions that will be ironed out smoothly by the end. Bogdanovich, however, did not incorporate his excerpt from the Minnelli film into the context of *The Last Picture Show* to make any ironic comment: "My reason for using *Father of the Bride* was more pragmatic. I really wanted to show a 1950 film in which there were some recognizable actors. I also wanted it to be a good picture, not just any old movie. And so I picked this one because Elizabeth Taylor is still well-known to audiences today, and yet they can see her and say, 'My goodness, look how young she looks,' and immediately we have the feeling of a period piece. Because we don't say anywhere on the screen that this is 1951; and so for the first reel or so you're not sure, if you haven't been told."

In this respect, he is right in line with contemporary cinema, and here we have a slight inconsistency in his veneration of the Hollywood past. At one time, a period movie would have begun with a caption on the screen giving the date. Bogdanovich doesn't go along with that: "It bothers me. I don't like writing on the screen if it's a talking film. There are certain old-fashioned things that I *don't* like. I don't like titles on the screen and I don't like wipes. I don't mind them as conventions of the past, but I certainly don't want to revive them. Just like I enjoy a lot of good music in other people's movies, but I can never get myself to use it. I can name you any number of movies that had the most brilliant scores, from *Citizen Kane* through the Hitchcock movies, but I'm embarrassed to have a movie scored: you know, an orchestra playing in the background that isn't source music. In other words, as in *The Last Picture Show*, whenever you do hear music it's because it's playing in the room or in the car or somewhere."

The social aridity depicted in both of his first films does not necessarily denote a primary concern: "I'm not a particularly socially conscious person. I wouldn't say that every place in America was the way that Anarene, Texas, looked in 1951. But Anarene, Texas, looked that way in 1951. I wouldn't say that all of America was like Los Angeles in 1968 when I made *Targets*, and I wouldn't say that everybody is like that boy. But a great many people live in that way; and since I was telling a story about that boy, that was what I had to portray. I don't like to make microcosm stories, and say that something is symbolic of the rest of the country. I didn't mean them really as criticisms of America as a country, although it is true that they reflect a certain aridity in American life; and what more can I say about that than—there it is. So what I meant was to criticize only the specific segments of the nation that I was portraying."

There is a pretty sharp distinction here between Bogdanovich's films and those of the veterans whose work he loves. John Ford might have observed prejudice with a critical eye in *The Sun Shines Bright*, but in the long run a sentimental glow of goodness settled upon the scene. Aridity was hardly the word; although, as Bogdanovich points out, "*The Man Who Shot Liberty Valance* shows rather a bleak future. He shows that what the West becomes is not what he would like it to become. But I'm glad you have said that my films are different in this way, because a lot of people have said that *The Last Picture Show* is very much a John Ford film, or very much a Howard Hawks film; they'll say anything, because you've given them the clue that you like a certain director. I think perhaps, though, that you could relate certain things in *The Last Picture Show* to Ford—the longshot at the end of the funeral scene is very much of a Ford composition, because of the big sky and all that. I know that I was thinking of him, because I said, 'We've got a Ford sky—let's shoot it.' But the placement of the longshot is at the end of the funeral scene rather than at the beginning of it. The standard way to use an establishing shot, of course, is to start with it, and then go into your close-ups. Well, we do the whole funeral scene in close-ups and then go into the longshot. That's something I learned from Hitchcock. I never noticed Ford particularly doing that. But the shot itself is very much thinking of Ford, while the impact of it is very much thinking of Hitchcock.

"Those are things that you learn, you know. It's not a question of being influenced. It's a question of looking at movies, and studying the craft of movies. I'm making movies, after all, in 1970; not in 1909, you know. And since everything came from Griffith, of course we're influenced. A painter is influenced today by centuries of art, as a musician is by everything since Bach. I don't think there's much that's original under the sun. That doesn't seem to me to be a criterion of merit—originality. Certainly not originality in technique."

Unsurprisingly, Bogdanovich wishes he had been born twenty or thirty years sooner. He doesn't remember at what time of his life the wish began. "I certainly don't remember thinking it when I was a teenager. But it's something I've wished as I've grown older. I mean if I'd been born sixty years ago I would have been able to direct Cary Grant. On the other hand, probably if I'd been living then I'd have said what a pity it was that I wasn't working in films around the time Griffith made *The Birth of a Nation*. One always wants to be back somewhere else—or ahead somewhere else. Nobody's ever happy where they are. That's part of the human condition, isn't it?—the grass is always greener, and all that."

Bogdanovich's documentary film about Ford, which he has called *Directed by John Ford*, was edited at the same time he was editing *The Last Picture Show*. "There are four interviews in the documentary, with Wayne, Stewart, Fonda and Ford himself. And those were all shot between 1968 and 1969, but then I couldn't begin cutting the film, because none of the clips that I wanted to use had been cleared. It took forever for the studios to come up with them. When Ford saw the completed film, his comment was that I'd done a good job on a dull subject."

Making the transition from film historian and critic to director was, to hear Bogdanovich tell it, no great effort of persuasion on his part, but something that came about by good fortune and circumstance. "I never tried to make a film before Roger Corman offered me the chance. I was a would-be director, but I was in the cupboard. I wasn't coming around saying, 'I want to direct movies.' I didn't try to put together projects or anything like that. Except one project: from the time I was about nineteen I tried to buy the rights to a short novel by John Galsworthy, *The Apple Tree*, and I always wanted to do that, but never could get enough money to buy it—though it was rather cheap. And, oh, I tried to write a script here and there—I didn't really get anywhere. I never like to do things on speculation. I like to get a job, or be offered something. I never had much incentive for doing things with the hope that they might work. That's not my nature. I never wrote for myself or anything like that—I did it for money. I was just barely earning a living by writing about movies. And I was getting a little help from relatives. I never thought of myself as a critic, really; because I began in the theatre when I was fifteen as an actor. I studied acting for four years with Stella Adler. Then at nineteen I directed my first play, off-Broadway, a play by Clifford Odets, *The Big Knife*. Followed a couple of years later by some other stage productions in summer seasons in New York State: Agatha Christie's *Ten Little Indians*, and *Camino Real* by Tennessee Williams, Kaufman and Hart's *Once in a Lifetime*. In fact, later on, I brought *Once in a Lifetime* back to off-Broadway. So the only reason I was writing criticism was because it was a way to get into movies free, frankly, and it was a way to make money until I could do what I wanted to do.

"Then I moved to California in 1964, after the calamitous disaster of *Once in a Lifetime*, which was a big flop off-Broadway and lost all its money. I continued to write feature articles, and some books. And I met Roger Corman at a screening. He had read my stuff in *Esquire* and he said, 'You're a writer—do you want to write for pictures?' So I said, 'Sure I'd like to write for pictures—what do you want me to write?' He said, 'Well, I'd like you to write me a combination of *The Bridge on the River Kwai* and *Lawrence of Arabia*—but inexpensive to produce.' So I said, 'Oh, well, that's not too much of a problem. I'll think of something.' So we thought up a story based on a real event in the Second World War. I wrote, I think, a rather good script. It was called *The Criminals* and it was about an actual happening during the Nazi occupation in Poland. Big picture. And probably not inexpensive. But it hasn't been made, and the screenplay has reverted to me, and I know that if I wanted to make it myself I could get to make it now, but I'm not interested in it really. So it's available for anybody out there who'd like to buy it. Good script.

"Then, before I'd finished writing that script in fact, Roger asked me to work with him on a new picture he was starting called *The Wild Angels*, as a general assistant. So I worked on that for what began as six weeks and turned into twenty-two. And really it was a paid—not very highly paid, but in fact a paid course in the making of films. I'd never worked on a picture. I'd been on a set only a couple of times, and then I hadn't observed very much. But on *The Wild Angels* I did just about everything you can do in a movie, from rewriting about 80 per cent of the script—for which I didn't receive credit—to finding locations, helping the casting, setting up certain sequences and designing certain things, making sure the lunches were there on time, acting in the picture, and then ultimately directing the second unit. Roger fell behind schedule because the Hell's Angels in the picture didn't like him and kept sabotaging their own motorcycles. So Roger said, 'We're going to have to create a second unit.' And I said, 'Who's going to direct that?' He said, 'I don't care who directs it. My secretary can direct it. You can direct it.' He was rather angry that day. So I said, 'All right—I'd love to direct it.' And then he was pleased with the work I did on that and he gave me the opportunity to make *Targets*. The financing came right out of his own pocket, $130,000. He got his money back. I don't know that he made much of a profit, but he didn't lose anything.

"Between *Targets* and *The Last Picture Show* I worked on two projects, and tried to fool around with several others. I got paid to not make three pictures. And then I read *The Last Picture Show* and tried to put that together. It turned out to be fairly easy, because Bert Schneider, who had produced *Easy Rider*, liked it very much when I went to him with it, and he agreed to do it immediately. But before that there had been almost a year during which I'd been trying to buy the rights to it myself, and failed."

What's Up, Doc? was instigated very quickly, by comparison. "Barbra Streisand and John Calley, the head of Warner Bros., saw *The Last Picture Show* in a rough cut in early May of 1971 and they liked it very much. Barbra told me that after the first reel she turned to Calley and said, 'I want him'—meaning me. So they asked me to direct a script which they had, and which Barbra had committed to do; and I read it and said I didn't want to do it. Well, they were a little bit upset, but I said, 'Look, let's do something else.' This script they had was a kind of a comedy-drama with a lot of social overtones, and I didn't like it at all. But I said, 'I'd love to work with Barbra. It'd be fun. And we all like each other, so let's do something different from this.' And they said, 'Well, what do you have in mind?' I said, 'Well, I'd like to do kind of a screwball comedy.' And I gave them a two-sentence idea, which had just occurred to me. Barbra strikes me as the first person we've had on the screen who's a little bit like Carole Lombard, and I thought she could play that sort of thing—and yet I was thinking of a movie that doesn't have Carole Lombard in it: *Bringing Up Baby*.

"So we had to work fast on the script. Because of Barbra's commitments, and Ryan O'Neal's, we had to start shooting in August and this was May. We got a script done with two different sets of writers—first, Robert Benton and David Newman who did *Bonnie and Clyde* and then Buck Henry. Both of them went through three drafts. So there was quite a bit of work."

There is, surprisingly, no animal in it. "No, well, it's not that close to *Bringing Up Baby*. It's quite close—but no animal. There's not even a dinosaur. In fact, I asked Howard Hawks to read the script and he said, 'You haven't got anything as good as the dinosaur.' I said, 'No—we couldn't steal that, Howard.' He said, 'You haven't got a leopard. Nor a dog.' I said, 'No.' He said, 'Well, it's all right—just don't let 'em be cute.' I followed that advice as best I could."

An Interview with Peter Bogdanovich

Martin Rubin / 1974

From the movie tie-in edition of *Daisy Miller*, by Henry James (New York: Warner Paperback Library, 1974). Reprinted by permission of the author.

Peter Bogdanovich's film credits include *Targets* (1968; director-producer-writer), *The Last Picture Show* (1971; director-co-writer), the feature-length documentary, *Directed by John Ford* (1971), *What's Up, Doc?* (1972; director-producer-co-writer), and *Paper Moon* (1973; director-producer). His sixth film, *Daisy Miller*, was shot on the actual locations referred to in James's story; principal photography began August 20, 1973, in Rome and was completed November 8 in Vevey, Switzerland. Mr. Bogdanovich has also written several books on the movies, the latest being *Pieces of Time*, a 1973 Esquire–Arbor House publication. He contributes a monthly column on Hollywood to *New York Magazine*. The following interview took place at Mr. Bogdanovich's home in Bel Air, California, February 18–19, 1974.

Q: How did you come across *Daisy Miller*?
A: Just one of those things I read. It's interesting, the way this has worked out, because I was going to do *The Apple Tree*, a story written by John Galsworthy in 1916. Actually, the story is similar to *Daisy Miller* in many ways: it's a love story about missed opportunities, it's about class differences, it's about an unwillingness to commit oneself emotionally to something that is alien or different.

But Galsworthy's story is much more sentimental. The girl in it is completely different. She's a little like Rima in *Green Mansions*, an innocent savage. Her name is Megan, a Welsh girl in the hills of Devon. This Englishman up from Oxford falls in love with her one summer, and she with him. He goes to town to buy her some clothes so he can take her away, and he doesn't have the nerve to go back. Twenty-five years later he comes to the area again and remembers. At that point he finds out that after he left the girl committed suicide.

I had been planning to do this story since I was about sixteen. For years I tried to get the rights, but they eluded me. At one time, they were owned by Jesse Lasky's widow—Lasky had meant to make the picture in the forties with John Mills and Elizabeth Taylor. Finally, when I went to Warner Bros. to make *What's Up, Doc?*, it turned out that Warner now owned the rights, and I was free to make it. So I hired Gavin Lambert to write the screenplay, and it was quite a good script, but I just didn't want to make it. Like many beloved projects, you want to do it for so long that by the time you do get to do it you just don't want to anymore. It's almost as though you'd made it already and so there's no longer any challenge left.

Then I was developing yet another story based on an incident that happened to an Italian friend of mine when he stayed at the Plaza Hotel in New York: he came out around two in the morning, it was so hot, and found an absolutely stunning girl lying on the fountain, asleep. In the story, she turns out to be this girl from Texas, a real Amazon, who hits him every time he makes a pass at her. Then it went into a cross-country trip—what I really wanted to do was to make *Lolita*, but it was not possible. I thought it would be funny with, say, Cybill Shepherd and Marcello Mastroianni. We tried to develop it, but it didn't work out, probably because it was just one good incident that wouldn't develop into a script.

So I didn't have a picture. Around about here, somehow or other, I read *Daisy Miller* again, not having read it for many years. And it seemed exactly the right thing to do, like a sign from heaven, because there was the whole idea of an Italian versus American background, which I had become interested in after going to Rome in 1969. And it also had the same basic idea as *The Apple Tree*, the same theme of missed opportunities, yet done better, much more elegantly and less sentimentally. And a great part for Cybill Shepherd, with whom I had wanted to make another picture ever since *The Last Picture Show*. So there we were.

Q: What's most immediately striking about the film *Daisy Miller* is how faithful it is to the book. This seems a very different problem from, say, *The Last Picture Show*, where you were more involved in adaptation: selecting and cutting it down. In this film, it's more a question of interpretation than adaptation. Why did you decide to stick to the original so closely?

A: Actually, when I first decided to do the story I thought it wasn't enough for a movie. So originally Frederic Raphael and I developed a much longer story and took a lot of license with Henry James. The dialogue, for instance, was very different; it was almost all new. There were several additional incidents—such as Winterbourne sneaking up to Daisy's room and going through her things when she was out.

Q: So that it became more like an obsession. . . .
A: Right, like Jimmy Stewart in *Vertigo* or Dana Andrews in *Laura*. He was sniffing around her stuff—it became sick in a rather obvious way. And then when Winterbourne saw her with Giovanelli at the Colosseum, he rode off on a horse to the seashore, where he went into a kind of fit—his money was stolen—and it became very Dostoyevskian. Everything was also made much more explicit in terms of Daisy; she became aggressive in what was not an 1878 manner. I'm afraid I collaborated in this somewhat, and I condoned it.

I really didn't get a chance to read the original story again until I was on my way over to Europe to make the picture. But when I did, I suddenly realized that the story had been lost, that what was delicate and subtle about it had been lost behind a kind of Russian-Jewish adaptation. And I started going through the story and saying, "My God, look at all this good dialogue that's not being used!" There was a lot to do in terms of making the dialogue just a little bit easier to say, but the *ideas* for the dialogue that James wrote were wonderful. The more I read the story, the more I saw that anything obviously overlaid on it would destroy it. It was a fragile tale, and if I was going to change it in any way, it had to be done in terms of interpretation rather than in the actual sequence of events.

But frankly, it wasn't my main concern that the picture be faithful to Henry James. I didn't think, "I must be faithful to the story, or else Leon Edel and all the James scholars will be up in arms." If I had been able to think of something that was better than Henry James, in terms of telling the story, I would have done it. It's just that I thought his original stuff was better than what Raphael or I had invented. So where the movie does do something different, it's because I thought it was an improvement, or a way of fleshing out and interpreting the story or visualizing something that wasn't dealt with.

I think it's a terribly good story; however, I do feel that it is a sketch rather than a finished canvas. When James originally wrote *Daisy Miller*, he subtitled the story "A Study." Some people have wondered what he meant by that. I think perhaps James himself wondered what he meant by it, since he dropped the subtitle for the New York edition. I interpreted it this way: when a painter does a sketch for a larger canvas, he often calls that a study. In his later career, James did much larger canvases—*A Portrait of a Lady*, for one—on the same theme.

So, to me, *Daisy Miller* was always a sketch. Now I'm not doing a short movie or a sketchy one. I'm doing a feature, and I can't afford to be sketchy. But for the same reason, I would prefer to do *Daisy Miller*, as opposed to *A Portrait of a Lady* or *What Maisie Knew*, because I've got somewhere to go with it. It seemed to me there were enough hidden ambiguities that could be given some fleshing out, simply by putting actors in the roles and interpreting it a certain way. When Orson Welles made *Othello*, he didn't care so much about literalizing Shakespeare as he did about visualizing a lot of the things that in the play were spoken. I didn't do at all the same thing, but I do hope that the movie of *Daisy Miller* can stand on its own, and won't be forever stapled to the book.

Q: It would seem that your experience directing on the stage was more useful for this film than any of your others. You mentioned that your attitude in the film would have to come through mainly in interpretation rather than changing things, and this strikes me as somewhat like stage direction. For instance, one of the most important scenes, both in the book and the movie, occurs when Winterbourne talks to Daisy at Mrs. Walker's dinner party. There are three very important exchanges in that scene. In the first one, Winterbourne tells Daisy, "Your habits are those of a ruthless flirt," and she says, "Of course I'm a flirt. Did you ever hear of a nice girl that wasn't?" In the next one, Winterbourne says, "They don't understand that sort of thing here," and Daisy replies, "I thought they understood nothing else!" Then, at the end of the scene, he says, "I've offered you excellent advice," to which Daisy comes back with, "I prefer weak tea!" All three lines are very important in the book, but in the movie the second one is the least emphasized, while James makes a big thing out of it, even adding a line about Daisy's "startling worldknowledge." And this is what you're doing throughout the film, picking what to emphasize and what to underline.

A: I don't like to spell out anything for an audience. In fact, that scene is done in the movie without a cut, until Daisy stands up. I think it's terribly important, particularly in this movie, to pay attention, because there's a lot more going on than you think there is. It's the cumulative effect of the scene that's important to me, rather than each individual moment, because otherwise you can start cutting in and emphasizing every line. But it seems to me you just have to play it like a scene and the way people are.

People never react in normal conversation. I may say something that shocks the hell out of you, but you wouldn't show it on your face at all. Now James says that Winterbourne was struck by her world-knowledge. But he doesn't say that Winterbourne's face reflected that shock. I'm always surprised at how little people react in life, in normal conversation. So it seemed to me that if it was going to be an honest scene, you didn't want to overemphasize anything. Let the audience discover the meaning of it.

It was important to me that the audience should watch the scene, pay attention, and then at the *end* of it, when Daisy says, "I prefer weak tea," and walks away, you're left with Winterbourne's reaction to the *whole* scene. He's left watching her walk away—as he does through the whole picture—watches her walk away, until she doesn't come back again. And he watches her with this expression of "What? I don't understand what just happened." It isn't just the "weak tea" line he's reacting to—it's the whole scene, the point of which is that Daisy knows a lot more than you think she does.

Q: There's another emphasis you use, when Winterbourne meets Daisy at Hadrian's Villa. (In the story, it's the Palace of the Caesars.) He says, "I do want to say something," then he hesitates—"I want to say that your mother tells me she believes you're engaged."
A: Yes, that moment is pretty much invented by me; it's really not exactly that way in the story. To me, the whole movie is right in that moment. It seems to me that if Winterbourne had said anything at that moment, it might have been all right, at least in terms of their relationship. And you can see that Daisy is terribly disappointed that he doesn't say anything. You see, he's just unable—that's why he's so pathetic, apart from being reprehensible. He's unable to come out and say it to her because of his jealousy, because of his repression. And then he's left perplexed, which is how that silly ass is left every time throughout the picture.

Then some people say to me, "Well, why was she like that?" or "Why didn't he just come out and tell her he loves her?" They don't understand the mystery that goes on there, that terrible repression. And they don't understand *her* any more than Winterbourne did, which only proves that the story's still timely.

Q: Although Winterbourne is not that sympathetic in the movie, I felt he was much more unsympathetic in the book.
A: He *was* more unsympathetic in the book. So was Giovanelli. I felt that Winterbourne was a man who's dying at the beginning of the story, and he lets himself die all the way, so that by the end there's no hope for him. It takes him a long time to die, and it only takes Daisy a reel. I found Winterbourne sad and pathetic. I couldn't hate him—although I tried to, because he stands for everything I loathe. He's a coward, he's a judge, he's mean-spirited.

Q: Is it true that at one point you considered playing the Winterbourne role yourself?
A: Yes.

Q: Why?
A: Because it's very difficult to find an actor in America who looks as though he has read a book. In the history of American movies there have been very few actors like that. Orson Welles had it, in a way Bogart had it, and Jimmy Stewart, when he was younger. Montgomery Clift had it—he would have been very good casting for the part of Winterbourne, except that he would have been a little bit *too* sensitive. But I can't think of a young actor in America today who gives you the feeling that he's read a book—whether he *has* or not.

Barry Brown *looks* as though he has—he looks intelligent. So do I, but I decided not to do the part and I'm glad I didn't.

Q: The opening scene of the movie, with Randolph switching the shoes in the hotel corridor, is not in the book.
A: Well, Orson Welles once said to me, "If I were doing that picture, I'd begin with the little boy." And it stuck in my mind. So when I was discussing the script with Raphael, I quoted that line to him. He said, "Welles is a pretty good fellow to take a cue from, so why don't we do that?" And then we came up with the switching shoes business.

Q: Except for Mrs. Walker, the boy is the character with whom you take the most liberties and improvise the most. He becomes more sinister and self-asserting than he is in the book.
A: Yes. I think one of the mistakes made with children in movies is that they're too sweet—something I tried to correct in *Paper Moon*. Children are not sweet—they're savages who are slowly being tamed to live in

society. I think adorable children are either not real, or if they *are* real, you want to hit them.

I think in the book James starts Randolph off as a little bit more of a typical child—he's too sweet in the beginning of the story; then he changes, becomes nastier and funnier later. I think James never bothered to make him less sweet in the beginning, so we rewrote that and made him tougher.

I also liked the idea of there being this element of foreboding about Randolph, as if he somehow knows what's going to happen. Children do have, I think, a sixth sense, because they're closer to their feelings than adults. In a subtle way, I wanted Randolph to feel what was happening between Daisy and Winterbourne, which is why I added that abstracted little moment where he's up in the tree and goes "Bang" with the fake rifle after Winterbourne. Then, later, we see Randolph fooling around with a noose. Children are obsessed with death anyway—they're more ghoulish than grownups—and I think that fits in with the story. Of course, it all leads up to the final rejection of Winterbourne by Randolph, which was my idea of how to end the picture.

Q: Yes, that's definitely different from the book, where you feel that Winterbourne is almost patronizing the child.
A: Yes, as he does everyone else in the story.

Q: In the movie, the Miller family always talks very fast, almost comically so. Why did you do that?
A: Well, the story is full of these long, long speeches which were written by James as one huge paragraph. And it just seemed to me in reading them that that's the way they would sound: just rattling on quickly and talking about this and that. I also thought it would be funny if we meet Randolph and he talks fast, interrupts all the time, and then Daisy does it, and then the mother does it. So we finally realize where it all comes from—the mother. It's a rather amusing way of finding out that all these Millers just talk and interrupt, and they're all rude.

Q: In the movie, our first introduction to Mrs. Costello, Winterbourne's aunt, is in a steambath.
A: That was Raphael's idea. I was nervous about it for a time, and the actress was very much against it. This was the first time that her character appeared, and Millie Natwick felt that there was no way that she could

recover from the ridiculousness of that position—pouring tea in a bath. I felt that she had a point.

However, I finally decided it would be more effective if she *did* start out as a figure of fun, or at least a figure of more humor than she is in the original story, so that as the story got darker in Rome, there was a definite change. The only other way you could have shown her was in a hotel room in Vevey, and it would have been an awful lot like the scene in her room in Rome—closed, Victorian surroundings. I thought ultimately that when we see Mrs. Costello at the beginning, even *she* should be in a little more relaxed atmosphere than she is in Rome.

But when she says, "You've lived too long out of the country. You'll be sure to make some great mistake"—which I think is a very important moment—I made sure that they were out of the bath. That's the main reason I had them get out at all.

Q: A main difference between the movie and the book is that the movie is definitely more nostalgic. The idea of the lost moment is made much more explicit—for instance, in the Chillon scene, which you expanded and which ends with a very nostalgic shot of the castle receding through the carriage window.
A: Well, it was very important to me that Chillon be something that the audience remembers with some degree of pleasure. Did you like the man playing the harmonica in that scene? Some people think his music too mournful. I believe it has the advantage of making the sequence both present and past at the same time.

You see, there is this moment between Daisy and Winterbourne at Chillon, there's a possibility of something happening and it doesn't quite. Now, my feeling is that whenever there's a joyous time, there's also an inner knowledge that this time is going to end. The music gives you both things at once, because at the same time that everything they're doing is gay, the music is implying that this is going to be over. And when it's over, it will be in the past, something you remember with pleasure or regret.

Q: The character of Mrs. Walker is somewhat changed from the book.
A: Yes, she's more sexual. In the story, she was the one character who seemed to me a bit ludicrous. I felt her motivation needed an edge to it because James doesn't explain why she is so upset by Daisy, except perhaps because of propriety, which I don't think is enough.

If I'd cast Mrs. Walker the way she was written, it would have been like that lady next door in Welles's *The Magnificent Ambersons*, who tells Tim Holt, "You'll be pleased to leave my house!" But Eileen Brennan projects a quite sensual quality. And I thought if she *played* the role very much the opposite, it would be a wonderful contrast—this sort of sensuality coming out underneath. Then we invented the character of Charles, Winterbourne's friend, because I thought it would be nice to show somebody whom Mrs. Walker makes a pass at after she fails with Winterbourne.

Q: Throughout the Rome section, Daisy is associated with mirrors.
A: Well, you, being an old Douglas Sirk[1] fan, could probably tell me what that means more than I can. But one of my reasons was that using mirrors would enable me not to have to cut. It made things smoother because I could show Winterbourne in closeup and also see what he was looking at without having to cut to his point of view.

But if you want to analyze it on a more dramatic level, the mirrors tie in with the whole voyeuristic aspect of Winterbourne: he'll look but he won't touch. He'll examine with his eyes, but he won't make a move to really grasp it, except perhaps obliquely. Even at the Pincio, when he sees Daisy and Giovanelli behind the parasol, you'll notice that the way he steps forward is very much like a voyeur, he sort of tiptoes up, watching to see something, hoping that something terrible will happen.

Q: There's a very mysterious moment in the Pincio scene, when Winterbourne glimpses a lady in the background. What was that?
A: That was a remnant of something in Raphael's script that I thought worth keeping. She's an unattached woman, alone, obviously a whore or a loose woman. And she gives Winterbourne a look. He notices her—he's afraid to look at her, but he's interested, he's tempted. I thought it was necessary to show just a little bit of his sexuality and his hypocrisy—he's tempted by her just as he's tempted by Daisy in another way. It's just one of those small ambiguous moments of which the story is so full. And I also liked what happened in the Punch and Judy show during that scene.

Q: Why did you put that in?
A: It was Raphael's idea, but if you've been at all to the Pincio in Rome, it's the thing you would naturally think of for atmosphere because there is a Punch and Judy show there, and it's probably been there for hundreds of years. The man we found who did it was remarkable and I just photographed his act and used the parts of it I thought most appropriate.

What I particularly liked was the moment when Punch slays Death. I thought that was interesting, particularly in relation to how Daisy reacts to it: she just laughs, and they all laugh. It's wonderful, the idea of Punch slaying Death; it's a sort of comic contradiction of the ending.

Q: There's also a parallel in the music when Winterbourne learns of Daisy's death—it brings back the atmosphere of the Pincio.
A: Yes, I used that same organ-grinder music—"La Donna e Mobile" from Verdi—three times in the picture. The first time is when we first see Rome outside of Mrs. Costello's window, and then at the Pincio, and then when he hears of her death. Each time it's a little louder, a little closer. The song actually, if you want to get into it, is from *Rigoletto*, and it's also used there two or three times. The last time, it's heard off-scene while this terrible, tragic scene happens on-stage.

Q: The photographic style of *Daisy Miller* is much more painterly than in any of your other films. Was there any particular painter you had in mind?
A: My father, if anyone. He was very influenced by the French school, particularly the Impressionists, and yet he came from a Byzantine tradition, which means his colors were far more vivid and vibrant.

By the way, I think it's also very important to remember that this is the first movie I've made in which the time period of the story exists prior to the invention of movies.

Q: No marquees in the background.
A: Definitely not. All my other movies were set in a time when movies were a part of what people did. I think movies have had a tremendous influence not only on me but on the characters in my movies, on life in general. But since *Daisy Miller* exists in a time when there were no movies, I thought it was especially important that this be the simplest movie in terms of the way it's shot. There's very little attempt to be in any way what is called "cinematic." I don't ever try to be, but in this one I tried to be even less.

Q: How did you feel about the use of the Roman fever in the narrative? Did you ever feel uncomfortable with it? In the book it struck me as a little too deus ex machina.
A: Well, I thought it had to be very carefully set up; otherwise we would be in a lot of trouble. There was, in fact, a Roman fever, which was

malaria—malaria is Italian and means literally "bad air," *mal aria*. At that time, it was something you caught if you went to the Colosseum or places like that, which in those days were near the swamps. But I still tried to prepare the audience for it as much as possible—for instance, when Daisy says, "I guess we'll stay all winter if we don't die of the fever!" Of course, James tries to prepare you for it too.

Q: But was this the only thing that could happen when one went to Rome? It's like someone going to New York City and saying, "I guess I'll stay all winter if I don't get mugged and raped in Central Park," and then they get mugged and raped in Central Park. The End.
A: Well, I was aware that it might appear that way to a modern audience, but I liked it. It's not necessarily realistic—rather a symbol in James's mind for the stuffiness and the bad air of the Old World, which kills off the New World. On the other hand, there was an outbreak of cholera while we were in Rome and tourists stayed away in droves and it's all anyone talked about—and a bunch of people died from it. Now this is a hundred years later in the history of medicine, so perhaps we are underestimating the danger of the fever in its day.

Of course, James was very ambiguous about the Old World–New World business. Personally I'm not sure it's the Old World killing off the New, but it's a complicated point. I was going to say that America obviously has vulgarized a great part of the Old World. Whether or not that's something bad, we can't say yet. Certainly we've brought a vitality that was important—new air and vigor. I think for the first fifty years of this century, the American influence in Europe and the world has been positive. Whether or not it has been for the last twenty-five years, I don't know. But it is true that the New World brought a sense of vitality and life, which Daisy symbolizes. I think the picture as it's made is generally rather pro-American.

When Pete Hamill saw the film, he said it looked to him as if Henry James had been rewritten by Mark Twain—it does have somewhat more of an energetic American quality than James's story. On the other hand, a French critic for *Elle* said that it was a completely European film—she couldn't imagine that an American had made it.

That's one of the things that confuse critics about me—they forget that I have a European heritage. Although my parents were living in America, I was brought up in a household that was completely European rather than American. In fact, I learned to speak Serbian before I spoke English. I think that's one of the big dualities in me. Although I embraced and continue to embrace America, very much like a first-generation American, I do have an artistic background which is totally European—my father being a Serbian painter, and my mother a Viennese.

Q: Not just you—one of the curiosities of American film history is that it seems like half the directors have foreign backgrounds—Hitchcock, Lang, Lubitsch, Von Stroheim, Kazan, Chaplin, Borzage, and so on.
A: It's true, but then that's part of American history too. As Hitchcock once said to me, "America is full of foreigners." It's one of the reasons why American movies have always been the most universally appealing—because there's always been this mix. And it's what has kept them healthy, I think—until recently—perhaps we need some foreign blood.

Q: Would you ever want to make a film about your background?
A: You mean like *The Quiet Man*—going back to the Old Sod. No, I haven't yet felt the urge. I don't know that I've come to terms with my own background. I just know that it must be what makes me feel out of step with so many other American filmmakers in my age category.

Q: You've said that the final scene of the film presented the most problems.
A: Yes, it's the only thing that was changed four times in the cutting. The big problem is that the story is basically very subtle, very reserved, and yet we're stuck with an ending which I find terribly moving. To me, the powerful moment is when Randolph turns his back on Winterbourne—an idea I had long ago. I wanted the scene to be very smooth and quiet and simple—there's no cut up till then, when Randolph breaks it all. Because as far as Winterbourne is concerned, until that moment he can handle it all. He's upset by what Giovanelli tells him—"She did what she liked," and "She never would have married me." But it doesn't all come together until Randolph looks at him that way. I think it's the final moment of realization—something penetrates that thick skull.

Q: The book ends with the implication that Winterbourne goes back to that woman in Geneva, but that's not really implied in the movie.
A: No, it isn't. I didn't see how to get that across in the movie. And I didn't really care about it that much. That's why the last shot leaves him where it does—in the graveyard. I think that's where he ends up, spiritually; it's all over.

Q: It's a shot of paralysis, like the last shot of a Hitchcock film.
A: I suppose you're right—like the end of *Vertigo*, which I think is so intensely sad.

I find that some people react to this movie by not understanding Daisy almost as much as Winterbourne doesn't. I think that speaks well of the movie, actually, because it shows that Daisy's problem, and the problem of a girl like that, isn't confined to the nineteenth century. The movie could easily be a metaphor for a girl of today. In fact, if you care to look at it that way, it is. Women still don't have the freedom to be what that girl was. There's still a double standard in terms of how men deal with women and what they think about women—how easy it is for a man to put a woman down. Part of what I think is so reprehensible about Winterbourne is the fact that he thinks nothing of Daisy's so-called indiscretions when she's with *him*, it's only when she's with somebody else that he judges her as a loose woman.

Q: Exactly. I don't know if that came out clearly enough in the movie, because in the book, when Winterbourne and Daisy go to Chillon, it's mentioned that people were looking at them. Then, when Daisy goes out on the Pincio to see Giovanelli, it's the same thing—everybody stares. And James writes that Winterbourne is "rather oddly rubbed the wrong way by this." What "oddly" refers to is: why should he be upset this time?
A: Yes. I didn't tell it that way. I decided not to tell it in terms of other people's reactions on the street. It seemed to me that Mrs. Walker was the one who was reacting badly, and if you generalized it, then it would become a social story, which I don't think is terribly interesting. If everybody is stopping to look at her, it becomes a story about how this just isn't done in this society. I don't think it's about society condemning her, it's about one or two people condemning her. I think that's always an easy way out, to say, "Well, society . . ." Society is made up of a bunch of people, and it's the one or two you know that screw you, not the whole world.

I also thought Winterbourne's hypocrisy is implicit in the way he behaves on the Pincio and before, when he asks her to go out on the lake with him in Switzerland. He's ready to take her out in the middle of the night, which is exactly what Giovanelli does at the Colosseum. I don't make too much of it, but I feel it's clear that Winterbourne is jealous as opposed to simply proper. Actually, James makes no mention of jealousy in the story.

A couple of friends of mine who have seen the film had, I thought, rather dense reactions. They said, "Well, gee, we didn't know until the last reel that she was really innocent." And I said, "But what does that matter?" I think it's a very important point to make that, as far as the director of the movie is concerned—I don't know about James—it's not important whether Daisy is, in fact, innocent. The fact that maybe she is, which is what Giovanelli tells Winterbourne, is an interesting point, but I don't think it matters. It's as though if she weren't innocent, then Winterbourne's reactions would be correct and justified.

It's like making a movie against capital punishment, and the man who's going to be executed is innocent. The point is not well made then because it becomes a story about a man who's unjustly murdered for something he didn't do. If you're going to make a plea against capital punishment, the man has to be guilty as hell. *That's* the point. So if you're making a movie about a girl who's a flirt—who, as Giovanelli says at the end, "did what she liked"—then it isn't a question of whether she is innocent or not. We're saying, "Why shouldn't she do what she likes?"

Note

1. Director of such films as *Tarnished Angels*, *Written on the Wind*, *A Time to Love and A Time to Die*, and *Imitation of Life*.

Dialogue on Film: Peter Bogdanovich

American Film Institute / 1978

From *American Film*, December–January 1978. © 1978 American Film Institute.
Reprinted by permission.

An inquiry into the arts and crafts of filmmaking through interview seminars between Fellows and prominent filmmakers held at Greystone, under the auspices of the American Film Institute's Center for Advanced Film Studies. This educational series is directed by James Powers.

To be a hot young director is to tempt the gods and the critics both—a formidable combination and often confused, especially by the critics. In 1971, Peter Bogdanovich was officially a hot young director, and stars like Steve McQueen and Barbra Streisand were beating a path to his screening room. *The Last Picture Show*, a modest, lovely movie about coming of age in Texas, had opened to strong reviews and long lines.

In rounds of interviews Bogdanovich, with some justification, glowed with confidence and pride. He told the *New York Times* he hoped to make fifty films, worried about what he would do when he had made all the films he wanted to make, and dropped the names of great directors as if he were already in their company.

Six years and six films later, the gods and the critics agree that Bogdanovich is no longer a hot young director. As everyone in the Western world knows by now, his recent movies—like *Nickelodeon*, *At Long Last Love*, and *Daisy Miller*—have not done well. Like a Greek chorus, the critics have gathered around each recent film to piously tut-tut about the wages of hubris, the debilitating effects of Hollywood insularity, and the ravages to genius invariably incurred from knowing Cybill Shepherd. (Notice that the insularity of critics leads to stock movie insights, like the lesson of *The Blue Angel*: Beauty always vanquishes talent.) In a headline, the *New York Times* now plaintively inquires, "Will *Nickelodeon* Be His Last Picture Show?" The writer portrays a Bogdanovich chastened, humbled, sadder but wiser—a sort of King Lear wandering on the heath, attended by Sue Mengers, his agent.

Is Bogdanovich about to abandon the movies to take up pottery-making? True, he no longer sounds like the king of the hill, but neither is his humility these days of St. Theresa proportions. He's now busy producing *The Big Red One*, directed by the no-nonsense Samuel Fuller. He has a half-dozen *small* films—his emphasis—planned for the next few years. He's resuming a movie column for *Esquire* because he misses writing and because he wants to bring to public attention young directors he admires. He's considering directing in the theater again. The recent defeats have given Bogdanovich a new perspective on the movies and moviemaking, but his love for the art is abiding.

It's a love that got an early start. Bogdanovich's father was a well-known painter, and the family lived in New York, where the son doted on movies and the theater. He went to the respected Collegiate School, wrote a movie and stage column for the school newspaper, but never went to college. (If there were any ill effects from that denial, it doesn't show in Bogdanovich's eclectic reading; in a recent week he made his way through works by Isak Dinesen, Nikolai Gogol, and Shakespeare; movie scripts, though, he loathes to read.) As a teenager he studied acting with the admirable Stella Adler; he was not yet out of his teens when he directed off Broadway Clifford Odets's *The Big Knife*; soon he was programming revivals for the New Yorker Theater and the Museum of Modern Art and writing MoMA monographs and pieces for everything from *Cahiers du Cinema* to *Esquire*.

A move to Hollywood was an exuberant risk; something might turn up. It did. A chance encounter with the colorful producer Roger Corman in a screening room led to a job on a Corman film, to his first film, *Targets*, and to a brief career as a hot young director.

Now cooler, more ironic, and pushing forty, Bogdanovich has lost none of his exuberance or cutting wit, as his answer to the Dialogue's very first question demonstrates. Bogdanovich talks about his hits, doesn't neglect the flops, considers the trials of working with a young Tatum O'Neal, gives his views of comedy, finds solace in the silent comedies, Lubitsch especially, and addresses himself to the pressing question, Is there a movie life after *Nickelodeon*?

Question: You started off by making two extremely successful films, and you followed up by making three extremely unsuccessful films. What happened?

Peter Bogdanovich: You ought to get your facts straight. My first picture was a financial failure; my second picture was a popular and critical success; my third picture was a documentary that almost no one has seen because the American Film Institute, for whom it was made, has kept it a secret. My fourth picture and my fifth picture were popular with audiences but made the critics uneasy. My sixth and eighth pictures got some marvelous notices, and no one went. My seventh picture was poorly received by everyone. Oh, it's a stupid question. Frankly, I think they're all reasonably interesting in various ways. Next.

Question: Your first movie, *Targets*, was a flop?
Bogdanovich: Yes, almost nobody saw it. Paramount made eight 35mm prints of it, of which I got one. It got some fair reviews and some terrible ones. My second movie, though, was *The Last Picture Show*.

Question: You once said, after *The Last Picture Show* was released, that you thought of your career in the same terms as that of the older director. You hoped that during your life you could do fifty films on a wide range of subjects. Considering the state of the business today, have you tempered that view?
Bogdanovich: I've tempered the view perhaps in the number of films. I don't know if I can make fifty films today, but one can try. I've got about six cheap little films I'd like to do in a row. That ought to keep me busy for a while.

Question: But the trend today is expensive films.
Bogdanovich: Well, perhaps we're coming out of that phase. At the moment, bigness is equated with quality. That's happened before, and it's a big danger. While I was a sort of half-assed critic, I once wrote that George Cukor had made a pretty good picture out of *My Fair Lady*, considering the limitations of $15 million. And, from experience, I found, when I had $6 or $9 million, as I did on the last two pictures, that I had been right. It's a hell of a limitation. The production gets bigger and bigger, and finally you've got all these people on the set who don't essentially do anything because they're not needed. But you're carrying them around with you everywhere you go, like a goddamned army. You can't just say, "Oh, let's not shoot this today. Let's go over there," because it's like saying, "We're not going to land at Normandy; we're going to invade at the Sea of Japan." You just can't. Somehow the freedom goes, and at the same time, the fun goes, too. After all, it's only fun when you feel that what you're doing is a sort of crime, a caper.

Jean Renoir once said that when you're making a picture you should gather around you not associates but conspirators. It's not possible to have three hundred loyal conspirators. To half of them it's just a picture, and that's when it starts not to be fun. That's why I love shooting at night. It's the best time because everybody else is asleep, and you're really doing this wicked thing nobody knows about. You've got to keep that larcenous quality to your work in pictures. That's the trouble with big pictures—there's no larceny in them. They're essentially respectable, and respectability is an insidious enemy.

Question: Are you indirectly arguing for location shooting?
Bogdanovich: I prefer shooting on location, and it ties in with the conspiracy theory of filmmaking. When you're on location all the actors are stuck there. It becomes a kind of marvelous boys and girls camp, or a reasonably peaceful army of occupation. We took over Hays, Kansas, for *Paper Moon*, and it's amazing how sweet people are on distant locations. For *The Last Picture Show* we were in Archer City, somewhere in Texas. Some kids were playing across the street in one scene. For this particular shot it would have given the wrong impression to have kids playing in the background. I turned to the assistant director and said, "Get those kids out of there." So he went over and yelled, "Hey, you kids, get out of your yard!" The kids got out of their yard. That happens all the time. There was one old man in Kansas who came out of his home to see a 1935 Ford we had in a shot. His daughter said, "That's the first time Pop's been out of the house in six years." Strange, you know, movies. They have a magic outside of the big cities. People are thrilled to have you. They haven't been on a Universal tour.

Question: *Daisy Miller* was not one of your expensive films, but did you wonder if it would have any commercial appeal?
Bogdanovich: All the time we were making it I kept saying, "I don't know who's going to want to see this." But we looked at rushes and said, "Isn't it beautiful, though?" We loved it. At that point I had made three very successful pictures, and I figured I could make one for me. It didn't cost too much. Everybody thinks it was an expensive picture, but it only cost $2 million.

The script is very faithful to the book, it's a good story, and I think the film is well made. Some people find it difficult to accept a character like Daisy Miller in such a milieu. If I were telling a Western with the same basic plot—an eastern girl comes to the West, she doesn't understand the way you're supposed to behave, people don't understand her—nobody would have any difficulty at all believing the character. After all, the picture is set in the same period most Westerns are set, 1875 or 1880. But the minute you take this chattering American girl, sophisticated, highbrow, artistic, pretentious—some people find it hard to believe. Still, that's essentially the point of Henry James's story. If you'll read it again, you'll find that she's described as being crude, vulgar, chatty, annoying, naïve, flirtatious—everything as we tried to do in the movie.

In any event, I think in ten years you'll like *Daisy Miller* better. It's amazing how pictures change. I've seen movies I adored ten years ago and now find lousy, and others I hated ten years ago I now think are masterpieces. Actually, what changes is you. But it is true that films have a way of changing their shape and color. That's why I think it's so difficult to be a contemporary critic, since it's almost impossible to guess correctly what's going to last. I've made a study of some old pictures that were very popular, well acclaimed. You'd be amazed how bad some of them are. The first Western to win an Academy Award, *Cimarron*, is almost unwatchable today. But that's just one tiny example—there are so many more. Somehow when a picture is new one doesn't as easily realize how lousy it is.

Question: In doing *Daisy Miller*, were you influenced by anyone in your camera setups and in the color and composition?
Bogdanovich: Mainly my father, who was a painter. He died in 1970. He had a great sense of color and composition. I think I learned a lot about that from him—mainly through osmosis. It's my own favorite picture. It's the only one I can look at and feel I had nothing to do with, which is nice. You see, looking at your pictures is like looking into a mirror. It's a strange connection, but I was at the Plaza Hotel in New York about two years ago with Ryan O'Neal. We were both staggering out in the morning for an interview. There's always a mirror next to the elevators to let you know how you look before you get in. Ryan was already standing there when I ran up. I looked and said, "Oh, hell." He said, "What's the matter?" I said, "I always think it's going to be better." And he said, "That's funny. I'm always pleased at how much better it is." That's the essential difference between actors and directors. But it's also the way I feel about my own films—I always think they're going to be better. On *Daisy Miller*, however, my reaction is more like Ryan's—I'm pleased at how much better it is.

Question: In the final scene in *Daisy Miller*, the young man is standing over the grave, and then the camera recedes and the screen slowly drains of color until it turns white. What meaning did you intend to convey?

Bogdanovich: If I told you what I meant, it might limit its meanings.

Question: Was it just a pictorial effect?
Bogdanovich: Well, wait a minute. What are we making? We're making pictures. The whole thing is a pictorial effect. Everything you do in a movie is a pictorial effect of some kind—if you're making a good movie.

Question: Well, film is not a painting.
Bogdanovich: At least partially, it is.

Question: But it's more than a series of paintings.
Bogdanovich: Well, yes, they move.

Question: In other words, you're saying that this was a rhetorical flourish.
Bogdanovich: I'm not saying that—you are. You said it was "just a pictorial effect." I object mainly to the word "just." I thought it was the right thing to do. It seemed to me that it was much more moving and satisfying than the usual fade-out. It's a fade-out, but it goes to white instead of dark. When we saw it—because we actually did it in the camera—we said, "That's remarkable." The image sort of froze, and the color drained; yet it wasn't freeze frames. I thought it would be interesting that way and particularly effective. We were going to reprise the cast, and the shot of Daisy—the first—was very white. So we went to white and then came out of white into her. It never fails to affect me. But it's "just a pictorial effect."

Question: Do you think you'll ever try to make another film out of a Henry James novel?
Bogdanovich: No, I wouldn't think so. Henry James has had it with me, anyway. You wouldn't want to do a great novel of his, like *The Portrait of a Lady*, because you're never going to do it justice. *Daisy Miller* is just seventy pages, so you could do the whole thing and make a good picture. People don't always realize that almost all the dialogue in the picture is by Henry James. I changed certain words occasionally that were a bit too formal. "I wouldn't think so" instead of "I shouldn't think so," simply because I didn't think Daisy would say, "I shouldn't." But there were surprising words that came up which you wouldn't have thought

were used during that period. Daisy says, for example, "Did you ever see anything so cool?" You'd think that was a fifties expression, but it's right there in the book published in 1878.

Question: You've known Orson Welles for some time; you're in his new film. Was he an influence?
Bogdanovich: Of course you learn a lot from Orson. I did—about a lot of things. I think everybody who has made a picture since 1941 has been influenced by him, stolen things from him—but everybody steals. I was talking to Howard Hawks about the shot in *Red River* when the cloud came and cast a shadow over the funeral. I said, "That's a hell of a shot." He said, "Well, sometimes you get lucky and you get one of those great Ford shots." I said, "You mean you thought of it as a Ford shot?" He said, "Oh, sure. We all said, 'Let's get that Ford shot.'" I said, "Then you were influenced by Ford in making that Western?" He said, "Peter, I don't see how you can make a Western and *not* be influenced by John Ford."

Question: What do you think is the most important tool that a director needs?
Bogdanovich: A good script and good actors.

Question: The most important skill?
Bogdanovich: The ability to speak to actors, to communicate with them, and to get performances from them. Second, a sense of where the hell to put the camera. Finally, knowing when to cut. Some directors know how to talk to actors and don't know where to put the camera. That's not so bad, because somebody will suggest to them where it ought to be. Some directors know how to cut and know how to deal with the camera but have no idea how to talk to the actors. So you have very interesting camera work and good cutting, but some of the heart is missing from the picture, despite its formal interest. Some know how to work with actors and how to cut—they're usually all right; they make good pictures. Some know all three; they make better pictures.

Question: Do you rehearse your actors?
Bogdanovich: Always. At least two weeks. The more the better—up to a certain point. You can over-rehearse a picture. It's best to rehearse to the point where nobody knows exactly what he's going to do but he thinks he knows approximately what he's going to do. Then it's usually time to shoot. While I'm rehearsing, I have an idea or two about shots. I get a

sense of where the camera ought to be for the key moments in the scene. Then, before I come out to the set—the day before or the night before or on way to location—I map out exactly how many setups I need. If the picture is tight, you have to hurry—and I've found that even when you have a lot of money you have to shoot tight because half the money goes to the stars. On a $9 million picture, you're spending at least $4 million on four or five persons. You always have to hurry, no matter how expensive the picture is. Though I've heard that some people take their time; I can't—it's like sitting there while the meter ticks.

A director is usually shooting completely out of continuity, of course—shooting the beginning last and the end first. That's why the rehearsal has been valuable, because the actors essentially know the scene. Even if you jump in the middle of it, they know approximately where they are because they've rehearsed it all without stopping, and they know what they're going to do. The set itself gives you ideas, particularly if you're on location. There may be a wall over here, and a certain shot you had in mind won't work. You find another shot. On real locations the place is like one of the actors. Certain actors can't do something, so you don't force them to do it; you think of a way to get them to do something similar or something completely different. If a room is a character, you just can't shoot because a wall is there. You find another angle.

Question: We're discussing acting, and I think one of the finest moments in *The Last Picture Show* is the last shot with Cloris Leachman. It's an incredible moment. She's trying to talk to Timothy Bottoms, but she can't quite get anything out. How did you work with her on that?

Bogdanovich: The camera was in front of her, and I was right next to it, and she was looking at me playing the scene. I was talking to her. I was telling her what I thought she should be trying to do. Essentially, the character was trying to say something; she had an answer to the situation. She seemed to glimpse the sun through a cloud, and she was trying to find the words to describe what she'd seen. But the character wasn't an eloquent woman, so she lost the way to express herself. I was telling Cloris all that as we were doing it. She was great in that whole scene. This was the scene that the producers wanted me to cut; they wanted to cut the entire last scene between Cloris and Tim Bottoms. They thought that the picture should end with him on the road. I said, "I made the picture only so I could have that scene in it." I think it's probably the best scene in the picture. It should be, since it's the last one—you might as well end a movie with something good. We kept it in, but I had to cut some other things out as a sacrifice. You have to give them something so you can keep the stuff you like. That's often true in life, too.

Question: How did *The Last Picture Show* come about?
Bogdanovich: People kept giving me Larry McMurtry's novel to read. Sal Mineo, a sweet, dear friend, gave it to me, and so did two or three other people. I finally read it about two years later, I liked it very much, and I wanted to do it. But I didn't know how to make it. I mean, having done a thriller I figured I could just spend the rest of my life making thrillers. It was something that I at least had the feeling I know how to do. But what I felt that *Targets* lacked was a solidity in the performances. Boris Karloff was good, and the boy—Tim O'Kelly—was good, but everybody else was iffy; they could have been better. So what I really wanted to do on the second picture was to concentrate on the actors, to get some performances. I came to feel that this was probably the most essential thing you can do in pictures, to have really good performances—not necessarily really good actors but really good performances. That was one of the main intentions when we made *The Last Picture Show*. A lot of other things, too.

Question: Where did you find Timothy Bottoms and the other performers?
Bogdanovich: Tim was doing a picture with Dalton Trumbo called *Johnny Got His Gun*, and I heard that he was good, so I asked to see him. He had these extraordinary eyes which looked as if they carried the sorrow of the ages in them. The truth of the matter, when you got to know him better, was that he was just feeling sorry for himself. But it looked at first, and I think in the movie, as though he was feeling sorry for the world. His eyes had an epic sorry; I thought he would be good for the picture. I came somewhat to regret that decision, but he's good enough in the picture.

Jeff Bridges just came into the office looking for the Sonny part. As soon as we'd talked a minute, I said, "He's not Sonny, he's Duane." Seeing Jeff gave me the idea of how the part should be played. The character in the story was essentially unpleasant. I felt that he should be cast and played as attractively as possible, because he was as much a victim as any of them. As it was, I think he was terribly touching in the part. But if you read the script you'd say, "That guy is not very nice."

Cybill I saw on a magazine cover, and I thought she'd be right for the part. I met her and she was. She also gave me a sense of how the part should be played. If an actor, by his presence or by his manner, suggests to you how a role should be played, that is almost certainly the actor for the part. Ben Johnson I just wanted. I thought he should play it, and it took me three or four months to convince him that he should do it. John Ford intervened for me. Almost everybody tried to convince him to do it. He just didn't want to. I told him he would win the Academy Award if he did the picture, and he did.

Question: How about the older women?
Bogdanovich: Ellen Burstyn read for the coach's wife, the part she played, and the waitress, and she read them all equally well. I said to her, "You cast it. Call me tomorrow and tell me which one you want to play." The next day she said, "I want to play the mother." Cloris Leachman and Eileen Brennan came in, and both seemed right. Clu Gulager's part is the only one that wasn't cast exactly as I wanted. I would have preferred Jimmy Dean, the country-and-western singer, but the producers didn't think it was a good idea. All the other parts were cast in Texas.

Question: On the pictures that you've made so far, what aspects particularly excited you creatively?
Bogdanovich: Everything. I haven't made a picture that I haven't wanted to make in some way or another. It's a lot of hard work, and you complain all the time while you're making a picture. You're always saying, "When is this picture going to be over?" Then it's over and you sit around and say, "I wish I was back making that—it was so much fun. No critics. No Hollywood." Particularly if it was a location picture. I saw a rough cut of the new movie by John Cassavetes, *Opening Night*. It was only about six hours long at this point, and I enjoyed it. I can just sit there and watch six or eight hours of John's movies. I don't care. I get into what he's doing and I'm happy. Anyway, Ben Gazzara was in the picture, and Ben and John and some other people and I had a drink afterward in a Chinese restaurant. There were a lot of people around, and Ben was talking loudly—as he often talks—about the Russian invasion of Czechoslovakia. He had been there shooting a movie. He said, "These sons of bitches come into Czechoslovakia—I don't *understand* these people! I don't understand these *people*! John, do you *understand* these people?" Then somebody from another table yelled out, "Shut up!" Ben didn't seem to hear. "I don't understand—Damn these people! Is that guy talking to me?" I said, "I think so." He said, "Oh, screw him." And I

thought, Ben behaves as though he were on location, and that's a good way to go through life—as though you own the town.

Question: What do you look for in cinematographers and editors?
Bogdanovich: Just somebody I like to be with. For ten or twelve weeks you have to sit with the same people and talk to them every day. Of course, liking them has to do with their being good. All the cameramen I've worked with have been good, I think, and pretty nice to work with—Bob Surtees was a little cantankerous on *Picture Show*, but he was over sixty at the time, and I was a kid. Also, he didn't approve of some of the sex in the picture—he thought it was a bit much. The dogs screwing on the front lawn put him off quite a bit. "We'd never have shot this stuff over at Metro!" he said. Actually, we got in a lot of trouble for that shot. You don't see much of it in the picture because I took most of it out. I thought that was just enough of a hint of it. But that shot was lighted on the front lawn of the real schoolhouse. The camera was shooting from the inside, and people driving by couldn't even see us. It was just these two dogs, and a lot of lights. Nice Texan people driving by said, "What the hell's going on? This picture company's gone too far." Luckily, it was the last shot in the school sequence.

Question: To return to actors, how did you work with Tatum O'Neal in *Paper Moon*?
Bogdanovich: With considerable difficulty.

Question: Did you have to overcome some difficulty with her father?
Bogdanovich: Oh, God, no, not with her father. I just had to keep Ryan from killing her. He will shout, "Goddamn it, Tatum, would you learn your lines? I'm not going to do it again. We've done it twenty-eight times! I did five thousand 'Peyton Places,' and I never went through anything like this." This is on a road in the middle of Kansas with nothing anywhere but Kansas and a car they're riding in and a rig pulling the car with a camera on it and about twelve people hanging on. It was a narrow road, and we couldn't turn easily. This was a scene between Ryan and Tatum which played without a cut. It was at the end of the second act where they have a big argument. A lot of things are implied about their love or need for each other—but all through indirection. It's one of those scenes where they don't say what they mean, but you hopefully get the point. I wanted it to be without a cut—about three or four minutes. We

figured that the scene would take about a mile and a half where the road was good and which fit the period.

Two miles down there was a place where we could turn around and come back. Just turning around took five or six minutes. Since the scene had to be without a cut, if they started down the road and after about three lines somebody blew it, we'd have to go all the way down two miles and then turn around and go back and start over again. The first day we did it twenty-five times. It was around the nineteenth time when Ryan was saying he couldn't do it any more. I remember putting my arm around him, and we walked up the road for about half a mile while I calmed him down. I got him to do it another few times, and we still didn't get it. The next two days it rained, then we shot some other stuff, and a few days later we came back and did it again. I think we got it on the sixteenth take that day.

Question: What problems were you having with Tatum O'Neal?
Bogdanovich: It was hard to work with Tatum then because she was only eight years old, and she didn't have any idea what the hell we were doing, and for half the movie she couldn't have cared less. She'd never had much discipline in her life. Also, eight-year-old kids have a world of their own. I like that world, but sometimes that world and the world we were trying to create didn't necessarily mesh. Like the time we were shooting the carnival scene at night. I believe we brought a small carnival from somewhere. You know, movie companies command these things: "Bring us a Ferris wheel." It was a cheap picture, but even on cheap pictures you can move a Ferris wheel. Tatum got there about five o'clock. It took us about three hours to light the scene. So she did what any kid would do at eight years old. She started riding the Ferris wheel, eating popcorn, eating candy corn, eating peanuts, and by the time we were ready to shoot she was sick. She was lying on the ground.

"I told you not to eat!" said Ryan. "Oh, Daddy!" "Oh, get up!" Ryan and I alternated yelling at her. Sometimes he would yell at her; sometimes I would yell. That was the night that I actually screamed at her at the end of the night. It was very cold, and it was about four o'clock in the morning. This shot was also without a cut—about two minutes of action and dialogue. It went all the way through the whole damned carnival. It was one of those dolly shots where you went here and there and way down here. We rarely got past the start. Finally, we were at the end. There was another minute there. Tatum's standing with her back to the camera, and she's trembling from the cold. And I cried, "Oh, hell, cut! She's shaking!" So we quit and had to come back the next night. I'm not usually that rough, but she was a wild little eight-year-old kid, and you had to scare her into doing it right. After about five weeks of shooting, she got into it and started to like it and was much better. She almost became professional, and then it was easier. Generally, that picture was hell because of a lot of problems. Still, it was just a lot of "pictorial effects."

Question: Every director must reach a moment during shooting on a picture where he doesn't know what he's going to do next. Has that ever happened to you?
Bogdanovich: It happened to me once on *Paper Moon*. It was the scene in which Tatum goes in to see her aunt right near the end of the picture. She goes in the door, there's a scene with her Aunt Billie, at the end of which she runs out of the house. It started to rain, and we had to jump into it. I didn't know what I was going to do because I hadn't had a chance to prepare it since we hadn't planned to shoot it. I had no idea what to do, and I tried to figure it out. I set up a couple of shots, and we didn't shoot them. Finally, I just said, "Fellows, we're not going to get this today. I just don't know what to do. Let's just go home." Welles once said to me, "If you really don't know where to put the camera, then you really don't know what to do in the scene." And I didn't know where to put the camera. That night I looked at the scene for an hour, and suddenly I thought of what to do with it, and the next day we shot it. But that's the only time it's happened.

Question: How did you get into directing? What were you doing before?
Bogdanovich: I started acting professionally in the theater when I was fifteen, and I did a little acting in New York in stock and in television between the time I was fifteen and about nineteen. I studied acting during that time with Stella Adler. The first thing I did as a director, when I was about nineteen, was *The Big Knife* by Clifford Odets, off-Broadway. I did another play off-Broadway about four years later called *Once in a Lifetime* by Kaufman and Hart. Neither production was successful. During that time I was also writing about movies because I didn't have any money and I wanted to get in to see them for free. There was a time in New York when I was on every screening list. I was on every list for theater tickets. I got all the film books from publishers. It was wonderful. I supposedly was writing for a little magazine called *Ivy*, a strange, short-lived little college magazine. I came out to California after writing several pieces for *Esquire*. About two years later, in a movie theater, I was introduced

to Roger Corman. He said, "You write for *Esquire*." I said, "Yes." He said, "I've read your stuff. Would you ever consider writing screenplays?" I said, "Sure, I would. Of course." He said, "Well, why don't you write a screenplay for me?" So I said, "What do you want me to write it about?" He said, "Well, I want a kind of a combination of *Bridge on the River Kwai* and *Lawrence of Arabia*—but cheap." So Polly Platt and I came up with a story, and then I wrote a script called *The Criminals*, which was never produced.

Around the same time, Roger was doing a movie called *The Wild Angels*, with Peter Fonda and Nancy Sinatra, and he asked me if I would like to work on the picture. I said, "Doing what?" He said, "I don't know. Just come on down and be with me. It's a short shooting schedule, only three weeks." I went to his offices at Fox and read the script as it came in. It was really a poor job. It was a motorcycle film, as you might remember, but the original script was written as if it were a Disney picture. There were shots that read: "The motorcycles roar by. Cut to frog on road as motorcycles roar by. Cut to frog's POV of motorcycles going by." Roger asked me to rewrite the script, and I redid about 75 percent of it—mainly improving the dialogue and strengthening motivations. George Chakiris, meanwhile, who was originally cast to play the lead, read the script. He didn't think it was bad—he thought it was immoral, and he quit. We decided that maybe Peter Fonda could play the part. Peter came into the office, and he had aviator sunglasses on, and he looked terrific. Then he took the glasses off, and his entire character changed—disappeared—the moment he took them off. In fact, if you see the picture, there's only one scene where he does take them off, and he's really no good.

Question: How did you come about directing some of *The Wild Angels*?
Bogdanovich: We had real Hell's Angels on the picture, and they didn't like Roger. He's got three weeks to make a picture, and he's saying, "Come on, come on! Let's go, let's go!" But the Hell's Angels didn't feel like hurrying up. There would be long waits while they tried to get their bikes going. We kept falling further and further behind schedule. A few days before we were supposed to quit, Roger said, "We're just going to have to throw out the rest of the script and piece it together the best we can. We've got about three-quarters of it." I said, "What about the other quarter?" He said, "I don't know. We'll just have to get a second unit to go out and shoot this junk." I said, "Well, I'd love to do it." He said, "We'll have somebody do it. It'll be easy. My secretary or you—it doesn't make any difference." I shot for three weeks, and that's how I learned to direct, by

doing it. When I finished shooting the stuff Roger said, "The cutter's got too much to do. You'll have to cut your own footage together." I didn't have any idea how to cut. But we got a machine and someone who knew something about it, and I started to cut, and I learned. I worked twenty-two weeks on the picture, from preproduction, through shooting, second unit, cutting, dubbing—it was an extraordinary twenty-two-week picturemaking. I haven't learned as much since. *The Wild Angels*, by the way, became a very big success. It cost about $300,000 and grossed about $5 million in America. Roger was pleased, and he asked me if I wanted to direct my own picture, which is how *Targets* came about.

Question: Has your acting experience, in *Targets* and elsewhere, helped your directing on your pictures?
Bogdanovich: Essentially, I think in some way you have to be an actor to be a good director. Also, you have to hear it in your head the way a composer or a conductor hears a score. He doesn't necessarily have to have all the musicians there to know how it ought to sound. In fact, what he's probably trying to do is to get the musicians to sound like what he already hears. When I'm working on a script I already hear it and see it a certain way, and then it's a question of getting the actors to sound that way and the crew to make it look that way. Sometimes an actor does something that's different, and I say, "Hey, I like that. Keep that. I hadn't heard or seen it like that." That's a gift. But, generally speaking, you're sort of trying to get them to do it the way you've heard it. There are a million ways to do this because every actor is different. So you beat a child on the head or scare her, or you indulge Burt Reynolds because he's nervous. I show the actor what I want by either saying the line the way I think he ought to say it or getting up and acting it out.

Comedy, for example, is very much a question of how the line is said, the pacing of the line with the next line or the line before it. Comedy is very musical, so is visual comedy. That's why I think you're cheating if the music punctuates the action. I think you haven't done a good enough job as a director. What I do like is when the music plays against the visual. Counterpoint, in other words. Somebody playing a funny song in a sad scene, or vice versa. When you're doing dialogue, it's very much a matter of how it sounds. You could even perhaps close your eyes on a shot and by the way it sounds tell if it's any good. That happened to me once during a scene with Eileen Brennan in *The Last Picture Show*. The shot was very complicated, and like most idiot directors I was looking at the camera instead of the actor because the camera had to get past an obstacle. When the shot was over, I said, "Cut," and I realized that I hadn't seen anything of what she'd done. I went over and sat in a corner, and suddenly I started to hear the scene. I had heard it and didn't even know that I'd heard it, and now that I thought it through it sounded pretty good. I said, "I think it's all right. Let's do something else."

Question: Do you pay attention to the reactions of audiences during preview screenings of your movies?
Bogdanovich: Oh, sure, but once the picture's finished it works for somebody. Not every joke in every comedy works for everybody, but there's always some joke in the picture that somebody is going to laugh at. Maybe just you or your mother. Orson Welles once did a production of a play called *Horse Eats Hat* in New York. It was not a big success, but one night there were two people really laughing. Everybody else was tittering but there was one person on one side of the audience who was screaming, and there was another person on the other side of the audience who was screaming. Because of them the performance played well, because everybody else thought, "Well, two people think it's funny." Laughter *is* contagious. After the first act the person over here went over to the person over there, because they had recognized each other's laughs. One was Thornton Wilder and the other was John Dos Passos. They sat together through the last act and screamed together.

Question: Did *What's Up, Doc?* present problems?
Bogdanovich: That was more fun than any picture I've made. It was heaven from beginning to end. First of all, I didn't give a damn if we ever made the picture. You must always not give a damn if the whole thing falls apart. That's the only way to do pictures, because when you start caring too much you get killed. *What's Up, Doc?* was a crazy situation because *Picture Show* hadn't opened. Nobody had seen the picture. My new agent at the time, Sue Mengers, was trying to impress me. She said, "There's a picture over at Warners that Streisand is going to do called 'A Glimpse of Tiger.' But the picture is closed down, and the studio has thrown all the footage out and the director and everything else. I think you should do it. But first Barbra and John Calley have to see *Picture Show*." In the meantime, there was another picture going with Steve McQueen called *The Getaway*, and another agent said, "We've got to get Steve to see this picture of yours because we want Steve to use you as the director of *The Getaway*."

A few days later, into this projection room over at BBS comes Steve

McQueen with about six or seven people. I say, "Hello, Mr. McQueen, I'm—" "Could you wait outside, kid? I've got to make a few phone calls, and then we're going to see the picture." So I went back to my office. A few hours went by, and Steve McQueen walks in the door with his hand outstretched and says, "You're a picturemaker, man. I'm just an actor, but you're a picturemaker." We started talking about art. He said, "You only made one mistake in that picture." I said, "What?" He said, "You cut away from that swimming pool scene too soon. I wanted to see more of that." Anyway, he wanted me to direct *The Getaway*.

The next day, armed with this information, Miss Mengers says to Warners, "Well, Bogdanovich is doing the next McQueen picture." So now, of course, Barbra and Calley are even more anxious to see *Picture Show*. But the head of Columbia Pictures—the picture was a Columbia release—hadn't even seen the picture yet. Bert Schneider, the producer of *Picture Show*, said, "We can't let the head of Warner Bros. see the picture before the head of Columbia has seen it. Let him see three or four reels and then tell him he's got to get out." John Calley and Barbra went to see the picture, and he left after the eighth reel and came to my office and said, "It's wonderful, Peter. Barbra's sitting in there crying, and I can't stand it that I have to leave but I have to leave."

Barbra came out later, and she was very complimentary. Her eyes were wet, so one knew she had been taken by the movie. We talked for about an hour, and I really liked her. We went downstairs to her car, and we stood there talking for another hour. I had read the script of "A Glimpse of Tiger," and I said, "It's not a good script, Barbra." She said, "You don't like it?" I said, "It can't make up its mind if it's a drama or a comedy. I don't want to do a drama; I want to do a comedy." She said, "I want to do a drama." I said, "No, I want to do a comedy. I want to do a farce." I thought Barbra would be terrific in a farce. I felt that her basic nature was comedic, and I didn't want to see her taking herself too seriously.

I won that battle and got to make the picture, although Barbra never really liked it. Unlike other actors that I've had to deal with since, however, she was sweet about it. And funny. Ryan would say, "Gee, I think it's kind of funny." But she'd say, "It's not funny! I know what's funny! It's not funny!" And I would start to laugh because when she said, "It's not funny," she was funny. She'd say, "What are you laughing at?" I said, "You—you're funny." She said, "I can't talk to this guy. I'm funny."

Question: Did location shooting in San Francisco present problems?
Bogdanovich: You know, San Francisco is such an extraordinary city. I

thought I had used it up, but I went back there recently because I'm going to make another picture there, and the city is inexhaustible. I could never imagine shooting another picture in Hays, Kansas, or Archer City, Texas, but you can shoot probably ten pictures in San Francisco and never use it up. We took over San Francisco and wrecked a couple of streets, and we got in a little trouble. We had a scare when all the cars went into the water at the end. The Volkswagen went in first and went down like a stone. It was very deep, and the driver didn't have an oxygen tank. We thought he'd come right up. A minute, a minute and a half, two minutes passed. Finally he popped up. What had happened was that the windshield came in on him, and he couldn't get the door open, so finally he got out through the windshield opening. He wiggled his way out. Luckily he was a stuntman in water, and he didn't panic.

Question: What happens if a shot like that goes wrong?
Bogdanovich: Well, we had seven or eight cameras on those particular shots. If one camera malfunctioned we would still get it. But I've never had anything happen on a stunt. John Ford gave me a very good piece of advice. He said, "Never rehearse action." I said, "Why not?" He said, "Somebody could get hurt." It's a slightly cryptic remark, as all of Ford's remarks were, but when you think about it, it makes sense. You talk out the action with the actor or the stuntman—very precisely. You try to discuss everything that can possibly happen and what you want and what you'll take if you can't get what you want, and then you do it. Usually you get an elaborate piece of action on the first take, because nobody wants to do it again, and they all work like hell to get it right.

I used the metaphor of a stunt as an example to my crew when I was doing *The Last Picture Show*. In one of the last scenes in the picture, the kid is lying on the ground dead, and everyone is standing around the truck in the wind, grousing. Tim Bottoms finally yells out, "He was sweeping, you sons of bitches!" and he picks up the body and carries it over to the steps of the theater. I wanted this done without a cut. From the moment he said, "He was sweeping," to the time he carries the body over and then walks away, I didn't want the camera to leave him. It was about fifty feet from there to the theater, so he had to pick up the body and carry it, and the camera was on a truck because we didn't have a good dolly down there. It was a complicated shot for the actor because of the emotion, and very complicated for the crew because there was a zoom involved which I wanted to hide. And the truck had to be driven carefully.

We set it up before lunch, and then I talked to Tim all through lunch. I was trying to find out what he was going to do without telling him *what* to do, because we had never rehearsed this line. I wouldn't even let him say it. In fact, I wouldn't let anybody else say it. I knew it was a line I only wanted to hear once, and I knew the actor should only say it once. It's one of those movie-acting things. It's not true on the stage. But there are certain lines in a movie that should only happen once because the minute you have to rehearse it or do it again, it becomes mechanical, or you might begin imitating what you did. That *first* emotion is very important for certain moments, and this was one of them.

The crew came back from lunch, and I said to them, in my sternest voice, "Now listen. We are not making a shot of a guy carrying a body across the street. We are shooting a bridge being blown up. There is only one camera, and we've only got one bridge, and if we don't get the goddamned thing we will never get it again because it's a cheap picture. We can't afford another bridge. I don't want any mistakes from you guys on this shot. And no excuses." We did the shot and we got it. To me it was like a stunt—it couldn't be done again. Luckily the actor was superb, and the crew got it right. As a matter of fact, to prove my point I did the shot a second time. The second one was technically better—it was actually less bumpy and smoother—but the performance wasn't there. It was all right, but it was a stock performance. The first one broke your heart. It's the only time I've ever been moved to tears on a set. I knew it must have been good because it killed me when I saw him do it.

Question: What happens to performances on those shots where, because of the mechanics of moviemaking, you blow it ten times?
Bogdanovich: What you're actually doing is rehearsing in front of the camera. You do it until it's right. Then you do it a couple more times in case something went wrong. You have to know your actors. There are some actors who get better the more often they do it, and there are some actors who get worse. So what you want is to get it before the changes are too extreme, which usually means around the seventh or eighth take. You have to be very careful. You have to know whether the actor is going to get better or not. You're hoping that you will have an accident, that something unexpected will make the shot great. John Ford said he thought the best things in pictures happen by accident. Orson Welles, in a similar vein, said to me, "A director is a man who presides over accidents." What you're really trying to do when you direct a picture is create an atmosphere in which accidents can happen—planned accidents.

There's a funny story which Henry Fonda told me. John Ford was directing *Mister Roberts*, and Fonda said, "We were shooting a scene with William Powell, and Bill hadn't done a picture in a few years. He was kind of shaky and nervous. He came out on the set. It was a long scene on a ship, about four or five pages, and Ford set up the camera, and we started to roll. Bill was just terrible. His hands were shaking, and he was just barely remembering his lines. I was thinking, When is Ford going to cut? But I went on playing the scene; I had done it so many times on the stage. We went on and on, and the scene ended. Ford said, 'Cut! *Print!* Did you see that cloud move in behind them? Wasn't that a hell of a shot?'"

Question: When you are doing comedy and pacing a joke, do you work at a series of payoffs—at a topper?
Bogdanovich: You've usually got to have three jokes and then a fourth on the same subject that's funnier than the other three. If you don't give the audience the topper, they slightly resent you. I think the best one I did was in *What's Up, Doc?* Obviously, the pane of glass scene is a great joke; Buck Henry wrote that, based on an idea of Benton and Newman's. That was like ten jokes building to the guy going through the glass. The glass had to break. If it hadn't broken I would have been shot, and the people would have stormed out of the theater in fury. But one day, while we were going through San Francisco looking for locations—we were about twenty in a bus driving around—I had an idea. I said, "Wouldn't it be funny if we had a Volkswagen bus, and the first car hits it and smashes it up, and then the second car hits it and smashes it some more, and then a third car hits it, and then finally the guy who owns it runs out, and the whole thing falls over?" Everybody laughed, so I said, "Let's do that."

It's just a very satisfying joke because the audience laughs every time the cars hit, and then on the last one, when the thing falls over, they're thrilled that we went all the way with it. It's not even laughter—it's relief. "Thank God he went all the way." But, there's another scene in *What's Up, Doc?* that didn't go all the way, and I'll always regret it. It's when all the cars go in the water, and then the police cars pull up. I should have had one of those police cars go in. I knew in preview the audience wanted that to happen, but I didn't have it. I should have had one of the police cars tear out to the edge of the pier and teeter over the edge, halfway. I should have had two cops jump out, and as they're hanging on above the water, their car topples in. Once it falls, they fall in. That would have been terrific.

Question: Do you think there's a market for that Keystone Kops kind of film?
Bogdanovich: It's not Keystone. It's not Mack Sennett. Look at Mack Sennett's stuff. He's not very funny. If it's influenced by anyone it's Buster Keaton. There have really only been two great visual comedy directors, Buster Keaton and Ernst Lubitsch. Keaton for chases, Lubitsch for everything else. And if you look at Keaton's pictures, you'll see the impeccable placement of the camera, the cutting, the timing. As a director of visual comedy, Chaplin was a klutz compared to Keaton. Keaton was dancing, flying, doing pirouettes, and Chaplin was plodding along. There was nobody else. The Keystone Kops and most of Sennett's stuff is mainly primitive, pretty grotesque running around. It was funny to people in that period; I don't find it funny today at all. So I don't really like to have *What's Up, Doc?* called Keystone comedy. I know what you mean, but I don't think it's accurate. God, I'm a pedant!

Question: Do you feel that great comedy survives?
Bogdanovich: I don't know if everything in a movie works a hundred years from now, but you hope that's what it's going to do. You hope that you're not making a picture that's only going to be a novelty, a seasonal item.

Question: Is *What's Up, Doc?* a picture, in your mind, that people will laugh at twenty-five or thirty years from now?
Bogdanovich: I don't see why not. Kids laugh at it, and older people laugh at it, and I get letters from people who have seen it fifty times. I don't see anything particularly datable about it. No topical jokes. No references to Johnny Carson or Jimmy Carter. There's nothing about it that gets too old. Good comedy doesn't date. I was in Berlin a few months ago for the film festival. I was asked, "What would you like to see while you're in Berlin?" I said, "I'd like to see some silent Lubitsch." So they looked through the archives and found seven silent Lubitsch movies, from about 1919 to about 1923. I was told, "We only have one problem. We can only get the projection room for one day, and we will have to run all the pictures on this day." I said, "Seven pictures in one day?" "When can you start?" I said, "I'll start at noon." I knew we were going to be up late that night before seeing Truffaut's new picture. And we were. The picture is called *The Man Who Loved Women*. We were all sitting around in the bar of the Kempinski Hotel—there's a Lubitsch name if I ever

heard one—and a young German scholar came up. He sat down and gave Truffaut a list on scratched-out paper with arrows and notes. Truffaut sat there with his glasses, turning it over and reading it. I asked what it was. The scholar replied, "I make list of every cross-reference in new movie with every other Truffaut picture. I find forty-eight the first time I see picture." So I said to Francois, "Is it correct?" He said, "Yes, every one is correct." That was stupefying to me.

The next day, at around one in the afternoon, Cybill Shepherd and I started looking at Lubitsch. Just the two of us, and Lubitsch. She loves him, too. The first one was *Madame Dubarry* with Pola Negri, and it's one of the best costume pictures I've ever seen. The second one was a comedy called *Die Bergkatze*, again with Pola Negri, which was never released in America, and it's among the three or four funniest movies I've ever seen. We were just sick from laughing. The third picture was called *Die Puppe*, also a comedy, also hilarious. They were each about an hour or an hour and a half long. Three movies, and it was as if we had just eaten three twenty-course dinners. I said, "Stop a minute." The projectionist said, "But we have to run all the pictures today." I said, "Could we just get something to eat?" They got us sandwiches, and we ate sandwiches while watching the next movie. Finally, around the sixth picture, I was sticking toothpicks into Cybill's leg to keep her awake. "You're not going to get a chance to see it anywhere else! Wake up!" I finally passed out, too. Still, we saw all seven pictures—all those hilarious, silent Lubitsch comedies—in one day in that screening room. But I can't say I saw all of them very clearly. I could tell they were all marvelous.

It's amazing how little we know about the silent era. It never ceases to amaze me how many treasures there are buried in those short fourteen years between 1915 and 1929 when sound came in and ruined everything. Since we began joking about purely visual effects, let me tell you what Mary Pickford once said. "If you looked at the history of motion pictures," she said, "silent pictures and then talkies, and you saw the difference in terms of visual quality between the silent pictures and the talking pictures, somehow you'd honestly think that they would have evolved the opposite way." With that gloomy thought, I bid you adieu.

Peter Bogdanovich Interview

Stephen Myers and Larry Estes / 1979

Interview conducted March 16, 1979. Previously unpublished. Printed by permission of the authors.

Stephen Myers: *Saint Jack* has an unusual history of acquisition. After the property was acquired, how did Roger Corman and New World Pictures become involved?
Peter Bogdanovich: I got involved with Roger because I wanted to make the picture as inexpensively as possible because I wasn't sure if it had a great commercial chance. I didn't know whether it did or not. I think now that it might. And also I just made a couple of expensive pictures that I'd been burned on and I thought it was ridiculous to try to make any more pictures that cost a lot of money. It's just too much responsibility and too much pressure. So the project, which was clearly not an action picture or an obviously commercial picture, I wanted to make it as inexpensively as possible so it would make back its money. I also wanted to make it with Ben [Gazzara]. I didn't want to use anybody else in the part but Gazzara. He was not at the time—and maybe that will change—a big box office name and the studios were going to give me a lot of trouble about why don't I use Gene Hackman or whoever and I didn't want any argument. So I just went to Roger because it was going to be easier that way. I thought it would be good for his company if I did a picture for him and it would be good for me if I did a picture with him because he certainly knows how to do pictures inexpensively. That's about it. Also, he gave me a chance to make my first picture [*Targets*, 1968].

SM: Shooting on location in Singapore must have been a little difficult. Did the local people know the novel and were they nervous about the filming there?
PB: We never told them what the movie was in Singapore. Some of them knew, but the government officially never knew that it was *Saint Jack*.

We called the picture *Jack of Hearts* over there. We even had a ten-page treatment that I wrote called *Jack of Hearts*, which had a completely different plot. We did that because they are pretty strict and because they didn't like the book. And they liked Paul [Theroux]'s subsequent book, *The Great Railway Bazaar*, even less because he had a couple of acerbic paragraphs about Singapore. So they're not too fond of him. So we didn't want them to know what we were doing. Some people knew, but we managed to keep it pretty quiet. It was kind of a nervous situation when we started the picture. We thought we might get thrown out at any moment, but we didn't. Also we had to keep our involvement with *Playboy* quiet because *Playboy* magazine is not allowed in Singapore. When I arrived at customs in Singapore, they said, "Do you have anything to declare?" I said, "No." And they said, "Do you have any copies of *Playboy*?" And I said, "No, I don't have any with me." But I was really amused. I said, "Why? They're not allowed?" And they said, "No." So it was a kind of B-picture atmosphere, you know. Kind of like some B-picture thriller. *Appointment in Honduras* or something. Trench coats. Actually, there weren't trench coats because it was so hot, you want to take off as much as possible when you're in Singapore. But we just had to keep a very low profile. The press got after me on the TV and I just didn't do it. I had to finally do an interview with the press with one dame from the *Straits Times*, which was the main paper there. It was government controlled. She was a nice lady, a young girl. I didn't tell her anything that was true. I had never given an interview in which I lied so consistently. My daughters were there visiting me and they saw this thing because it appeared in the paper with my picture. My older daughter read it and said, "Daddy, you're not thirty-five. You're older. Why didn't you tell the truth?" I said, "Because I wanted to be consistent. There isn't anything true in the whole piece."

SM: Was it a physically difficult location?
PB: Yeah. Sure. Well, Singapore is not a backward country in the sense that they have all the modern hotels and it's a developing country. They're constantly building. It's very small, you know. It's an island, maybe twice the size of Manhattan. And that's the country Singapore. People, when I call, I say I want to call Singapore and they say, "What city in Singapore?" I say, "That's it. Singapore is Singapore." People don't know that. So, yeah, it was a difficult location. But it wasn't difficult like when you're in the middle of Kansas and you have to drive fifty miles to get somewhere. It was just sometimes we would go places where there

would be no toilets or there would be no comfort. And we had nobody there who had ever worked on a picture. We had no crew. We only had about eight people who had ever worked on a picture before. We brought in a Dutch cameraman and his assistant, we had a French soundman and his two assistants, and we had three Dutchmen who worked on the crew like grips and gaffers. And we had a French assistant director. That's it. The rest of the people had never worked on pictures before. They were all Chinese, or Malay, or Indian. Except for the five or six main Caucasian parts—that means Ben Gazzara and five Englishmen and me, because I'm in it—all the other people had never acted before. They were all people in Singapore who had other jobs, because there's only about a one-half to two percent unemployment in Singapore. Almost everybody's working. So the people . . . we'd say, "Can you work?" And they'd say, "Well, what day? I'm working every day." They're all working. They're all shipping clerks or models or a couple of people are very successful businessmen. Travel agencies. One guy was a travel agent. He'd come to work.

SM: Which part do you play in the film, by the way?
PB: Have you read the book?

SM: Yes.
PB: The movie's not like the book. Hardly at all. But there's a character in the book whose name, I think, is Eddie Shuck. Toward the end of the book he's the Army guy who asks him [Jack Flowers] to work for the Army. That character has been totally rewritten. His name is Eddie Schuman in the movie. And he is Army Intelligence, but I don't think there's one line of dialogue that is the same. None of the scenes are the same.

Larry Estes: Are the five Englishmen you referred to known English actors?
PB: They're known in England, particularly. I don't know if they're known that well here. You've probably heard of Denholm Elliott.

LE: Sure.
PB: He plays the leading Englishman. He plays William Leigh. The other four are not as well known. James Villiers, Mark Kingston, Joss Ackland, and Rodney Bewes.

LE: I know Ackland and Villiers.

PB: Villiers has a big part. It's the biggest of the four. He's very funny in it.

SM: You said a minute ago that you never thought of anyone but Ben Gazzara in the role of Jack Flowers. When did you decide that?
PB: I don't know because I played around with a lot of other actors in my mind and I even talked to a couple of other actors about it casually. I never was happy with any of them. I guess it was when I was doing *Opening Night* with Cassavetes. I had a little thing I did for him in *Opening Night*. I went to the shooting and Ben was there. I had met him before but only casually at a party or something. I got to talking to him and we went out and had a drink—John and Ben and three or four others of us—as a matter of fact, we went to a Chinese restaurant in Universal City. Benny's very loud and expansive. I mean he's very garrulous. He just has a very strong voice. It's not that he tries to be loud, it's just that he has a strong voice and he always projects. It would be hard for Ben to whisper. So he's talking and people are looking around. I just liked the way he was in life. And I said to him, in fact, "You behave in life as though every place you are, you're on location on a picture; you sort of feel like you own the place." I don't know why that is. I suppose it's because you're constantly revising the streets or changing what's there. You say, "Get those people off the street!" or "Move those cars out! Get those lights going!" So you figure it's yours. And Ben behaves like every place is on location. I started to think that was a good way to be. It's a nicer way to go through life than to be intimidated by every place. Not that I am, but you know what I'm saying? I got him in my mind for the part then and I couldn't get it out. So that was it. It's just that once I get an idea on somebody, I just can't shake it. It's just like Ben Johnson in *The Last Picture Show*. I just wanted him. He kept saying no. And I tried everything to get him until I finally did. I just couldn't think of anybody else in it.

SM: Do you think you'll ever get Cary Grant?
PB: I almost got him. Almost got him for *Heaven Can Wait*. I was gonna do *Heaven Can Wait*, you know. And Warren [Beatty] and I talked about it for some time. It was his idea to use Cary and, of course, my main reason for wanting to do the picture was because I thought it would be fun to have Cary in it. And I almost got him, but . . . that's another story.

SM: Was that James Mason's part?
PB: Yeah. But it was going to be completely rewritten. It's rather a poor

part, actually. It's a dull part. It was dull and I knew Cary wouldn't do it unless it was rewritten. I haven't seen the picture. But it was a dull script. The part was dull in the script. I knew it had to be rewritten for Cary. I told him some of the ideas, which he kind of liked. But that's another story. That's a story of Warren and me. Anyway, I'm glad I didn't do the picture despite the fact that I hear that it's very successful and very good.

SM: I was wondering since you appeared in *Opening Night* if you were using any improvisational techniques in *Saint Jack*.
PB: No. We tried to make it look that way, though. Most of it was written down. Almost all of it was written, but we kept rewriting it. For instance, we would go someplace, a real place. We would talk to the people there. We would have an experience of some kind with prostitutes or transvestites, or pimps, or whatever. Then we would get back to the hotel room and we'd sit down and remember what happened and construct a scene out of it. We would all sit around and dictate it, get it down like that. And sometimes Ben would throw in a line during a scene that wasn't written, but it was unusual. It was all written down and then we would make it seem extemporaneous.

SM: You said that the movie is quite different from the novel. What changes did you and the screenwriter [Howard Sackler] make and did you have contact with Theroux during the writing?
PB: Paul and I worked together for about a month on the first draft or so, which was quite a bit like the book. Every draft that was done subsequently . . . first by me alone and then by Howard Sackler and me; and then later by Ben Gazzara; the associate producer, and old friend of mine, George Morfogen; and me in Singapore. All those drafts consistently kept moving further and further away from the book. It's very different in construction than the book, of course, because the book begins sort of in the middle and goes backward and comes around again. And it covers a period of twelve or fifteen years. We did it in two and a half or three years. In the book, William Leigh comes from Hong Kong once and dies. In our version, he comes three times. He comes to audit the books over a period of three years. That was Sackler's main contribution, figuring out how to construct the script so that it would have a first act, second act, and third act. That was very helpful. But really the biggest changes are subtler than anything to do with plot, although we did clear up the plot in many ways because it was murky in the book. It was really to do with character and trying to make a movie. What we kept saying

while we were there was, "Let's try to make this movie free of bullshit." We'd get ourselves into a movie situation and we'd say, "This is a movie situation. It's full of shit. Let's get out of it." That was the main thrust of what we did. What we tried to do in Singapore was to try to give it a kind of freshness. Everybody who makes movies falls into certain traps and certain ruts, and certain easy ways of doing things whereby characters say things in movies not because they would do them in real life, but because it's easier ... and moves the plot along or enables the other character to react in a way that you require them to react. We tried to strip all that away and say, "O.K. Let's have the people really talk independently for themselves. Everybody's on their own." It sounds easy, but it actually is hard because you have no convenient clichés to fall back on. Also we said, "Let's not underline anything. And if the audience doesn't follow it, fuck 'em." But we didn't go quite that far. In other words, we weren't trying to be obscure. What we were trying to do was not to spoon feed the audience, not to give them pablum like so many movies do. We tried to just tell the story as honestly and as free of bullshit as possible. I've said it. For instance, the character that I was supposed to play in the book was kind of a ridiculous heavy. I mean, he was ridiculous and a heavy. I think that Paul intended for him to be ridiculous, he made fun of him, made him a mock heavy. First of all, I couldn't play that if it was going to be me because it's not the kind of thing I can play. Also I thought it diminished Jack because Jack talks to him and deals with him and I thought he was diminished that way. What we did was we made the character of Eddie Schuman as strong and likeable as possible. If, in fact, he is presenting alternatives to Jack that would lead him on the road to perdition or Hell ... Well, you know, the devil is very attractive. It's only in Walt Disney pictures that the witch is ugly. Because the witches can be beautiful. And they're more effective if they're beautiful or attractive. You know what I'm saying. We made the relationship between Jack and me very friendly, actually. That's a good example of what I'm talking about. Also, the relationship between Jack and William Leigh was muddy in the book. They sort of half-assed became friends or it only happened in one or two days in the book. We had it happen over a period of years and we thought that it was important that that relationship be unspoken, but genuine and deep. And that's hard to do without spelling it out. It's hard to do without the people saying, "Gee, I really like you and I really want to get into you." A lot of the way it works—and I think it does work—is thanks to the certain something between Denholm and Ben that worked. It works particularly well on the screen when we see them together because they're such an odd couple and yet they work.

LE: When do we get to see it?
PB: Well, you're leaving in about an hour (laughs), so I don't know how you're gonna get to see it.

LE: Do you think it will be out before the end of the year to qualify [for the Academy Awards]?
PB: No. But you could see it if you're back here. We'll be running it. It's a rough cut. It's not rough, it's just a work print. It's pretty smooth by now, but the sound needs some . . .

LE: Is there music?
PB: There is music. Source music. Nobody's ever noticed that I never use scores. I never had a score. It isn't too conscious on my part. I just always think, maybe I'll have a score on this one and then I'm never able to figure out where to put the cues. I'm always embarrassed when the score comes into a movie. I mean, if it was my movie, I think I would be. I'm not particularly embarrassed by it in other people's movies. But it always seems to me like an admission of failure.

SM: The scene doesn't work. . . .
PB: The scene doesn't work so you put music in. I mean, music that underscores the scene. Like you've got an insert of someone reaching for that [reaches for matchbook]. You hear "Dah, dah." Hand comes in and takes it. "Dah, dah, dah, hmmm." All that shit. I don't know what it's for. A girl who's in love with a guy . . . "Dee, dee, dah, dah." I remember John Ford said a wonderful thing about that. I was talking about *The Searchers*. I said that I thought it was a great picture. He says [imitating Ford], "Yeah, there's too much music in it." I said, "There's too much music?" [Ford voice]: "Yeah." [PB]: "You didn't . . . ?" [Ford voice]: "No. I didn't put that music in. Too much music. You know, I always think you got a guy in the middle of the desert dying of thirst and there's the goddamned philharmonic soaring away behind him. It seems to me ridiculous." And that's sort of the way I feel about it. If I use source music, which I've done in every picture except *At Long Last Love*, of course, which was a musical, I always try to find music that is counterpoint to the scene, that doesn't underline visually what the scene is, but plays

counterpoint against it almost. Because I figure if you've got the visual doing one thing, the sound ought to be doing something else because if they're both doing the same thing, you're wasting one of your tools.

SM: I noticed that throughout *The Last Picture Show*, not just the music but other sound, particularly in the scene in which Cloris Leachman opens the door and there's this burst of laughter from the TV set.
PB: At the end. Good.

SM: You're not feeling laughter at the time. It's a really striking moment.
PB: That was the most dangerous use I ever did because that whole last scene is played with laughter and a kind of ridiculously silly song, kind of a "Hee Haw" song going on in the background. I remember when I first put it in, when I would see it with an audience I was always terrified that they would be listening to it and they would laugh. It never happened that they laughed. But I always thought, "Oh Christ, I'm taking a risk here because what if they laugh."

SM: Do you have another project?
PB: Several, but I don't know what I'm going to do next. I'm not giving you a glib answer. I don't know what I'm going to do next. I have no idea. I have got three or four things I'm thinking about, but nothing I'm sure about.

SM: By the way, I work at the AFI in the Film Library . . .
PB: Oh, you do?

SM: . . . and I just sent out *Directed by John Ford* to the Utah Film Festival.
PB: Yeah, I was up there. How many prints have you got in there?

SM: Two.
PB: Thirty-five [millimeter].

SM: Yeah. Two thirty-fives. How was the print? Did you see any of it?
PB: All I saw was a minute, really. It looked OK.

SM: It sounds crazy for me to ask you since I work there, but I don't know. Could you tell me why there aren't 35 millimeter prints theatrically available on *Directed by John Ford*?
PB: Yeah. Because the AFI, in their infinite wisdom, managed to get

permission from all the studios except RKO. With RKO, the only rights they could get was non-theatrical, non-playing. So the picture can't be shown anywhere where anybody can pay to see it. That's why it took so long to make the picture. I was asked to do it in '68 or something. I started working on it in '68 and shot most of it in '68, '69. It wasn't finished until '71 because they couldn't get the rights to anything. And they did it so slowly.

SM: I didn't realize when you had started.
PB: I think I shot the stuff with the people in the movie in '69. I was shooting *Picture Show*, I was preparing *Picture Show* in '70, so it was before that. I finally cut it. I said, "Fuck it. They haven't got me the rights, they haven't got me the clips, they haven't got anything. I want to make another picture." I cut it at the same time I was cutting *Picture Show*. Physically cut it at the same time. Cutting both at the same time.

SM: Now we're talking about the editing of *The Last Picture Show*. That was my next question. I thought there were two sequences that were really emotional for me. One of them was the fight between Duane and Sonny and the other was the death of Billy, when Sonny finally looks out the door and sees that broom. And then you see the broom closer.
PB: Yeah.

SM: Was that something you had decided on before you got on location, was it something you decided on during the shooting, or when you got into the editing room?
PB: Which? What do you mean to decide? How to shoot it?

SM: How it was going to look on the screen.
PB: Usually, almost invariably, the cutting and where the cutting goes I decide some time just before I shoot the scene. Sometimes it's planned out in rehearsals. On every picture I've made we've rehearsed for at least two weeks, sometimes longer. On *Saint Jack* we rehearsed three weeks. *At Long Last Love* we rehearsed eight weeks or something. But *Picture Show* we rehearsed two weeks. Some time during the rehearsals, where I was going to put the camera and therefore where I was going to cut. Like for the scene with Duane and Sonny when they go around the car and they have the fight, that was all worked out. The actors knew also where the cuts were going to come. What you see in that sequence on the screen is all I shot. There was nothing left over. There's just the slate and the tail

trim. So we never shot the whole scene each angle. There's about forty cuts there, thirty-five cuts or something in that sequence. And what you see is exactly what we shot. We didn't overlap anything. The actors had rehearsed it without cutting. We had rehearsed it several times all the way through. And I would tell them, "I'm gonna cut here and you're gonna have to pick it up." So they knew the flow of the scene and they could jump into it anywhere because they knew what the emotion was. The cutting of that was worked out in rehearsals. The thing with the broom, I couldn't tell you how or when I decided on that. It was certainly before the cutting room. I don't leave many decisions for the cutting room and the older I get and the more experience I have, the less I leave to the cutting room. Which doesn't mean that you don't have things to do in the cutting room. Things change your mind and you think of better things. But essentially when I'm shooting the picture, I know the cutting. For the broom thing, we did two set-ups. It wasn't something you could decide in the cutting room. We needed a long shot and a slightly closer shot, the same exact angle. It was really a zoom with the zoom taken out. Normally you would do that with a zoom, but I don't like zooms.

SM: It wouldn't have worked the same way.
PB: No. It was a good effect.

SM: It reminded, not at the time I saw it, but later when I saw *The Birds* again, it reminded me of the sequence when . . .
PB: . . . where he sees the eyes.

SM: Right.
PB: Yeah. I think it reminded me of it, too. I think I stole it from him. It's an effective way of punching something. It's really like a double take. You're looking at something and you're looking at it closer, which you do in life. One does sort of zero in on something.

SM: Actually he (Sonny) had done that previously, just in hearing it. He had heard the brakes squeal.
PB: That's all.

SM: And he hadn't really noticed it. Then he heard something else. Then he looked.
PB: He looked out because he heard the brakes. He saw the truck was stopped and then he came outside. He was turning to leave and then he

noticed the broom. That usually got an audible reaction from an audience, that shot. They would gasp. Nice to know that it worked.

SM: It must have been very gratifying then when you went to the New York Film Festival.
PB: It was surprising because one had no idea at all. I never thought the picture would do any business at all. To tell you the truth, Steve, I don't remember thinking about it. I don't remember thinking about whether this is going to be successful or not successful. I remember some people told me they didn't think it would be. And some people said they didn't think I would get much out of it because it was an actors' vehicle. In fact, Orson Welles said that. He said, "You're not going to get anything out of this. All they're gonna say is how good the actors are, if they're good." Well, it didn't work out that way. One of the reasons for doing the picture is that I had made *Targets*. It was a thriller. I thought the action sequences were quite good in that picture. In fact, they were good. But I didn't think the acting was as good as it could have been. Of course, we only shot it in twenty-five days. But still, I was not as happy with the acting in it. I thought Boris was good and I thought that Tim [O'Kelly], the boy who played the killer, was good; but I didn't think anybody else was all that hot. And I wanted to do a movie in which the performances were everything just to see if I could do it. Because I had already done the action. So now it was time to see if I could really get some good acting.

SM: Well, you did. It's probably the most perfectly cast film I can think of.
PB: There was only one part in it that was miscast. He was all right in it, it's just that it wasn't my original idea. The character that Clu Gulager plays, Abilene. I had wanted to use Jimmy Dean, the country and western singer. I thought he would have been wonderful. And the producers were against it. I'm sorry I didn't fight for that more.

SM: Apparently there were cuts made in the script as you were doing shooting . . .
PB: . . . which we didn't shoot at all.

SM: . . . and then there were things that you shot that were cut out. Could you talk about what they were?
PB: There was a lot of stuff. When the picture was finished, originally, it was about twenty-five minutes longer. A lot of that stuff shouldn't have

been in it. It was just long walks and stuff. But there were a few scenes, probably a total of three or four minutes, that should have been in the picture that aren't. Everybody was worried that it would be too long. It was a long picture and it wasn't a picture with any action. It wasn't a conventional movie in any way. It was in black-and-white. It was kind of depressing. The producers felt it was too long. They kept wanting me to get it under two hours. Finally did get it under two hours. Then when it opened, nobody ever said it was too long. So about seven or eight months later I said to Bert Schneider, "Listen, I want to put a scene back that I feel we never should have cut." Because a lot of people kept asking me where Duane and Sonny lived. How come you never dealt with their mother and father? There was a scene that had dealt with that early on and it was one of those scenes that they said didn't matter. And I always thought that it did matter. So I did put it back into the negative and it was in subsequent prints and it's always been on television. I think it's a scene between Sonny and the waitress.

SM: Genevieve the waitress.
PB: Genevieve the waitress. You remember the scene.

SM: Very well.
PB: That was cut out. Then there was a really interesting little scene between Sonny, Duane, and Jacy when they're driving away from school. They're kind of kidding around, racing another car. And they sing the school song, putting it on. They're kind of kidding around, joking. And the three of them are in the front seat of the car. It was kind of a nice scene. It preceded the scene with the French fries when they're in front of that place and the mother comes up. And it was a nice scene because it paid off at the end when he [Sonny] is at the football game and you hear the school song. It would have had an additional meaning there which it now doesn't have. I always was sorry that I cut that scene. Even though it wasn't brilliantly acted, I've been sorry that that scene isn't there.

SM: Did you also shoot the class picnic before they go to the motel?
PB: Yeah, that was shot, but that wasn't very good. I'm glad I took that out. It was all right. It was long. I didn't mind losing that, but we did shoot it. We also shot a scene on the pool table when Jacy gets seduced, or allows herself to be seduced by Abilene. That was an effective scene. I cut that out myself. I didn't want to have it in the picture because I thought it was redundant.

SM: You shot *The Last Picture Show* and *Paper Moon* in black-and-white and it had been a few years since there had been a commercial Hollywood picture. Since then there has been *Young Frankenstein* and *Lenny*. What did it take for you to convince the producer or the studio to go with black-and-white?

PB: Well, it was easier than you would think. I told Bert Schneider that I wanted to do the picture in black-and-white. This was late. We were about ready to go shoot it. He said, "Why?" I just said that I thought the picture should be in black-and-white. I thought it would give us the period quicker without any problems. I thought we would be able to get better photography. I had been down to Texas and I had photographed a lot of those little towns in color. Sixteen millimeter just to remind me of what I had seen. These were bleak, sad little places you'd drive into and you'd think it was the end of the world. And then when you saw it on the screen in color, they didn't look so bad. Because color has a way of glamorizing things, romanticizing. I said all this to Bert. I said that I felt the acting was everything in this picture and that the actors would seem better in black-and-white. (Which is true of acting.) Now Columbia had had a big success at that time with a picture called *Easy Rider*. And I think that because of that, the studio (the head of the studio at that time was Bert's brother), more than likely if Bert Schneider had come to them and said, "I want to make a picture in eight millimeter," they probably would have said that he's got to know something we don't know. So I don't think he had any trouble.

SM: Did you have any difficulty finding cinematographers who could work well in black-and-white?

PB: Well, I used an old guy named Bob Surtees. I talked to a whole bunch of photographers about it and I ended up with Bob because he had done good black-and-white before and because Laszlo Kovacs was not available. (He was shooting some crappy picture that he always regretted having shot and which I told him not to shoot. But that's another story.)

SM: Do you have problems with labs with black-and-white since they don't do very much of it anymore?

PB: No. You have to sit on them, but you have problems with labs on every movie. They have to be sat on, often.

SM: When Polly Platt was at AFI a few months ago doing a seminar, she said that on *What's Up, Doc?* when you came on the set for the final party before the chase begins, that you suddenly had ideas about gags to use, like the huge foot that falls down and kicks somebody down the stairs. Does that happen very often with you, to just have a moment of inspiration on the set?

PB: Well, often seeing a set or a location for the first time or walking onto it and knowing that you're going to have to use it, is like finding an actor that you're going to use. You get inspired looking at an actor. You think of things you'd like them to do or think of ways you'd like them to behave. So you see a set and you say, "Wouldn't it be funny if . . .?" or "Wouldn't it be nice if . . ." Yeah, it happens often. It better happen. Otherwise you're in trouble. Well, in the script in that sequence, all it said was, "And now ensues a fight which will be staged by the director." That was all it said. Buck Henry wrote, "A brilliant fight ensues which will be staged by the director." So I had nothing to do but just make it up.

SM: In all the criticisms I've read about the film, there is always the obvious connection made with *Bringing Up Baby*.
PB: Which they wouldn't have noticed if I hadn't said it. I'm the one who said it.

SM: The thing that strikes me, though, particularly at the end of the film is that really Barbara Streisand is Bugs Bunny and Ryan is a scientific Elmer Fudd.
PB: Sort of. That's really what it is. It's a cartoon more than it is a movie.

SM: It seems more Chuck Jones, in a way, than Howard Hawks.
PB: Well, the chases are influenced most by Keaton. But it's a cartoon. I always thought of it as kind of a comedy version of *Targets* (laughs) in which the element of destruction is positive as opposed to negative. That's all. You know, Tim [O'Kelly] goes around shooting people and Barbara goes around stealing and trying to inveigle her life into other people's lives. It's sort of the same idea as *Targets* (laughs). Also, people ask me why the picture is so ugly visually. I say it's on purpose because the whole picture is supposed to look like a Holiday Inn or a Hilton Hotel. That's where we shot it.

SM: In lobbies and airports.
PB: Lobbies. Airports. It's all sort of awful urban sprawl. Also, San Francisco is kind of a silly city. I mean, I love it, but it has its silly elements

that seemed to me a good reason to shoot it in San Francisco. Those hills, those ridiculous hills you have to walk up.

SM: *Paper Moon* is a very funny picture, but it seems to me that there is also an undercurrent of great sadness, particularly with the little girl Addie.
PB: I think so. I'm glad you say that. I always thought so. People say, "What a funny, charming movie." I thought it was one of the saddest movies I made because this girl is nine years old and she's put through the mill. All she wants is for the father to say that he loves her and that he's her father. He won't do it. It's only because she's witty and has some guile at the end that she's able to pull off the ending.

SM: The only reason he keeps her as long as he does is because he finds that it's profitable.
PB: He uses her. It's profitable. That's right. It *is* profitable. I don't think there's any question in the fact that he kind of likes her. . . . Not likes her, but he feels guilty and he has a certain attachment to her. But the audience reads in all the sentiment, you see. The audience is so used to sentimental attachments between fathers and daughters, and besides the fact that Ryan and Tatum *are* father and daughter, that they are reading into it what is not in the script and not in the movie. Very carefully not in the movie. Because I feel the ending is very sad. She loves him. She'll do anything to be with him, as some daughters will for their fathers.

SM: The saddest scene for me was the one in which she and Imogene—really it's the first contact between two children in the film. They have both had to be adults all this time. Then in order to get what each wants, they have to concoct a scheme which necessitates that they will be split up. That scene in which Addie runs down the hall and the girl is just standing there waving.
PB: Yes. It's the last time you see her. Yeah, that was nice.

SM: It's really sad.
PB: I think the picture is sad. People have, generally speaking, never pointed out the blacker aspects of that movie. Like that scene right after that. I think it's the next shot when they're riding in the car and we're on their backs. Ryan says, "I don't know why that woman did such a thing to me. I would have done anything for that woman. Has this been going

on a long time?" She says, "Oh yeah. From the beginning." He says, "You promise me something, Addie." She says, "What?" He says, "Promise me when you grow up you'll never be the kind of woman that goes around deceiving men." She says, "I promise, Moze." I think it's such a devastating scene, that's why I played it on their backs. You couldn't see their faces for that scene. I *had* it the other way on their faces. People miss the point of that movie. It's all right, though.

SM: Also, Trixie is a pathetic character. You laugh at her, but . . .
PB: Oh yes. But she's so touching. That scene on the hill, she'll just break your heart. Yeah, *Paper Moon* and *At Long Last Love* are two sides of what happened in 1936 (laughs). There was the Depression and there was New York. There were the rich people and the poor people. The poor people were in the middle of Kansas and the rich people were fucking around and throwing away food in the middle of Long Island.

SM: You have interviewed several directors and you even watched John Ford direct some of *Cheyenne Autumn*.
PB: I've watched a lot of directors. I watched Hawks work too on two or three pictures.

SM: Oh, really? Which pictures?
PB: Oh, *Man's Favorite Sport?*, *El Dorado*, *Rio Lobo*.

SM: Is there anything that you think you took away or think you learned from watching them direct?
PB: I learned a lot from all of them in terms of how to deal with people. I couldn't say exactly. It was just a question of osmosis. I never sat around taking notes saying, "Now I'm learning this." I just watched and kept my eyes open and my ears open. I never really studied movies, either, which is a misconception people have about me—that I sat and noted shots and all that. I never did any of that. I just went to a lot of movies and sometimes looked at them more than once. I never was really aware of shots. I didn't like to look at them because it would sort of ruin the movie for me.

SM: Speaking of problems that would come up while you're shooting, I read that you didn't get along very well with Timothy Bottoms . . .
PB: No.

SM: . . . and I understand that he didn't get along well with all the other actors, but . . .
PB: He hasn't gotten along with anybody, before or after. Nobody seems to get along with Tim.

SM: How do you handle on the set a problem with an actor? A personality problem?
PB: It never really flared up on the set so that it was particularly noticeable. It was just sort of a quiet tension and Tim was too young and inexperienced to make a lot of trouble or anything. He just had this sort of unpleasant attitude, superior attitude, born of insecurity. So we dealt with it. He's all right in the picture. People like him in the picture. I thought he was OK. In other words, what I'm saying is that it wasn't anything like big scenes. It wasn't anything you might imagine. It was just sort of a subtle undercurrent of displeasure.

SM: I think he's good in the film, too. I wouldn't have thought, until I read later, that there was any problem.
PB: He is good. We had to work hard to get him to be good, but he was good. He was young. He was just nineteen, you know.

SM: Oh, I didn't realize that.
PB: Yeah, they were all young. They were all nineteen—Cybill, Jeff, Tim. They were either nineteen or just turning twenty.

SM: It's amazing when you think about all the actors who were in that picture and the careers that that picture started for them.
PB: Almost everybody.

SM: Ben [Johnson] had had a career.
PB: Ben's career was over.

SM: It started all over again.
PB: Cloris's career was nowhere. Yeah, I know. It's amazing. It's very gratifying because I thought they were all good actors. Plus there were some kids that we found in Texas who came up and did pretty well, like Randy Quaid. John Hillerman was in that picture. It was his first picture.

SM: He's a funny, funny actor . . . in *What's Up, Doc?*

PB: Wasn't he good in that? And in *At Long Last Love*, I think he's wonderful. He was in *Paper Moon*.

SM: He played a dual role of the sheriff and the moonshiner brother.
PB: He was so good, nobody ever noticed it.

SM: It was the second time around before I noticed. After the credits, I had to go back and see it again.
PB: It's amazing. He's a very good actor. I've known him for years, you know. He's one of my oldest friends. I mean, I've known him for twenty years or more.

SM: You knew him from New York?
PB: From New York, yeah. We acted together.

SM: How did you become involved in producing Samuel Fuller's *The Big Red One* and when did you leave the project?
PB: When I first met Sam in 1964, he told me about this project and I said why the hell didn't he make it. He told me a litany of postponements and things. I begged him from then on to please write it. And when I got some money in . . . I don't know really what year it was. After *Daisy Miller*. I got him some money, an advance to write it. And he did. We took it around. We had some problems with the studios and finally we found Lorimar was interested. Lee Marvin wanted to do it. I was involved in it for awhile until it became apparent that I really didn't want to go and be the line producer and do all that. I just wasn't interested.

SM: Were you still thinking about acting in it at that time?
PB: Well, he wanted me to act in it. Sam really wanted me to play that part. I didn't want to be the line producer, but I thought I would be there on the set anyway if I was going to act in it, so I could help out. But it became more apparent and more apparent that I was going to be doing another picture at the same time, that I really wanted to do another picture and not just sit around for ten weeks acting. And also I was worried, frankly, about playing a soldier. I told this to Sam. I think people know me and I have a personality that enough people know that I think it's going to be too hard for people to believe that I'm a dogface. I don't even know how to hold a rifle. I mean, I do know how to hold a rifle, actually. But I don't seem like I'm the type to run around with an M-1. I just felt uncomfortable with the thought of it. I thought it would be stretching

and asking too much of the audience. I really was afraid that it would hurt the believability of the picture, that Peter Bogdanovich was going to be a dogface. I was looking at it objectively. In other words, if I were directing it, I wouldn't have cast me. Finally, it worked out that I couldn't anyway because of *Saint Jack*. I'm glad because he's got Lee and he's got unknowns, really. I mean, Mark Hamill, I suppose people know him, but he's not a real familiar face. I think that's the way the picture should have been done, and I'm glad it's the way he did it.

SM: Have you seen any of the footage?
PB: Not a foot, but I hear it's super. But I always knew it would be. I brought Gene Corman into it. I put the whole thing together and brought Gene and Sam together, worked that out. And Lorimar. Then I stepped away from it. I retain some interest in it. Really the main idea was to see if I could get it on for Sam because I thought it would be a good movie. I kept saying, "I want to see this movie. If I have to get it fucking produced, I will, because I want to see it." That's really the truth. I wanted to see the picture. And I'm sure it will probably be the best picture of next year.

SM: Do you have any idea when your book on Orson Welles will be completed?
PB: Well, it's been completed two or three times, it's just that Orson would prefer it not to come out now. He's working on other things he's written: his memoirs and so on. So it's sitting around somewhere. It will come out eventually. I have no idea when it will come out. It certainly won't be in the next two or three years. The material is there. It's very powerful and, I think, very good.

SM: Everybody is waiting for it.
PB: Well, it can be a wait. I could write a hell of a book about Orson, but it's going to be awhile.

SM: What about the movie?
PB: The movie? I don't know. *The Other Side of the Wind*. I don't know. I've seen a lot of it. He's shot 95 per cent of it. An awful lot of it is even cut together. But he needs that last little bit of money to finish it. The last I heard from him he said that there was a light at the end of the tunnel. He said that about a month and a half ago and I haven't heard from him since. In fact, I must call him. I don't know what's happening. But

it's an extraordinary piece of work. And it really deserves to be out and seen. Wonderful. What he did is extraordinary and how he did it. . . . It's a miracle that any of it has been done. [John] Huston is brilliant in it. All the acting is very good. I've got a big part in it, you know. I'd really like to see it. I don't look that good in it because I look twenty-five pounds fatter in it, but I'm good in it, I think. And John is extraordinary. All the performances are.

SM: It's really sad that he can't find the financing. I understand that the major reason he went to the AFI Salute was really to show pieces of the film and to get someone interested in it.
PB: That's right. To try to get some money. It was a naïve hope.

SM: Richard Wilson even said that that night he felt that there was a lot of animosity in the audience. Did you feel that too?
PB: Oh yeah. Well, it was an unpopular award. The town was not pleased that Orson Welles was getting that award. A lot of people didn't come for that reason.

SM: That's really sad.
PB: Well, Steve, it's a shit-eating business. Let's face it. We all write about him, me included. I say "we," I mean "me." We all write about the wonderful days of Hollywood, but it was always shitty. People were always going through hell. And they're always going to when you have an art that is essentially ruled by money. And it's so expensive that it has to be. It's not like a guy who wants to sit down and write a book and he can write it on toilet paper if he has to. A guy wants to paint a picture, he can paint it on a wall. You can't make a movie without some money. Even a little movie costs more than most of us have. It's always going to be like that because there are people who are interested in money and there are people who are interested in art. And the two of them usually aren't the same. There's nothing new about it. There is no art without patronage. Artists don't live in vacuums. I don't believe that artists should live in ivory towers. I believe that artists should pay their way. But there are always exceptions to that rule. And there are always the ones who are special and who have to be treated differently. And there's not room for them. And there should be room for them. In fact, there was more room for the mavericks when there were more movies being made than there is now. There was more room for an Orson Welles in the forties and even in the fifties than there is today because there were more movies being

made. Imagine. A studio, if it made forty-five movies in a year and one of them was a crazy, artistic triumph and nobody went to see it, what the hell, they could afford it. You'd be amazed at some of the movies that lost money. Garbo's movies never made much money. Neither did Lubitsch's. *The Merry Widow* lost money. That wonderful one with Chevalier and Jeanette MacDonald—one of my favorite movies that I've ever seen.

SM: It's interesting that some of the ones that made the most money, now you haven't even heard of.
PB: The ones that made the money are the bombs today. That's right. You couldn't pay people to go see them today. Sure. That's the way it is. That's the way it always is. Come on, let's face it. When Beaumont and Fletcher were writing plays and Shakespeare was retired, everybody said, "Well, that old has-been, William Shakespeare. It's Beaumont and Fletcher. That's what's playing. Let's go see Beaumont and Fletcher." You got to get used to that when you make pictures or do anything. In any kind of endeavor, if it is completely understood, appreciated, and applauded in its own time, the likelihood is that it won't survive other times. That's why I'm always happy if my pictures don't make a fortune. I think there is something vulgar about making the kind of money that *Jaws* makes. Too accepted, you know (laughs). That's too much. I'm happy if they make their money back and make a nice profit and enough people go see it. *Paper Moon* had a nice gross. *What's Up, Doc?* already was getting to be too popular (laughs). No, I'm kidding. I think it's wonderful when people go to see your pictures and have a good time. It doesn't even matter if they understand it. You know, you said you had a feeling about *Paper Moon*, a certain sadness. I said a lot of people didn't get that. It doesn't matter if they got it or not. You got it. That's one. If there's one out there, maybe there's another few. And that's all you really can expect. In an audience of a hundred, if one person gets what it's really about, that's plenty. Other people enjoy it on another level. Movies are primarily, like any art—and particularly movies which are such a mass medium—there should be several levels on which they work. It's those movies that only work on one level, whether it be an artistic level or an entertainment level, I always think there is something missing. Because they should work on at least two or three levels. There's an exchange about that in my book on Fritz Lang in which he talks about that, the various strata of the audience.

Peter Bogdanovich: "What Is the Point of Making Pictures?"

Michael Ventura / 1982

From *L.A. Weekly*, May 28–June 3, 1982. Reprinted by permission of the author.

Peter Bogdanovich has made many very good movies and at least one great one. *The Last Picture Show* was a classic as soon as anyone saw it. Add to that *Paper Moon, What's Up, Doc?, Saint Jack, They All Laughed*—and argue about *Daisy Miller, At Long Last Love,* and *Nickelodeon*. He's discovered excellent actors and a few stars: Tatum O'Neal, Ellen Burstyn, Jeff Bridges, Cybill Shepherd, Timothy Bottoms, Cloris Leachman, Randy Quaid. Others have done their best work in his pictures: Barbra Streisand, Ryan O'Neal, Ben Johnson, Ben Gazzara, John Ritter. And, of course, Dorothy Stratten (in response to whose murder he's taken a hiatus from films to write a book about her). Or, at least, a hiatus from making films. Bogdanovich's company, Moon Pictures, is buying and producing properties while he writes about Stratten.

I'm summarizing his work because after a name becomes as well known as "Peter Bogdanovich," one forgets what he's actually *done*—forgets that, with his eye for talent, his influence has gone beyond his own films. It's also largely forgotten that during the 1960s Bogdanovich was, with Andrew Sarris, a very important film critic. Sarris was mostly responsible for Americans recognizing the importance of John Ford, Howard Hawks, Alfred Hitchcock and many other names taken for granted as "great" now, but not taken very seriously before the mid-sixties. After Sarris's breakthrough, Bogdanovich's writing and interviewing preserved as much of the feel and technique of these men as could be put into words—his *Pieces of Time* is one of the most important, and certainly one of the most gracefully written, of all the books about the movies.

So much for history. I went to Bogdanovich because he's the conscious inheritor of everything that's been best in American movies. And because it seems to me that the crisis in American filmmaking now—and with American film production halved this year, and American production values becoming more and more shoddy, it is no less than a crisis—is primarily a crisis in technique.

Ezra Pound has said, "Technique is the test of a man's sincerity." In days of belief—whether it's a belief in Christianity or in making movies—the cathedrals are better built, the paintings are more meticulously painted, and even a "B" film is superbly lit. (Look, for instance, at the Basil Rathbone *Sherlock Holmes* series for camerawork and lighting that shames almost all our $30 million productions today.) Talking about belief is airy and abstract—but what *is* technique in film, that measure of belief in what one is doing? What is it, and where has it gone? I asked Bogdanovich about the basics, and he gave me what amounted to a Master's class. For I think that only a more thorough grounding in technique by the people most intensely interested in film—from the passionate intellectual movie buff to the director, from the actor to the producer to the studio lawyer—is going to give us, once again, a film culture instead of simply a film market.

Michael Ventura: In general in the film business, I've found a great ignorance of the history of movies. I don't mean in a scholarly way. I mean in learning to look at the quote-unquote "old masters." Do you find a squandered heritage?
Peter Bogdanovich: Well, we certainly have gone backward. In terms of the technique of making movies we've been going backward for some years. They used to make pictures better, and more economically, and faster, there's no question about it. We're having to learn all over again. After I finished *Nickelodeon* somebody said to me, "How do you feel?" I didn't like the picture, and I said, "Well, I think now I know how to make pictures, maybe I can make a few." Because it takes a while to learn. Ford directed for years before he made *The Iron Horse*, which is his first known masterpiece. Hawks was directing for some years before he made *Scarface*—he'd made seven or eight pictures, none of them that hot. Hitchcock, the same. All the best directors made a lot of pictures before they made that *one*.

But they worked a lot more than we get a chance to. They were shooting all the time. I mean, Allan Dwan was shooting six days a week for ten years every fucking day. And so was Griffith. Ford would shoot three pictures a year. In 1939, the year I was born, Jack Ford released three movies, and each one is a masterpiece: *Stagecoach, Young Mr. Lincoln,* and *Drums Along the Mohawk.*

Ventura: What do you call well directed?

Bogdanovich: So you don't see the seams, you know? So you can't tell it was directed. In other words, to me the best pictures are the ones where you may feel the director but you don't notice him. Except through a kind of inference. I don't like movies where you say, "Oh, that was a great shot," "Isn't that a great camera-move?"—if you're noticing it, I'm not happy about it. Just tell the story and stop fiddling with all that, was John Ford's attitude. People used to say, "John Ford never moves the camera." I have *looked* at some John Ford movies: he moves the camera quite often; the thing is you don't *notice* it—that's why it's good. Same thing with Hawks.

Ventura: Have you found a big difference in making studio pictures and independent pictures?

Bogdanovich: There hasn't *been* a studio since I've been directing. The reason the old studios had an image, so to speak, was that there was one guy who ran it for a long time—he *owned* it! Warner owned Warner's. Metro-Goldwyn-Mayer, Mayer was *there*. Harry Cohn's studio was Columbia. Now the people who run it are employees and they come and go. So essentially it's all become sort of one studio—there're just different addresses.

Ventura: What about "studio" meaning sound stage as opposed to on location?

Bogdanovich: Of all my pictures, the only two that for me don't work anywhere near the way they were intended to were *At Long Last Love* and *Nickelodeon*, and both of them were heavily made in studios. The best parts of *Nickelodeon* were made on location, the rest of the stuff had that studio feeling I hate. We can't do it anymore. I think the reason we can't do it anymore is simply: black-and-white and color. You can't shoot color in the studio. You never could. Color is distracting. The only reason they got away with it in the old days was that the public didn't notice and didn't give a shit. They hadn't read twenty articles and fifty books about movies. And they didn't go on Universal Tours, where they tell 'em how not to make pictures. Now the public knows that there are studios, there are fake rocks, there are stunt men—people didn't think about that back then. So all we've done is to take them backstage at the magician's show and made it tougher for the magician.

A good example, *Only Angels Have Wings*, a completely studio picture *but* it's in black-and-white and there's a lot of fog. So you don't see the phoniness of it. If it was in color it would be no good, I'm sure. The minute you have color you've got to do it more carefully. You can't cheat. It's much tougher to cheat in color.

It's like John Ford said, "A good dramatic story, give me black and white." Orson Welles said, "Black and white is the actors' friend." That's another reason the performances looked so good in the thirties and forties, it's easier to be a good actor in black and white. You're not looking to see has he got freckles, has he got pimples. You can see the make-up in color. Black and white you don't need it. You don't need it in color, either, but they don't know that.

Ventura: Why don't they know that?
Bogdanovich: I don't know! They think you have to have make-up. Actors never wear make-up in my movies. Never. Actresses, sometimes, they want to put on stuff, and I say "Don't."

Ventura: We—meaning, American filmmakers—seem to have forgotten the most basic things about film directing. What would you say they are?
Bogdanovich: How to talk to the actors. That's the most important thing, really. Of course, if you know cutting you're in much better shape, because you can shoot what you need instead of just shooting what you think you're going to need. After knowing about actors, the most important thing, I think, for a director, is to know what the hell he's doing in terms of cutting.

Ventura: Could you talk about that in more detail?
Bogdanovich: For example, you have a three-page scene between you and me sitting at this desk, like we are, with a tape recorder between us. Now, it's three pages, we both know the dialogue, and we're gonna shoot it. Average director will come in on an establishing shot: the two of us at the desk. Shoot it from the door over there. So we see both of us; see the room. Move in now to a tighter two-shot—see the both of us. That's two shots. Then he has another shot over my shoulder, onto you. That's three. Another shot over your shoulder onto me—that's four. Then probably he goes and gets a close-up of you and he gets a close-up of me. That's six. Six set-ups for three pages. That's average. Oh, and maybe he'll get an insert of the tape recorder for cut-aways, in case they want to take something out, or whatever—that's seven. Okay? Seven set-ups for three pages.

Now, generally speaking, the average director will not only shoot those seven angles, he will also shoot *the entire three pages* in each of those angles. Except *perhaps* the long shot, he might not. And of course he won't on the inserts. Now you and I don't know, at this point, as the actors—we don't know exactly which angle is gonna be used when we're playing the first, last or middle lines. We don't know. He might use any one of the five angles when you say "I don't like you." It might be over my shoulder, it might be on *me* when you're saying it—you don't know, right? Okay. So you gotta play each of those times, try to be just as good, each time.

Well, you know, maybe they do your close-up last. So that's when you *really* want to be good, in a close-up, and they're doing it last, you've already done the lines now five times—and maybe each one of those setups you had to do it more than once, because the director said, "Well, why don't you do that again," so maybe you do two, three, four times in each angle maybe.

Now, every time you move the camera there's a rule of thumb: it takes about an hour. [Note: At present studio budgets, the average film costs approximately $15,000 an hour to shoot.] Unless you're moving very fast. On television, you have to move fast; but on the average feature, it takes about an hour. So there's seven hours. Forget the insert: six hours. That's almost the whole day. For three pages. Well, they say three pages, on the average film, *that's pretty good* these days. So we're not doin' *bad*.

However, there's another way to shoot it. What if you, the director, come in and you know exactly where you want to be, where the cutting is, for the whole three-page scene. So you've got on a piece of paper that the first ten lines are a two-shot. So you shoot the first ten lines in your two-shot. That's all you shoot in the two-shot, because you know the next three-four lines are going to be over-shoulder shots. So you shoot the next part of the scene, just that, over the shoulder. Now, the actors *know*: "This part is going to be in this angle, I don't have to do it again." Now the last part of the scene we do in close-ups, that's the only place I'm going to use close-ups, for the end of the scene. Let's say, just to make it simple, I'm only going to shoot the last three lines in close-ups. Just before we go for the gun, all right? And that's all we ever do. You only need to say "I don't like you" once. In the close-up. Well, aren't you happy? Plus, it goes faster. Much faster. Because you don't have to do it *all* perfectly *each* time. It'll take a lot less time because you're shooting a lot less.

Now, when people say a person spends millions of dollars to make a movie, I say he doesn't know what he's cutting. Doesn't know what he's shooting. Because you don't have to shoot so much if you know what you want before you get on the set.

Of course, some directors I know who are very good will shoot an awful lot of coverage, an awful lot of footage, and they're still damn good. Cassavetes, for example, is to me a marvelous director who breaks all the rules and he's still very good. There are no rules for talent. But it certainly moves faster this way.

Ventura: You said cutting is the most important, after knowing how to talk to actors.
Bogdanovich: The *main* thing, the main thing is how to talk to actors. Because I'll tell you the truth: somebody can teach you about cutting, you can have a cutter on the set, there's no crime to it—Billy Wilder had a cutter on the set all the time, always did. You got a cameraman to tell you how to light it if you have problems. Get a good writer, he'll tell you how to write it. But somebody's gotta talk to the actors. You can have ten good actors, and they're still not gonna be that good unless somebody's there. Because the difference between actors on the stage and actors in the movies is that on stage there's an audience, and no matter if the stage-director is a schmuck, if the actor can really work with that audience he'll know where he is. In the movies there's no audience. There's just the director. He's the only audience. That's why so many actors feel adrift in the movies.

I asked Cagney once—and he said he'd worked with about seventy directors—I asked Cagney what did he think was a good director, and he said, "Well, I only worked with five. A good director for me is a guy who if I don't know what the hell to do, he can get up and show me."

Ventura: In most arts you hear about "self-expression," but in this town that's a dirty word. When you're making pictures, is that there for you, does it go through your mind?
Bogdanovich: I think so. When I'm working I'm thinking, "What's the point?" Is it just to make another movie, or make money, or what? I've tried never to make a movie to make money, I've tried never to do a movie that I didn't think was about something. It may have been misguided, and I maybe didn't pull it off, but it started out with an intention of being about something. Even that musical *At Long Last Love*, which didn't work—but the *idea* was to try to show the very tenuousness and difficulty of a relationship that's based on what we all think is "falling in love." What *is* falling in love? That's what the movie was about. I don't

think it ever answered the question, but at least it was asking the question. It just didn't work.

Ventura: Seems like you asked that question again in *They All Laughed*.
Bogdanovich: Yeah, I think what I did in that picture was to accept it. And to try to define more what it was. In *At Long Last Love*—that's an ironic title, because nobody really gets what he wants in that picture. In *They All Laughed* Ritter does get what he wants. And it's based on trust. Totally. Because none of them *discuss*. Neither does he ask her nor she ask him what it's really about. She in fact asks him and he lies to her and she knows he lies, and *still* likes him. So there's two people who essentially say, "Well, we love each other, and that means we just trust each other, 'cause that's *it*." On faith.

In fact, Dorothy's [the late Dorothy Stratten] character in the movie is totally on faith. 'Cause the audience—interesting thing is, that the audience accepts it on faith, too, because there's no idea of what she does. You don't know whether she's really having an affair with Sean Ferrer, which she doesn't seem to be. Or why she doesn't like her husband. But you take her side in it, and that's partially because Dorothy annihilates disbelief. You don't believe that there's anything wrong with her—she doesn't seem like she would be doing anything wrong.

Which was true of Dorothy. That was her personality. And that comes out, you can't hide that. She had more natural star presence on the screen than anybody I've ever worked with. You didn't have to do much with it, really. The thing to do was to get her back to the way she *looked*, as opposed to the way she was supposed to look. In our picture she wore *no* make-up at all. And we got her hair back closer to its natural color. Without any frills. And then you just had this amazing translucent quality she had. That's what Audrey Hepburn commented on to me, how Dorothy looked as though she were translucent.

And then, of course, when Dorothy got murdered it changed everything. About . . . [his voice trails off]. The meaning of things falls into a different perspective when somebody you love dies, or gets killed. When my parents died it seemed more in the nature of things. Parents die before you do, supposedly. At least that's sort of the way it goes. But this was different. This was a murder. And it wasn't a movie. It was life.

You know, we all make movies about murder—we all make movies about a lot of things—but we don't really know what it means. We just think we do. But when something *happens*, and it's real, and there's no way to change it, no way to rewrite it, no way to recut it or reshoot it, you suddenly say, "What *is* the point of making pictures? What is the point of doing anything? Because *this* is *real*." And how do you deal with it? What *is* important? You start asking a lot of questions. At least I did. About anything you've ever done, about anything anybody's ever done.

And that's one of the reasons I'm not going to be directing for a while. Because I'm just trying to get a company together where a lot of people are working toward a common goal and quality. That's the only thing I can do at the moment. I'm not able to do much more than make pictures—I wish I could. But that's the main thing I know. So I'm putting together a picture company. Try to show them a world that does exist. Or that could exist. Or that shouldn't. There has to be some point to a movie beyond simply the money. I've always known that, but never more so than in the last couple of years.

Dialogue on Film: Peter Bogdanovich

American Film Institute / 1986

From *American Film*, June 1986. © 1986 American Film Institute. Reprinted by permission.

An inquiry into the arts and crafts of filmmaking through interview seminars between Fellows and prominent filmmakers held under the auspices of the American Film Institute's Center for Advanced Film Studies.

In the late fifties and early sixties, Peter Bogdanovich was known as a New York theater actor and director, but his writings on film—critical pieces, profiles, monographs—were already among the most influential American works on the cinema, at a time when the French critics, and Andrew Sarris, were focusing attention on the auteur theory. Bogdanovich's pieces on such classic directors as Howard Hawks, Orson Welles, Alfred Hitchcock, John Ford, and Fritz Lang not only earned him the reputation of the "American Francois Truffaut" (a credit he refutes), but also brought him a wealth of background information about film that was put to good use when he turned to work in the movie business.

For he had always wanted to direct films, and in 1964 he took Frank Tashlin's advice to "go West." In Hollywood—like many then-aspiring, now-famous young filmmakers—he first worked as an assistant to Roger Corman, who subsequently gave him the opportunity to direct his own feature. *Targets* (1968) brought him to the attention of the Hollywood community; his continuing work in film kept that attention. *The Last Picture Show* (1971) was a critical and commercial success, and, together with his next two features, *What's Up, Doc?* (1972) and *Paper Moon* (1973), established him as one of Hollywood's bright young stars. He received the New York Film Critics' Award for Best Screenplay for *The Last Picture Show* and the Writers' Guild of America Award for Best Screenplay for *What's Up, Doc?*

The next years, however, saw only a flickering light from that star. *Daisy Miller* (1974), *At Long Last Love* (1975), and *Nickelodeon* (1976) were not well received, and Bogdanovich withdrew from directing. "I'm tired, and I want a rest," he admitted in a *New York Times* interview.

His return to film, with *Saint Jack* (1979) and *They All Laughed* (1981), brought him renewed critical acclaim, but the box office was not as enthusiastic. Personal and financial setbacks marred the next years, but with *Mask* (1985), Bogdanovich released a brilliantly conceived and executed film, and recaptured the critical *and* commercial approval that Hollywood considers necessary for any stellar designation. The Academy of Motion Picture Arts and Sciences awarded *Mask* an Oscar for makeup in 1986, a fact Bogdanovich was not aware of when he made the following remarks, excerpted from a two-hour seminar.

Question: You've always emphasized how much you've learned from other filmmakers. Can you give us some examples?
Peter Bogdanovich: With Roger Corman, which is where I began directing—although I had done a lot of writing before that, and also directed and acted in theater—there were practical lessons: You learned how to move fast, and down and dirty; get in and get out quick. And that was great, because that knowledge and way of working, that somewhat informal and guerrilla kind of filmmaking, should be the way everyone learns. You steal the scenes, you con locations, you do anything you can to get the picture in the can fast.

I learned a lot from Hitchcock, who always insisted that you have a point of view in the scene. That's really important to remember when you're directing, because it's going to affect everything—the framing, the size of your image, what you're showing and when. And it helps to tell a story because it puts the viewer into somebody's place.

Camera placement has a lot to do with the point of view in a scene. For example, if you have a close-up of me, and a wide shot of you, it's my point of view. If I have a close-up of you, and a shot of me from there, it's your point of view. Most pictures don't have a point of view in scenes; they just have shots.

Question: What do you look for when you're casting?
Bogdanovich: Well, I don't know if I look for anything—I think it looks for me. On *Mask*, we had a helluva time looking for someone to play the boy, Rocky. We saw people in New York, and in L.A. Michael Chinich and Universal Casting saw kids all over the country. There wasn't anybody you could just snap up. The person who gave one of the best readings was Rob Lowe. I was so distracted by his good looks that we actually

put a stocking over his head and cut eyes out. We did this for almost every actor who read for the picture, because we knew we weren't going to see anything but their eyes, so what was the point of all this expression which we weren't going to get on the screen.

Anyway, very late in the day—he was the last person to read for me—Eric Stoltz comes in. And I've heard this scene read thirty times by now—it's a scene where Rocky's talking to the blind girl. She says, "How'd you get the name Rocky?" And he says, "Well, when I was a kid I used to rock a lot in my crib, and my mom called me Rocky." And Eric said the line, but when he got to the word "Rocky," he did it with a kind of singsong voice—"Raaa-keee"—and I got shivers, and I thought: This is the kid.

Something happens, and it's usually in the eyes. It isn't really how you look, it's what's in your eyes, and that's something that is impossible to manufacture. I often like to use people who haven't worked before, because they don't know what *not* to do, nor what they *should* do. They haven't got bad habits; they're fresh.

Question: Do you usually rehearse before shooting?
Bogdanovich: I've rehearsed every picture. On *Picture Show* we rehearsed for two full weeks—one week in L.A. and one week in Texas. On *They All Laughed* we rehearsed two weeks in New York, sometimes on the real locations.

Question: With a two-week rehearsal schedule, do you worry about over-rehearsing actors?
Bogdanovich: You never let them really get it perfect. Cloris Leachman in *The Last Picture Show* has that big scene at the end where she throws the coffeepot. I never let her say the words to me until we shot it. She said, "Can we rehearse the end?" I said, "No, I don't want to hear it." She said, "I want to say—" I said, "I don't want to hear you say it." She said, "I'm going to do it in front of the mirror." I said, "I don't give a damn—I just don't want you to do it in front of everyone else until we shoot it."

Whenever I see the picture now, that moment when Cloris starts to yell is very moving to me—it was the first time she had ever done it, and you can feel that in the way she's breathing; she gets out of breath, and it's wonderfully touching.

That's an extreme example. There are other times when we've rehearsed things down to the comma, but even then, even when they're getting it right, I won't let it quite happen. Even if it's a little too well rehearsed, you can always change the lines just before you shoot the scene, just enough to throw the actors a bit. If it requires some kind of very big emotion, like Cher crying when the kid dies at the end of *Mask*, you can't rehearse that. It's like a stunt. You don't rehearse stunts, either, you just plan them out carefully and then shoot them.

Question: Why do you give line readings to actors?
Bogdanovich: It's a way of communicating. Having been an actor, I found it very difficult to direct a scene unless I could walk my way through it. I didn't know how to direct any other way. James Cagney said to me once, "A good director is a guy who, if I don't know what the hell to do, he can get up and show me."

Question: Did the scene in *Mask* where Cher and her father toss a ball back and forth start out with dialogue?
Bogdanovich: Originally, the grandparents were not in the picture at all. I said, "Some 'normal' family would be great—doesn't he have normal grandparents?" Yes, he does. Well, let's get them in the picture. After we got a hint of what they were like, I said, "How about after they come back from the ballgame and Rocky gives Cher the ball, she looks at the father and throws it at him." [Screenwriter] Anna [Hamilton Phelan] said, "That's good, what does the father do?" I said, "He kind of grins lightly and throws it back at her. And she kind of looks at him and then throws it at him again." She wrote it down that way and that was it. It was tricky to shoot because every one of those cuts was a different angle. It was kind of an action sequence—or, rather, a *re*action sequence. *They All Laughed* is full of those. I like to make sequences like that—it's really silent pictures, and something you can do in movies that you can't do in any other medium.

Question: Do you always know exactly how you're going to shoot a scene?
Bogdanovich: I don't feel comfortable if I walk on the set and don't know how I'm going to shoot the scene. If I don't know that, I feel I'm in deep trouble. Usually, I have a breakdown of what I need, and then I'll often eliminate things, rather than add. I like to shoot as little as possible. So I might have written down in the script: Close-up Harry, medium-shot Fred, Fred's point of view, insert gun, close-up Fred, medium-close two-shot, and out. Seven shots. I don't draw it, there's no storyboards, and I don't shoot masters. Unless we're going to play the scene in the

master, then we do it and don't cover. I prepare that the night before or that morning.

The main thing, I think, is that I look at a scene and think to myself: Where do I have to cut? Because if I don't have to cut, I won't. Otto Preminger, who's an often overlooked director these days, and shouldn't be, because he made some extremely good pictures, said to me once, "Every cut must have a purpose. If you don't have to cut, then don't—because when you're cutting you're interrupting the audience's flow even though they don't know it." I think if the cast can sustain a scene, and you don't have to cut, try to play it out. Of course, playing out a scene is a bitch. It's tough to do.

Question: How do you approach the use of music in your films?
Bogdanovich: I've always thought it better if you can somehow play against the scene a little with the music. So it isn't on the nose. The music ought to be in counterpoint to the scene. I think a score shouldn't explain the scene to the audience, or nudge the audience, as if to say, "Do you get it?"

Question: Could you say a little about the differences between working with the studio and the independents?
Bogdanovich: I have found it doesn't matter if they are independent producers or studio heads or television executives—sometimes you run into good ones and sometimes you run into bad ones. Sometimes they're dumb, other times they're very smart. Just luck of the throw. Of course, there are certainly good and bad directors, too.

I think a lot of directors put us in bad shape because they spent too much money on pictures that didn't do any business. And you can't expect an industry to be run for pictures that lose money. John Ford said to me, "There's two things that're important making pictures—one of them is that you have fun making it, and the other is that the picture makes money." And Howard Hawks was even more succinct; he said to me, "Just remember, make pictures that make money."

Now, if you make nothing but pictures that make money, you're probably not much of an artist—I don't know why, it just turns out that way. But in order to be a functioning artist in this business, you've got to have a few movies that make some money. It's not as bad as it seems sometimes: I had three commercial hits in a row in the seventies and then I didn't have a box-office success for a long time, maybe ten years—and yet people kept offering me pictures. If I didn't work, it was because I didn't *want* to work. Once you've had some amount of success in the movie business—if it wasn't just a fluke—you can get work again. But you've got to make something eventually that does a little business. Personally, I've always felt it was important to make pictures that make their money back. To me, anything over that is gravy.

Question: You make references much more to older directors and movies than to newer ones. Why?
Bogdanovich: Well, it isn't just that pictures were better crafted then, with a dexterity and flexibility that was extraordinary, but they also told more. Not like today—most movies are thirty-minute stories told in two hours. When you go to the movies now, you're lucky to get the hors d'oeuvres, much less the meal. Maybe you get hors d'oeuvres and a soup, sometimes you get a salad, sometimes you get nuts, sometimes you get just nachos. I think it's important to give an audience a full meal.

The reason it's so hard to make pictures sometimes—especially in real locations, which is the best way to work, however—is that you are taking your reality and trying to impose it on everyone else's—the world's. And that can be pretty difficult.

Peter Bogdanovich Interview

Thomas J. Harris / 1988

From *Literature/Film Quarterly* 16, no. 4 (1988). Reprinted with permission of *Literature/Film Quarterly* at Salisbury University, Salisbury, MD 21801.

A few streaks of grey hair are all which betray the fact that Peter Bogdanovich is now forty-nine years old. Despite numerous career setbacks—partly related to personal problems—over the past fifteen years, the director manages to retain, despite a certain world-weary air—hardly unexpected—much of the youthful enthusiasm and vigor which characterized his former *Wunderkind* self. It is understandable that he would have felt the consequences of success and failure more intensely than his contemporaries (Scorsese, Coppola, Spielberg, Lucas, De Palma) and that his outlook (evidenced particularly by 1985's *Mask*) would have matured correspondingly. After all, Bogdanovich, one will recall, was the forerunner of all the above-mentioned directors: his 1971 *The Last Picture Show* had put him on the map before anyone had even heard of *Mean Streets*, *The Godfather*, *American Graffiti*, or *The Sugarland Express*.

Granted, the chronological time span which separates the release dates of these other films from Bogdanovich's is very small, but the fact is that Bogdanovich had, long before his first commercial success, been closer in *spirit* and *inclination* to such great American auteurs as Ford and Hawks (having started his career at the tender age of twenty-one by writing books and monographs on them—in addition to Hitchcock, Lang, and Welles). He had even befriended both veterans (coercing them into participating in documentary tributes to their careers which he wrote and directed), and they had supported wholeheartedly his ambitions.

However, as Bogdanovich's output, along with that of certain of his fellow directors, particularly Coppola, began to become more and more personal—and less and less successful, both critically and commercially—throughout the seventies and into the eighties, it seemed that the influence of the masters had died out for good (Ford passed away in 1973 and Hawks in 1977, followed by Hitchcock in 1980). But happily in the case of Bogdanovich, after a long period of silence, a quirk of fate caused a script to come his way which not only appealed to his newfound personal sensibilities but also enabled him to exhibit once again that same superb visual-narrative sense which had characterized such earlier works as *Picture Show* and *What's Up, Doc?* (1972) and which was one of the hallmarks of the great American films of the past. The considerable commercial and critical reception accorded *Mask* has brought Bogdanovich back into the forefront of American picturemakers, a position which he seems eminently suited to fill. The director's next scheduled project is the long-anticipated sequel to *Picture Show*, *Texasville*, which he plans to have before the cameras in May of 1989, with most of the original ensemble reprising their roles.

The following interview was taped at Mr. Bogdanovich's home in Bel-Air, California, on March 11, 1988, and is excerpted from Thomas Harris's upcoming *Bogdanovich's Picture Shows*, which will be published by Scarecrow in late 1989.

Question: How did it feel coming back to filmmaking after your absence on *Mask*? Did you go into it with a positive attitude?
Bogdanovich: I don't know if I did or not. I think I was not quite ready to make a film, and there I was making one. Because after Dorothy Stratten was killed in 1980, I didn't really want to make any more pictures. And it wasn't a pose; it was a complete lack of interest. I realize now looking back that it was a kind of shock that it took me a long time to get past. I remember giving away projects, saying "You direct this, I'll just sort of produce." And when *Mask* came along—we were very tight on money at that point—and I was asked if I wanted to direct it. I said I didn't really want to get into it, but the more I did, the more I found it interesting, and I thought it had something to say, particularly about the transcendence of a certain kind of death. Unfortunately some aspect of that has been lost because the biker funeral scene (wherein Red, played by Harry Carey, Jr., is laid to rest) and the "Little Egypt" scene were cut out. The "Little Egypt" sequence—where Rusty and Rocky sing together—was particularly important in terms of the sense of fun of the movie and the sense of the characters really getting along and the fact that she was in fact talented as a performer. It was very moving, touching, funny. But getting back to your original question, I don't know if I was quite ready to direct, but I had to, and I jumped into it. I would say about two, three weeks into it I really got interested; part of me felt it would be good to just

do a picture as a professional, to just make a movie, like they used to, so that was the way I approached it at first.

Question: What aspects of the film did you and Cher disagree on?
Bogdanovich: Not much, really. What's been said was all stuff she made up afterwards, when the studio took her aside—they were angry with me because of the fuss I made over the Springsteen songs being cut from the film—and whispered a lot of things in her ear that supposedly I had said that I didn't say. She had never played the lead in a motion picture, and she didn't know what I was doing, because I don't cover scenes, and the other directors she'd worked with do. She thought I was trying to trick her, and I tried to explain it to her, but she really didn't understand the principle. It was a very difficult role for her. She needed to be very carefully handled. I couldn't coddle her. I know she was upset sometimes that I wasn't more doting and conciliatory, but I was spending most of *my* time rewriting the script.

Question: Did you give her line readings?
Bogdanovich: A few times, and she objected to that, but she'd listen. I would tell her to do certain things, and she didn't like that, and I insisted. Also I had to cut a lot more than I normally would with her because she couldn't sustain the scenes.

Question: There are an awful lot of close-ups of her.
Bogdanovich: Yes, because she's very good in close-ups. She has great eyes. That was the trick of the performance, to get close, so the eyes convey the real meaning of the scene.

Question: What problems did you have with Anna Hamilton Phelan's script? It was her first effort.
Bogdanovich: It originally told the story over a period of ten years. So she and I and Starger worked on it, and I eventually said, "Let's just make it the last year of his life." Also, Anna had a lot of good ideas, but they didn't necessarily always happen in the right place or to the right people, so we did a lot of rewriting in that way.

Question: The way you introduce Rocky is very clever. The revelation of the disfigurement is very matter-of-fact.
Bogdanovich: I wrote that whole opening scene. The picture originally began when Rocky comes to the school. I said, "We have to have a

scene where the audience is alone with Rocky, absolutely alone with him before anything else happens." You didn't really see him very clearly at first. You see him go by, you see him in the mirror, but you don't really see him—boom—close-up until the mother's there. That way the audience is able to deal with their reaction to it, so that by the time you get other people into it, the audience has already gotten over the shock. In other words, "This is it, this is what it is," and they kind of say, "Well, it's not so bad." I thought if the audience felt like they knew him after this, they would accept anything, and as it turned out I was right.

Question: There was a scene in Anna Hamilton Phelan's third draft where Rusty has a seizure and has to be taken away. The scene is not in the final cut.
Bogdanovich: We shot that, and it was quite a good little scene, but it just didn't work in the context of the picture. It was too "heavy."

Question: Some critics complained that the bikers seemed softened and overly sentimental.
Bogdanovich: That's because they [the studio, Universal] cut out all the good stuff with the bikers. The funeral scene and the "Little Egypt" scene were really biker scenes. They were shooting it up with guns and beating each other up. We handled them kind of comically, but still there was a serious side. In the funeral scene, you saw them lowering a bike into the grave, then a guy pulls out a gun and starts shooting, and they all get drunk. Bikers are like modern cowboys really. But it wasn't just because of the bikers that the funeral scene was important. In that scene, while everyone is gathered at the gravesite, Rocky is sitting far away, and Cher looks at him and goes over to him and says, "Aren't you gonna throw something in the grave?" and he says "No. He's not there anyway. He's everywhere now," which was Rocky's attitude toward death. Because this was cut out, the last line of the picture (which I also wrote). "You can go anywhere now, baby," loses a lot of its impact. That was the whole point, that once the spirit is released, it can go anywhere, and that aspect—which, as I mentioned before, is what interested me most about the picture—was considerably muddied.

Question: You're not exactly sure what kills Rocky at the end. Is it entirely physical or partly emotional. There was a line in an earlier draft where he said to the dog, "I don't think I want to make myself well anymore." Did he have any control over what was happening?

Bogdanovich: He just died. It wasn't anything he planned. He felt like he was going to die and he did, that's all.

Question: What about the look of the film? It's unusually bright and sunny.
Bogdanovich: That's all wrong. Laszlo Kovacs and I worked harder that we'd ever worked trying to obtain a certain depth of focus with color. What happened was the producers got so angry with me over the mess I was making about the music that they went to the Technicolor lab and told them to print the picture five points brighter all the way through, which ruined everything we did. So when Vincent Canby wrote that the makeup didn't look convincing, I called him up and said, "You're damn right." That's why everything looks so out-of-focus in the background.

Question: So it was originally a much darker picture, more melancholy?
Bogdanovich: Oh, *much* darker. More like *Daisy Miller*. People said to me, "Why did you make it so bright? It looks like TV." I said, "*I* didn't."

Question: Do you think that the fact that the Springsteen songs were removed hurt the picture a lot? Critics have said that it's a film about some people and the music they listen to.
Bogdanovich: You see, people don't understand. Look . . . a movie should be like a dream. It washes over you, you don't know what's affecting you, you can't do anything about it; you're taken away. Movies are like visual music. They have an abstract, visceral effect on you. Now, we had *fifteen minutes* of Bruce Springsteen music all the way through the picture. The music was having a visceral effect on the audience. Without it, several key scenes don't make sense. For instance, after the dissolve to the truck coming toward the cemetery at the end, you were supposed to be hearing "Born in the U.S.A." on the radio, to signal to the audience that it was not 1980 any longer but *now*, four years later. Without that transitional device, a lot of people thought it was Rocky's funeral and wondered why there weren't more people there. So the emotional impact of the picture was damaged as a result. Also, the picture was damaged commercially, since it premiered just as Springsteen's national tour was at its height of popularity. Instead of $40 million, it probably would have grossed $100 million. Also, the original cut that I had was much more of a working-class picture.

Question: In the final print it is never explained how Rusty and Rocky were subsisting.

Bogdanovich: Exactly. You could tell that the Sam Elliot character supported Rusty with the money he got from his bike shop. But you weren't sure where she was getting her money. That was something that was fudged in the script because they didn't want to deal with it. But it was a lot clearer that she was into drugs—and maybe selling them—in the other version. My original version—two hours and eight minutes, including "Little Egypt," the biker funeral, and the Springsteen songs—was a much more accessible and likeable film.

Question: On *They All Laughed*, did you originally have one composer in mind, like on *At Long Last Love*?
Bogdanovich: No, it was an assortment of popular songs.

Question: Were you consciously trying to make another picture with the same type of framework as *At Long Last Love*?
Bogdanovich: Well, I like that kind of story, yes.

Question: Did you have *La Ronde* in mind when you came up with the idea? Some critics have compared your film to Ophuls's.
Bogdanovich: *La Ronde*? No, I just thought it would be fun to make a movie about people that I knew and relationships and their complications. Although it was going to be a personal picture, I wanted to cloak it in something impersonal, because I wanted to play by the rules of the old Hollywood game. And so I came up with the concept of a group of detectives falling in love with the people they've been hired to follow. Incidentally, I recut the picture after it was all finished. Practically no one has seen that version—I own the only print—but again it's a much more accessible picture, not as sad, not as down. And there's Springsteen music in it too.

Question: You've said you like to have scenes planned out on paper before you get to the set. Did you do that on the musical, *At Long Last Love*?
Bogdanovich: Oh, sure. Very much.

Question: What do you think your biggest mistakes on that picture were?
Bogdanovich: What went wrong with that picture was in post-production. The picture was all right in production, and I thought it was gonna be pretty good. What happened was that afterward we got rushed. We had one disastrous preview in San Jose, and I recut it, and we had another preview in Denver that was 100 percent better. And *then* we screwed it

up. Bad advice. And I agreed with the critics when it came out. I didn't like it either. I went back and paid Fox about $70,000 to let me recut it again myself. The final version that circulates on TV now I think is really quite a good little movie.

Question: It's not quite as bad as its reputation would indicate.
Bogdanovich: No, it's quite a nice movie, especially considering what it's supposed to be about—a group of people who can't communicate, who have to sing in order to say what they mean because they can't really say what they mean because they're basically superficial and kind of frivolous. It's also about the difficulties of maintaining relationships, and how you like one person for sex and another person for something else.

Question: Most people who don't like the picture have commented that although it seems like you all had fun making the picture, that fun somehow doesn't translate to the audience. There's a distance there. You've said that while you're making a film, you don't have the audience in mind, but is there any way to judge that sort of thing?
Bogdanovich: Well, the thing is if you can get the audience on the right wavelength on a picture, they'll buy anything you do. The picture came out with the worst kind of reviews and general reaction, and unfortunately when that kind of thing happens, it's almost impossible for anyone to be objective. The only way that picture will work is one hundred years from now after everybody's dead, and somebody uncovers it and says, "hmmm. This is kind of interesting."

Question: When you made *Saint Jack*, were you concerned that it make money?
Bogdanovich: The two pictures I made that I thought would not make a lot of money but that I thought would probably make their money back if properly exploited were *Daisy Miller* and *Saint Jack*.

Question: Did you ever consider shooting *Saint Jack* in black and white?
Bogdanovich: Yes, and I changed my mind after having a conversation with Jean Renoir. He said, "I think if the audience goes into a picture knowing it was shot in Singapore, they would like to see the color of Singapore."

Question: Some people thought the ending was implausible—that Jack Flowers would suddenly turn moralistic after demonstrating that he had no moral scruples whatsoever over the preceding two hours.
Bogdanovich: I don't think that's true. I think that's exactly what he *would* do. At the end he just says, "Fuck it" and throws the film into the river. There's a point beyond which he won't sink. That's the factor that attracted me to the book the first time I read it.

Question: Now that you've become accustomed to making pictures set in the present, will you ever go back to the past again? Also, is there anything in terms of subject matter that interests you now but that wouldn't have say, ten or fifteen years ago, during your "cinephile" period?
Bogdanovich: Oh, yes. Several of my favorite projects are set in the past. Two are based on Robert Graves's novels. One is *The Golden Fleece*, the story of Jason and the Argonauts. That's set in 1225 B.C. And there's another called *Seven Days in New Crete* which is a kind of utopian story set way in the future. There's no technology in it, so in that sense it's not a science-fiction picture, but it is really. It's a kind of *Time Machine* story. Those wouldn't have interested me at all ten years ago. I wouldn't have read them ten years ago.

Question: Hawks said to you once, "Just remember to make pictures that make money." But there's really no way to tell whether a picture will make money before it opens.
Bogdanovich: Well, you can certainly tell when you're making *What's Up, Doc?* that it's going to be a commercial film, because of the stars and the kind of picture it is, just as with *Daisy Miller* you think to yourself, "This is beautiful, but who's going to want to see this?"

Question: Does directing come easier to you now?
Bogdanovich: Well, sure. The more pictures you make, the easier the technique comes to you. I couldn't have made *Mask* or *They All Laughed* when I started. Those are very complicated pictures. There's a definite break in terms of style after *Nickelodeon*. But then both *At Long Last Love* and *Nickelodeon* weren't released the way I intended. Only four films of mine have come out exactly the way I wanted—*What's Up, Doc?*, *Paper Moon*, *Daisy Miller*, and *Saint Jack*. The rest have been compromised either one way or another before shooting or after. *They All Laughed* is my favorite picture to date.

Question: Are you more content with yourself now? Are you able to deal with success better? What do you think it means to be successful?

Bogdanovich: Success means a lot of invasion of your privacy. It means that your life is no longer your own. Success is a lot more difficult to deal with than failure, because it's insidious—you don't think that you *have* to deal with it.

Question: Do you think what happened to you in the seventies—the three hits followed by the three flops—was inevitable in any way?

Bogdanovich: No, the success took me completely by surprise. I thought *Picture Show* was just a small movie. I never thought it would do as well as it did.

Question: Now that the old masters are gone, do you feel you're competing with your contemporaries?

Bogdanovich: I don't feel I'm competing with anybody. I don't like competition. It's a deadly male invention. I'm just trying to make pictures the way I like them to be.

Between Action and Cut: Peter Bogdanovich

John Gallagher / 1997

From the National Board of Review website, August 2004. Reprinted by permission of the author.

In 1997, director-historian-actor Peter Bogdanovich richly deserved the National Board of Review's first William K. Everson Award for History of Film for his book of his classic filmmaker interviews *Who the Devil Made It* (1997, Alfred A. Knopf). The late Professor Everson, a long-time NBR member and contributor to *Films in Review*, was one of our leading film historians, educators, and authors.

John Gallagher: Bill Everson was a very generous guy. He loaned me a print once of William K. Howard's *White Gold* (1927) and I'm on the subway thinking I'm holding what is very possibly the only existing copy of this film.
Peter Bogdanovich: I remember going up to his apartment on West End Avenue. I never saw so much film. Everywhere you looked, cans of film, in the corners, on the shelves, in the bathtub.

JG: He told me the management of his building had to reinforce the floors in his apartment.
PB: The floor would buckle. Film is heavy, heavier than books.

JG: You must have read *Films in Review* when you were a kid.
PB: Oh sure.

JG: It was one of the only film history magazines around.
PB: I used to collect the career indexes, the issues that had a career article with a list of the person's films. I had a whole bunch of them. I got rid of all my film books a few years ago, sold some, gave some away. I've gone

through like four libraries. Every so often I want to periodically eliminate and start over again. The only thing I miss having is *Cahiers du Cinema*; I used to have a run of those that disappeared. Somebody stole them.

JG: I devoured *Who the Devil Made It*. You had such a rapport with these directors—Hawks, Walsh, Cukor, Hitchcock. The Howard Hawks interview is spectacular; your sessions spanned ten years with him.
PB: Yes, from '62 to '72.

JG: He was one of the veteran directors you were closest to.
PB: Yeah, as close as you could get. He was very encouraging to me and very kind, and tough in his way. He liked me and I liked him a lot. I miss him a lot. Thing is, my father (the artist Borislav Bogdanovich) was an older man, he was forty when I was born, so I grew up with an older father than most people. He died at a young age, at about seventy, and I think I gravitated towards older people just generally. The consequence of that is all these directors that I interviewed didn't seem old to me, really. So many of them have died and I feel bereft of a lot of friends, because the age thing didn't mean much to me. I feel sometimes like a whole part of my life is gone.

JG: I was very moved by the poignant picture you painted of Allan Dwan—"The Last Pioneer," as you call him—living in this little house in the San Fernando Valley owned by . . .
PB: His housekeeper. Well, Allan was one of the sweetest men you ever could ask to meet. He was so kind. I think he was the nicest to me overall of the directors in the book. He was very warm, extraordinarily encouraging, interested in everything I did. He was just really fun and buoyant all the time. He never felt sorry for himself. He seemed very jolly and wise.

JG: Is the interview in *Who the Devil Made It* the same as the book you did on Dwan, *The Last Pioneer*?
PB: It's the same interview. It's just slightly shorter actually.

JG: *The Last Pioneer* is long out of print, so it's great to have it in the new book.
PB: Yeah, that's difficult to find.

JG: As is *Fritz Lang in America*.

PB: *Fritz Lang in America* is virtually all in the new book, a little bit cut but not much. It's in a different order because in *Fritz Lang in America* we didn't deal much with the German films, but it's basically the same interview. Very little was cut from that interview and very little from Dwan. The book was so fat so we took some stuff out.

JG: It's interesting in your prelude to the Fritz Lang interview to read about your relationship with him.
PB: It was rocky. But he was like that. I've hardly heard of anybody saying anything nice about him, except Kevin Thomas (of the *Los Angeles Times*) who got along with him very well. Fritz was threatened by people and also competitive as hell. He reminded me a lot of the European intellectuals I grew up with. My father would have a dinner party and these kinds of people would come over. I met a lot of people like Fritz when I was a kid growing up here in New York, so he was familiar to me as a type. He wasn't too nice after a while but I try to remember the good things because he was extraordinarily generous and warm in the beginning.

JG: What was Josef von Sternberg like?
PB: Very warm in a cold way. He was just very reserved and not very outgoing. He didn't speak too much but what he did say had a lot of weight. He was sad, he was a sad man. I didn't understand a lot of that stuff when I was that age. I didn't understand what had happened and how rough it must have been. You don't when you're younger, till you go through some shit, you don't really know what they're dealing with and it must have been extraordinarily difficult for Joe. Very tough. I think his wife Mary kept him going. She taught, she was an archaeologist. I guess he had some money from the Directors Guild but I don't know how . . . had a nice house though, didn't seem to be broke but again I don't know how they kept going. He died four years after we met. I didn't know him that well but I saw quite a bit of him.

JG: I'm a huge Leo McCarey fan and of course I read your piece on him in *Esquire* so again it's wonderful to have the full interview finally available. It's such a gift to have this interview in print, the only extensive one we have with McCarey. It's like suddenly finding a career interview with Victor Fleming or Woody Van Dyke or Gregory La Cava.
PB: Yes it's too bad but that was really how it got done 'cause the doctors and the wife didn't want to have it done. They thought it would hurt his health. Jim Silke, who was at the AFI then, convinced Irene Dunne that

it was a good idea, and Irene Dunne convinced the doctors and the wife so I was allowed to go. Leo enjoyed it. There's no question he enjoyed doing it. It tired him out. After the first session I didn't see him for a while 'cause he had a kind of a relapse. It was very fortuitous that I was able to do it because he was very revealing and a delight, and very much like his pictures although he was pretty sick and was fading. He faded through the whole twelve sessions. I didn't get that much after the first two.

JG: It's interesting to learn that Cary Grant tried to get out of doing *The Awful Truth* (1937).
PB: Isn't that amazing? That was surprising. I never asked Cary about that but Cary was always a little uncomfortable about McCarey. I was very friendly with Cary Grant, he was very nice to me. The interview I did with McCarey went to the AFI as part of the Oral History Program, the full interview was there in their files. Somebody read it and did a piece about Cary Grant and I think in some book that was published it said that Leo McCarey didn't like Cary Grant, based on my interview. I remember saying to Cary, "I'm sorry about that thing with McCarey but that's what he said." He said, "Oh that's alright, that's alright." It was Garson Kanin who told me how much of an influence McCarey had on Cary Grant. You can see it in pictures.

JG: You can see it comparing *The Awful Truth* with other movies Grant did before that, with the exception of *Sylvia Scarlett*.
PB: *Sylvia Scarlett* was a kind of Cockney characterization and he was very good in that but it isn't like *The Awful Truth* at all.

JG: The Cary Grant persona really came out of *The Awful Truth*.
PB: It happened in that picture. It came together for him in that picture. Having met McCarey, albeit when he was not himself really, I could see where that came from because he had a very sophisticated dry wit, kind of mischievous, with all those little kinds of noises that Cary makes in the movie, that's very McCarey. I can see Leo McCarey giving him that stuff. You can see it in other McCarey pictures without Cary Grant where people react that way. In *Ruggles of Red Gap* (1935), Roland Young has that very dry quality. Well, the Laurel and Hardys have that kind of reserved humor, slightly laid back.

I think what is the key to the big movie stars—and I'm writing a book about that for Knopf tentatively called *Who the Hell's In It*, all the actor pieces that I've done, all being rewritten and I'm writing new stuff—and one of the main points I'm going to make in there is that the really big movie stars were all personalities of a certain kind and they were seen differently by major directors and those directors had an impact on those actors which they carried with them. Cary Grant is a perfect example. One of the things I left out of the book really by accident, it'll be in the next one, was that I asked Cary about von Sternberg. . . .

JG: They did *Blonde Venus* (1932) together.
PB: *Blonde Venus*. I said to Cary, "Does von Sternberg direct you much?" He said *(Peter does a flawless Cary Grant)*, "Not really. But the first day he saw me he looked at me and he said 'Your hair's parted on the wrong side.'" I said, "What'd you do?" He said, "I parted it on the other side and I kept it that way the rest of my career." There's a perfect example. If Joe hadn't said that maybe it would have been different. But that was a little thing but a big deal, parting your hair on the other side! And then, wow. Then you can see in *Sylvia Scarlett* that Grant, as George Cukor said, found himself in a certain way as an actor, he allowed himself to be free, 'cause he's kind of reticent in all the other pictures, kind of laid back. He had been a straight leading man up to that point but not very interesting. In *Sylvia Scarlett* suddenly he explodes into a characterization. It was Cockney that he had grown up with, though he was from Bristol, he knew people like that. Then with McCarey on *The Awful Truth* suddenly he took the sophistication and the slapstick—and Cary of course had been a circus performer, an acrobat—so McCarey used that and you can see how the character and persona changed from von Sternberg to Cukor to McCarey and then to Hawks who used him for the comedy stuff in *Bringing Up Baby* (1938) and added elements and then had him play a dramatic part for the first time in *Only Angels Have Wings* (1939). So really in the few years between 1936 and 1939, Sternberg was earlier, but in those three years he worked with Cukor, McCarey, and Hawks and then Hitchcock in '40 which gave him another thing. With all those things going through, he had a career. He knew what to do for the rest of his career. He knew how to play each aspect of himself. So his personality in those roles, with that fine-tuning the directors gave him, made him a movie star.

JG: Jimmy Stewart is another great example, from Capra to Cukor to Hitchcock to Mann to Ford.
PB: Yeah, Jimmy is a little less obvious than Cary Grant because he always had a certain persona. He had the Westerner and the Easterner that

he played. It's odd that he played both those things so effectively, and you see them both in 1939 with *Mr. Smith Goes to Washington* and *Destry Rides Again*. That was the rest of his career right there in those two pictures. The only thing that was different was that after the war he added a certain element of harshness and cynicism which was exploited not just by Anthony Mann but by Hitchcock and Preminger, kind of an awareness about himself. He told me about that, he said *(perfect Jimmy Stewart imitation)*, "I thought I better toughen it up." Somebody was putting him down after the war and he drew on the more neurotic aspects of his personality.

JG: I'm amazed by Jean Harlow—dreadful in *Hell's Angels* (1930) and *The Public Enemy* (1931), then she becomes a different performer in *Red Dust* (1932), *Red-Headed Woman* (1932), and *Bombshell* (1933).
PB: I think the first time you see that change is in *Dinner at Eight* (1933).

JG: *Red Dust* and *Red-Headed Woman* pre-date that.
PB: They do? That's right, they do. *Red Dust* is Fleming, who directed *Red-Headed Woman*?

JG: Jack Conway.
PB: Well, a lot of it depends on who the co-star is and who the director is, no question about it, because the actor has to feel a certain way in front of the camera. I've seen actors dreadful in a take and then you tell them something and suddenly it changes everything.

JG: You have to make a creative environment for them.
PB: It's an atmosphere in which you feel that you can't really do anything wrong. The actor should feel that he can't do anything wrong. You may not like it and say let's try it that way or this way but it won't be *wrong*. Orson Welles was extraordinary with that, at creating that kind of atmosphere, 'cause I acted for him, where you felt that maybe he wouldn't like it or he'd ask you to do it again but you didn't feel like, "Oh Christ I better not do that," and you could just do anything. You felt it would be alright, Orson would forgive you if it wasn't good. If he didn't like something he'd laugh hysterically and say, "That was pretty bad, we'll try that again!" It was always kind of fun and I think to varying degrees certain directors were like that. Certainly Hawks was very laid-back and very encouraging.

JG: It shows, doesn't it, in the naturalistic dialogue patterns in movies like *Only Angels Have Wings* (1939). I love that picture.
PB: It's very much like being with Howard, that movie. If you knew him you kind of felt, well, that was Howard. You could see him writing that stuff, having the actors do it. Yeah, it's very Hawks. I like it too. It's fun.

JG: Speaking of Orson Welles, what's the status of *The Other Side of the Wind*? Do you know where the footage is?
PB: Oh yeah. The negative is sitting in a vault in Paris. There's a stalemate, a Mexican standoff—is that politically incorrect?—well anyway, between Orson's heirs, which basically is Oja Kodar in this case, and the Iranian investor who put up money, and Orson put up some money and the French court decided that neither owned it, that both owned it and they'd have to agree before anything could happen. They've been not agreeing for years and it just sits there.

JG: What a shame.
PB: Yeah. And Orson asked me to finish it should anything happen to him. He said that to me in '73 or '74 one afternoon. He said, "You must promise me that if anything happens to me you'll finish it." I'd say, "Orson, for God's sake, nothing's going to happen to you." He says, "I know but you must promise." And I did and I feel the burden of it. All it takes is money, that's it. It just takes some money to pay everybody off and put it together. It's shot. There's very little to shoot, there's some trick stuff, there's no acting stuff, there's a few trick shots and some things, but very little.

JG: You'd think that Miramax and Fine Line would be falling over themselves to do that.
PB: You would think so but maybe they don't know about it. I haven't really pursued it lately, I've been having my own problems. Frank Marshall was involved in trying to help us get it together. Y'know, there are so many things going on in life, in one's own career, it becomes a problem but believe me it's on my mind and we're trying again now to see if we can make something happen.

JG: The Cukor interview in your book was originally for a TV special.
PB: I don't know what it was for, I can't remember but it never got used. It was for *something*. It was for a documentary or something. I don't know. It never got used, that's all I know.

JG: The Ulmer interview was originally published in *Film Culture* and then pieces in *Kings of the B's*.
PB: Todd (McCarthy) used most of it, I don't remember. What's there in the Knopf book is mostly there. It's not all there. His daughter is preparing a documentary about Edgar and she found they're restoring a lot of his films, I just spoke to her before. I'm meeting with her back in L.A. next week. The BBC is interested in doing a documentary on him and they found *Natalka Poltavka* (1937), they found a number of his old pictures.

JG: There are some wonderful stories in your interview about the making of Ulmer's Yiddish films, the nudist camp in New Jersey. . . .
PB: Yeah, some amazing stuff. I think you get a real sense of what he was like.

JG: In retrospect, seventies mainstream Hollywood was a golden age compared to today—*The Last Picture Show* (Bogdanovich), *Taxi Driver* (Scorsese), *The Conversation* (Coppola), *Five Easy Pieces* (Rafelson), so many great pictures. What happened?
PB: Well, what happened was that we all fucked up, really. What happened was the director became the superstar. People like John Cassavetes and some of my stuff, we all kind of geared it toward the director and that's pretty much what happened at the end of the sixties and early seventies. And then we had freedom to make what we wanted and most of us all made big bombs in various ways whether it was Coppola who went off the deep end or (Michael) Cimino, I made a musical that didn't work (*At Long Last Love*), Marty Scorsese made a musical that didn't work (*New York, New York*).

JG: In *Everyone Says I Love You* (1996) Woody Allen does the same thing you did in *At Long Last Love* (1975).
PB: Woody says he went to see my picture at the (Radio City) Music Hall five times and he loved it, but I didn't know that until recently! *(laughter)* But that picture was rushed into release. That was a disaster and unfortunately people say to me now, "Gee, I really like that picture, why was it so attacked?" But the people who are reacting to that now have only seen the recut version which was the one I recut after it opened, you see. It was an original musical comedy and we only had two previews. Two. The first one was a total disaster in San Jose and the second one in Denver was OK. It played. But then I made some more changes to

it because of pressure from the studio and didn't preview that version. So that version which had never previewed opened and it was the worst version there was. It was fucked. Then I saw that playing and I realized what I needed to do but by then it was too late. It was overconfidence on the part of the studio, because the studio really liked the movie, that was the funny thing. They liked it, they thought it was terrific but in a musical, well in anything, it all has to do with construction. And in a musical particularly, the balance between the musical numbers and the dialogue has to be delicate and I just was still too inexperienced to realize how critical that was, and so after the picture had opened it was declared a bomb. The only place it made money was at the Music Hall. Then I realized how I should have cut it after that and I immediately did cut it, they let me recut and I think I paid for that, and that version was then shown on television and that's the version that all release prints have been ever since. That was quite different from the opening version. Very different, but unfortunately it was too late.

JG: I always felt the critics at the time were incredibly harsh to you.
PB: Yeah, well they were. Judy Crist, the critic, was a friend of mine and when we were preparing to come into New York with *At Long Last Love*—which I always refer to as *At Long Last Turkey*—I spoke to Judy and she said, "How's the picture?" and I said, "It's OK, I guess." She said, "It better be good." I said, "What do you mean?" She said, "They're layin' for you here," and they were. It was just too much. I'd had three hits in a row and even though people think of *Daisy Miller* as having gotten bad reviews it was a critical hit and got quite good reviews.

JG: It's the best Henry James adaptation.
PB: Well, thank you, that's what Gore Vidal said.

JG: I didn't know if you've seen *Portrait of a Lady* (1996). It's a snore.
PB: *Daisy Miller* was a good picture but I probably shouldn't have made it at that particular moment. I remember when we screened it at Paramount, Frank Yablans, the new head of the studio, came over to me and I said "What do you think?" He said, "It's alright." I said, "Is that all you have to say?" "Well, what do you want me to say? I said, "It's just alright?" He said, "It's fine, it's good, but you are Babe Ruth and you just bunted." From a commercial point of view he was right. It was not a picture that was ever going to be a big hit unless you released it today. It got very good notices. People remember it as having gotten bad notices but

the truth is that *Paper Moon* got fairly mixed notices. The *New York Times* didn't like it, *Time* didn't like it. On the other hand the *New York Times* raved about *Daisy Miller*, but it was just not a commercial picture in its day plus at that point Paramount changed hands, Barry Diller came in, Frank was out, it fell between the cracks, and nobody really pushed it. I like the picture. I think it was pretty daring.

JG: Weren't you supposed to star in *Daisy Miller* at one point?
PB: I asked Orson if he would direct Cybill and me in it. He said, "No, you direct it. Cybill's born to play it." He encouraged me to do it which maybe was a double-edged sword but anyway Barry Brown was so right for the part that it was scary. But it was also a problem because he just wasn't very personable and the part needed somebody with a little more personality, but y'know, he was the part, he sure was Winterbourne. Poor Barry. He killed himself, really, with booze.

JG: He projected intelligence in the part.
PB: He had a kind of intelligence and he was a very bright kid but he was so self-destructive. But he was very much like Winterbourne, he was definitely "winter born."

JG: Let's talk about Raoul Walsh.
PB: Yeah.

JG: Were you going to do a Walsh interview book in the seventies?
PB: We were gonna do a big interview and then after that first interview he decided he was going to write his own book. He said, "Pedro, I'm going to do my own book, so we'll talk." I think he talked to Schickel after his book came out. He didn't do any more interviews until after his book came out. I think it made him decide, what the hell, I may as well write my own book.

JG: It's a fun interview talking about his pre-moviemaking days.
PB: You get a sense of what he was like, don't you.

JG: Absolutely. And you got him to talk about some of his lost films like *Lost and Found on a South Sea Island* (1923) and *The Spaniard* (1925).
PB: We got all the way up to *What Price Glory* (1926). After that most of his films got to be pretty known. I regretted that I couldn't get more but

I was very happy with what I had. I didn't know what I'd ever do with it, I never used any of it except in that piece I did in *Esquire*.

JG: "Paul Revere on the Trolley Tracks."
PB: Which was really an attempt to plug his book. It was published around the time his book came out.

JG: Did you stay in touch with him?
PB: Oh yes, we talked on the phone all the time. I didn't go out to see him much, he was way out in the Simi Valley but we talked on the phone a lot.

JG: Did you ever interview King Vidor?
PB: I knew him and I met with him a few times, and he was a lovely man, but Nancy Dowd did a great interview, very long, hard to get.

JG: Yeah, it's in the DGA Oral History Series.
PB: It's very complete. Coppola, Friedkin, and I had a company at Paramount....

JG: The Directors Company.
PB: It was a great fuckin' deal. Billy, Francis, and I could make anything we wanted under $3 million and not even show an outline to the studio. That's how *Daisy Miller* got made. Nobody read it, nobody saw it, we made it for 2.2 (million), substantially under three, and that was it. My partners weren't happy with it, they thought it was a kind of a vanity production to show Cybill off. If I'd wanted to do that I would have done something else. That was a pretty difficult role, and I thought she was awfully good in it. What some people didn't realize is that that was the way a girl like that would have been in 1875. She was from New York, she was a provincial girl. If you read the story that's what she is. If you read the original novel we hardly added anything. The movie is exactly the book. I added one sequence that I wrote that Freddy Raphael had nothing to do with. In fact, Freddy Raphael had nothing to do with that script, it was so funny. There's two things he wrote. One idea was the little miniature painter and the other thing was having that scene play in the baths.

JG: With Mildred Natwick.

PB: Yeah, that was his idea. Everything else was the book and I couldn't use his script 'cause it was really way over the top. Anyway, that's another story. We went to arbitration in England 'cause Freddy's English and so they were a little partial to him. They said I could have billing but it would have to say "Additional Dialogue by," and I said I'm not going to give myself that.

So anyway the deal at the Directors Company was anything we wanted to make under three million was fine. And if we wanted to produce a picture for another director it could be anything up to a million and a half. So King Vidor came to me and asked if we would help him produce a picture that he wanted to do very badly about what happened to the guy that played the lead in *The Crowd* (1928).

JG: Murray.
PB: James Murray. And King had a whole script prepared to do a movie about what happened to James Murray. I wanted to do it, I was trying to get it together but then Billy pulled out of the company and Francis kind of reluctantly pulled out of the company and there was no company. It was over.

JG: *The Conversation* was the Directors Company, wasn't it?
PB: Yeah. There were only three pictures made for the Directors Company. Billy never made one. I did *Paper Moon* and *Daisy Miller* and Francis did *The Conversation*. I had a deal on *Paper Moon* before the Directors Company came into being and I decided to throw it into the company as a way of kicking off the company, 'cause it was made for under three (million) too, it was 2.8.

JG: Did you ever hear about a company called Renowned Artists that John Ford, Tay Garnett, and Ronald Colman tried to start back in '37?
PB: No! I've heard about Renown, Harry Joe Brown and Randolph Scott's company.

JG: Renowned Artists had a deal in '37 with UA. Ford was going to do *The Quiet Man* and Garnett was going to do *Trade Winds*, but the company never got off the ground.
PB: I would think that the idea of independence during the studio system would have been very, very difficult because it was so much easier to do it with the studios. It would have been hard to break off. (William) Wyler, (George) Stevens, and (Frank) Capra did it after the war (with

Liberty Productions) and McCarey was supposed to be part of that and he decided to go on his own (Rainbow Productions), but they were still pretty much attached to studios. Although I think *It's a Wonderful Life* (1946) probably suffered because it was a Liberty Production. I think the studio (RKO) kind of fucked them a little on that one. That's why it wasn't successful. I doubt that picture, if it had been properly distributed, wouldn't have been successful. It probably was done for political reasons to screw him. They didn't like them being independent. I'm sure of that. They do that. They can screw you up. They can distribute it badly, and you have no control and you can't really prove it.

JG: Are you interested in doing independent pictures?
PB: Sure. I have a number of pictures that I want to make and I'll make them however I can.

JG: You were involved with Sam Fuller's *The Big Red One* (1980) originally.
PB: Yeah, it's a sad story. I should never have left the damn thing. I was going to do *Saint Jack*. That was a mess. What happened was, Yablans was the head of Paramount and I got Frank to make a deal for Sammy to write a script, and I think they paid him and he wrote a draft and then Yablans was out of there, I don't know what happened, but the next thing that happened was I got Lorimar to step up to it and I was going to be the producer. Sammy wanted me to play the Bob Carradine part. I didn't see myself as a soldier but I regret that I didn't do that and I regret that I didn't stay involved as a producer but for various reasons it didn't work out. I brought Gene Corman in (to produce). Gene took over and Gene wasn't as strong with Lorimar as he might have been, so unfortunately they kind of took the picture away from Sam. He was stuck with having to complete it their way. It was unfortunate. I didn't see the completed version till it opened in New York in 1980. Sam invited me, I remember Dorothy Stratten and I went to see it and that's when he met her. It was right toward the end of shooting here in New York (on *They All Laughed*). I just thought it didn't feel anything like what the original script was, what it could have been. That footage still exists. There's been an attempt to put it back the way it was and I've spoken to Joel Silver and a couple of people to see if they could get the money to let Sammy do it correctly. That's another problem, getting that money together.

JG: Is there more footage that exists for *The Last Picture Show*?
PB: Yeah. The original cut was about two hours and twenty-five minutes,

but it wasn't the right cut, it was too long. When we were preparing *Texasville*, Peter Guber agreed to let me recut *Picture Show* by adding certain footage to it. The picture had not yet appeared on video so the idea was to add some footage and make a new version of it and put it out in theatres prior to the opening of *Texasville*. That started to happen. I started working on it, I reviewed all the material and decided there were about seven minutes I wanted to put back in. Some stuff had disappeared, but very little. The sound had disappeared but the footage was there. The dailies were there so we had the dailies of the sound. I put back about seven minutes and then Frank Price took over at Columbia and Frank didn't like me because of the situation that happened at Universal on *Mask*, so Frank pretty much sabotaged that plan, which was to bring *Picture Show* out and then *Texasville*, so that was sabotaged and didn't happen. What did happen was that *Texasville* had to be totally recut because I had to lose certain stuff that wouldn't make any sense if you hadn't seen *Picture Show*. It wasn't available anywhere. So that was unfortunately very sad. *Texasville* came out and was perceived incorrectly because it wasn't what we made. It was perceived as too much of a comedy when in fact the original *Texasville* was more evenly balanced between comedy and drama. Subsequent to that the long version of *Last Picture Show* was finished on 35mm and on laserdisc and is available on Criterion laserdisc, seven minutes longer. There's a very good laserdisc that's been available a few years. Pioneer did a director's cut of *Texasville* so that also exists on laserdisc in a version that's twenty-five minutes longer. But the only way to see those two pictures the way we would have liked them to be shown one after the other is on laserdisc.

JG: You mention the balance of comedy and drama. People like Leo McCarey did that so beautifully.
PB: It's my favorite thing. Doing a comedy that becomes sad or the intermixing of comedy and drama, which when I was growing up had a name—it was called a comedy-drama. Now they don't do that anymore. It's either a comedy or a drama. It's very unusual now to have the two mixed. The ability to do that is the best.

JG: *Paper Moon* is a great example of that.
PB: That has it. Most people thought of it as a comedy but I made it as a drama. I thought it was fairly mordant humor.

JG: How did John Ford react to *The Last Picture Show*?

PB: I don't know if he ever saw it. He never said anything to me about it. He never said anything about any of the pictures. I don't know if he saw them. He came on the set of *What's Up, Doc?* and visited but I never heard him say anything.

JG: How about Hawks?
PB: Hawks did. I ran *Targets* for Hawks and I describe that in the book (*Who the Devil Made It*). He said, "The action's good and that stuff's hard to do." He was critical of it otherwise but complimentary. Dwan saw the pictures and he was very encouraging. Jean Renoir was the most encouraging. He asked me to run my pictures at my house once I got a projection room. Hawks was very proud of *What's Up, Doc?* though I don't remember him ever saying much about it. He went down to South America one time for some kind of retrospective and came back with some snapshots he'd taken of the marquee when *What's Up, Doc?* played in Rio. He was kind of proud of that.

JG: He had to be proud to see *Targets* where you use a clip from *The Criminal Code* (1931) and have dialogue about it with Karloff.
PB: Yeah, I say, "Howard Hawks directed that." Yeah, he liked that but Howard never said much about those kinds of things.

JG: What was it like working with Boris Karloff?
PB: He was so sweet, a wonderful man. He was a joy to work with, very encouraging. Loved the picture, loved the script. I first met him a few days before we started shooting. He'd flown over from London to do the picture, came out to my house in the Valley at the time to have dinner. He said to me, "As I was landing in Los Angeles I was reminded of one of the lines you wrote in the script, and I think it's the truest line I've ever read in a screenplay." I said, "My God, what is it?"
  "It's that line—'What an ugly town this has become.'"

JG: It's interesting reading your interview with Edgar Ulmer in *Who the Devil Made It* about him working with Karloff on *The Black Cat* (1934).
PB: Yes, and how funny he was and how charming. Boris was like that. I don't know anyone who's ever said anything against Boris. I think Hawks talks about him briefly in the interview too.

JG: Did you know Tay Garnett?
PB: I met him once, just shook hands with him at a museum screening

or somewhere. He wrote his own book (*Light Your Torches and Pull Up Your Tights*).

JG: I remember seeing your documentary *Directed by John Ford* when it first aired. Where can one see that now?
PB: The AFI has it. They've done nothing with it. They never did clear the rights to the clips so you couldn't show it anywhere except for free. I've been trying over the years to get somebody to finance an updated version of it but haven't managed to pull it off.

JG: That film has classic interview clips with Ford giving you answers like "Uh huh" or "If you say so."
PB: Well, that was just what we got. That was Ford *(laughter)* so we put it in.

JG: Did you work with his daughter Barbara Ford, the editor?
PB: She worked on *Mask*. She died right after. I knew Barbara for years. She worked with me as an assistant at the house, she was kind of the secretary at the house for a few years. She was really a sweet woman. She died of cancer shortly after *Mask*.

JG: She was very close to her father.
PB: She was very close with Jack. Yeah, he thanked me for helping her.

JG: In *Targets*, you also show a clip from Preminger's *Anatomy of a Murder* and you mention Ben Gazzara and of course you went on to work with Ben.
PB: He wasn't a friend then. I didn't know him. I met Ben through Cassavetes when they were working on *Opening Night*, that was the first time I met him. I went over to do that extra thing and we all went to have lunch and that's where I got the idea to use Ben in *Saint Jack* because he was very much like the character that I envisioned of Jack Flowers. At one point I thought of Cassavetes playing him, but I thought Ben was more outgoing, more the kind of character this guy was, plus he was Italian. The ironic thing about it all is the first review of anything I ever wrote was for my high school newspaper and it was about the off-Broadway production of *End as a Man*, which was the first time Benny had been seen in New York. It was a weird kind of coincidence that was the first thing I ever wrote about.

JG: That was filmed as *The Strange One* (1957).

PB: It was, but I saw it off-Broadway. It was such a hit it moved to Broadway. It was brilliantly done. Ben was extraordinary. I saw everything Ben did in New York in those years before I moved out to Los Angeles. I saw *Hatful of Rain* on stage with Gazzara, he was brilliant, and I saw him do *Cat on a Hot Tin Roof* which was magnificent.

JG: He's great, wonderful guy.
PB: Oh, you know him.

JG: Yeah, his daughter Liz worked on the editing of my film *The Deli* (*author's note*: I subsequently directed Ben Gazzara in the feature *Blue Moon* [2000]).
PB: Liz worked with us on *Saint Jack*.

JG: How did you handle directing yourself in *Saint Jack*?
PB: I'd walk through it myself and stage it, which I do often even when I'm not acting. I'll step into it just to figure out how to do it. I began as an actor and I will very often have to step into the role to see how I'm going to stage it. People I work with let me step into it and figure out how to do it. On *Saint Jack* it was no different except in this case I was going to play it. So I'd stage it and walk through it with Benny and then I'd have another actor step in and I'd watch it and then I'd shoot it.

JG: Did you do that on *Targets* as well?
PB: No, I didn't have the luxury to have somebody else on that one, which is tougher.

JG: Would you mind talking about your experience with Sergio Leone?
PB: No, I don't mind. It was doomed. Sergio had liked *Targets* and he decided he wanted to have an American director direct the picture (*Duck, You Sucker!* a.k.a. *A Fistful of Dynamite*). He pretty much thought he was going to be able to push the buttons and tell me how to shoot it. I worked on the script for about three months with Luciano Vincenzoni who was a terrific guy and a terrific writer, and had written Sergio's best films, the two after *Fistful of Dollars*—*For a Few Dollars More* and *The Good, the Bad and the Ugly*. For me, those are Sergio's best pictures. I went over there (to Italy), I didn't know anything, I was arrogant and I didn't get along with Sergio because he wanted to direct through me. I didn't want to particularly do that. It just didn't work out and I quit or was fired after I came back for Christmas, and I never went back. Before I even left we had been

told by BBS that we would make *The Last Picture Show*. It was just a question of clearing the rights and eventually they were cleared. We got the rights and I went right into preparing that when I got back. So it was just as well. The Sergio Leone picture came out and it was called *Duck, You Sucker!* The title we were going to call it was *Johnny and Johnny*, because one of the characters was called Sean and the other was Juan. They both mean John so they were going to call each other Johnny.

JG: Was it cast at the point you were working on the script?
PB: I think it was going to be Rod (Steiger) as Juan. Who ended up playing Sean?

JG: James Coburn.
PB: Yeah, I think they were both cast. After I left, Sergio tried to bring another director in but the two actors wouldn't go for it and it ended up that Sergio *had* to direct it. I don't think he wanted to particularly but he did though. He did it alright.

JG: Didn't you also try to set up a picture with Howard Hawks?
PB: Hawks had a Louis L'Amour Western that he wanted to put together and it just didn't work out. He wanted to produce it and I was going to direct it. I should have probably done it. I don't know that I said I would but I think he just couldn't get it put together. I got busy with *Picture Show* and one thing led to another. I wish I'd done it now. At the time . . .

JG: Do you think there was more respect then for the veteran Hollywood directors than today? I've had meetings with producers and executives who have literally never heard of John Ford.
PB: Oh yeah, I'm not surprised. Then it was closer to the beginning, it was twenty-five years ago, all those guys were alive, it was closer to when they made pictures. The people who are running the movies today don't know pictures. They just don't know them. They have no film culture at all. So many of the young people making pictures don't watch the old pictures. It shows in the work. A lot of the American independent films and even the Hollywood films made today show an amazing lack of film culture. It's almost as if everyone's trying to invent the wheel all over again. The technique of pictures seems to me very old-fashioned, old-fashioned in the sense that it's primitive. Today it's cut-cut-cut-cut-cut, that's all it is.

JG: That's the whole MTV influence.
PB: It's just cut-cut-cut. That's pretty easy to make pictures that way.

JG: Have you seen *Sling Blade*?
PB: That was different. That was good. I thought Billy Bob Thornton was amazing. I told (John) Ritter to tell Billy Bob I thought he had gigantic balls to just put the camera down and watch some of that stuff. He didn't feel he had to cut it up into a thousand pieces.

JG: It was almost shot like a Biograph film.
PB: It's very good, very effective. Very well done. Woody Allen shoots a lot of stuff in one master shot. I saw him the other night and I said, "Do you like to do them in masters?" He said, "Yeah, I do everything in masters. I hate all that coverage." He doesn't even bother to shoot it. That takes a lot of confidence and knowledge. I feel like in most American pictures today nobody's home. Nobody made this picture, which is why I used Hawks's quote for the title of the book. I asked Hawks who he liked and he said he liked almost anybody that made you know who the devil was making the picture. The director's a storyteller and he ought to have his own way of telling it. That just about sums it up.

JG: Would you tell the story about John Ford asking Ben Johnson to do *The Last Picture Show*?
PB: I had asked Ben to do it and he turned it down. He said, "There's too many words. Too many words, Pete." So I called Ford and I said, "I've got this really good part for Ben Johnson, he says, he won't do it, he says there's too many words."

Jack said, "Aw Jesus! I mean, Ben always said that. When we were doing (*She Wore a*) *Yellow Ribbon*, I mean he'd come on the set and he'd say to the script girl, 'Do I got any words today?' If she said yes he'd go out and sulk. If all he had to do was ride the horse he'd be happy. I mean, Jesus, where is old Ben?"

"I think he's in Arizona."

"Aw, give me his number, I'll call him."

I said, "It's really a good part."

"Well, I'll call him."

About fifteen minutes later he calls me back and he says, "He'll do it."
I said, "Did you talk to—?"

"He'll do it. I said to him, what's the matter with you, Ben, I mean, Jesus, Pete has got a good part for you, what do you want to do, play Duke's sidekick your whole life?"

So then about ten minutes after that Ben Johnson calls me and he says *(Ben Johnson drawl)*, "You put the Old Man on me."

"I really want you to do this."

"Oh, God, Pete, I don't know. . . . I'll be back in a couple of days, I'll come see ya."

So he came over to the office and he still didn't want to do it. I kept bugging him and bugging him. He'd been there about an hour and I said, "Ben, if you do this, you're going to win the Oscar for it." He got angry with me, he said, "Why do you say that! Why the hell do you say that!" *(laughter)*

I said, "I don't know if anybody else will get the Oscar, but you in this role I think will win the Oscar. You'll certainly get a nomination." Then we talked another forty minutes. He had the script in front of him and he slammed the script shut and said, "Oh alright, I'll do the goddam thing!" That's how he agreed to do it. And he did win the Oscar.

JG: You do a great Ben Johnson, by the way.
PB: Old Ben. I can't believe he's gone. That's weird.

JG: You also worked with Harry Carey, Jr., on *Mask*.
PB: And in *Nickelodeon*. He was very good in that and very good in *Mask*. Wonderful actor. I had him in another picture, that awful one I made for De Laurentiis, I don't even like to mention it, *Illegally Yours*.

JG: You took a lot of shit for *Nickelodeon*.
PB: Well, again *Nickelodeon* was not released the way I wanted it. I had two pictures in a row that were favorite projects of mine, the musical (*At Long Last Love*) and *Nickelodeon*. Both of them were very dear to my heart.

JG: *Nickelodeon was originally called Starlight Parade.*
PB: That's how it started, and that was a mistake, I should have never gotten involved, I should have done it myself. I'd been planning to do a big picture about the silent era, largely based on the interviews with Dwan, Walsh, and McCarey. I was preparing it and I got a call from my agent and she said they're preparing a movie called *Starlight Parade*, there's another director involved but they want you. I said, "Well, I don't really want to do their script, I'll have to rewrite it completely."

"They'll let you rewrite it, whatever you want."

Basically I rewrote the whole damn thing and never used any of *Starlight Parade*. The trouble was, again, the picture had a balance between comedy and drama and it was a comedy-drama, no question about it, and I had wanted to do it in black and white. It was very important to do it in black and white and Columbia, the studio, wouldn't let me. I had a big fight about that and they cancelled the picture. Then Barry Spikings at British-Lion came in and funded some of the picture, threw in a few million dollars. It ended up being a Columbia-British Lion picture but when it was all done it was a difficult picture. The previews were edgy and the studio wanted me to take most of the drama out, play it more comedy and turn it more into a *What's Up, Doc?*, which it really wasn't. So that threw it off and it got fucked up. Again, the picture came out not at all the way I wanted. I tried to recut that one and I couldn't get back to it.

I still would like to put some of that stuff back. There's about five minutes I'd like to put back that really makes a difference, some heavy stuff where you find out that Ryan O'Neal has an affair with Stella Stevens, it becomes very clear, and you see that John Ritter knows it. All that stuff. It was just much heavier and darker. So the picture got screwed up and that's why I took three years off and went away. I said I don't want to do this. Finally I did *Saint Jack* for that reason with Corman—I didn't want to compromise what I believed in anymore. We didn't get much money to make it, but *Saint Jack* was made exactly how I wanted to. People thought I *had* to go to Corman. I didn't *have* to. I just didn't want to deal with the studios. They said they'd make *Saint Jack* but not with Ben Gazzara and I wanted to do it with Ben. That's why I went off and did that.

JG: There's something you said about Raoul Walsh's directorial style in *High Sierra* influencing *Targets*.
PB: Well, the chase.

JG: What was it about Walsh's pictures that influenced you before you were a filmmaker?
PB: The energy is amazing, tremendous vitality and a very sure sense of action. He was a very good action director. *White Heat* is one of those very powerful action films. *High Sierra*'s a picture I love. Raoul had a real sense of the kinetic, and a recklessness that was very effective. Those films he made at Warners like *Gentleman Jim* and *High Sierra* in the early forties were very, very effective. I love even *Colorado Territory*.

JG: Remake of *High Sierra*.

PB: A very effective remake, with Joel McCrea, who was a dear man. I never really talked to him as much as I'd have liked to. There's a biography of him coming out, by the way. His daughter I think interviewed him and Knopf is going to publish it.

JG: He was an underrated actor.
PB: Very underrated. He really did some good ones. A really nice guy too. But Raoul was a lot like his movies. There was a recklessness and a vitality in the man that was appealing. An edginess. He was edgy. I like what Allan Dwan said about Raoul Walsh—"I always liked Raoul's on the edge kind of thing." There was that kind of on the edge thing with Walsh at his best.

JG: Did you know William Wellman?
PB: Never met him. I just never met him. I know he said a very nice thing about me on television one time, 'cause it was reported to me. He named me as one of the young guys that knew something. I was the only one he mentioned. He said he didn't like the new pictures but he thought this guy Bogdanovich knew something. Something like that. That was nice.

JG: What's your opinion of his work?
PB: He was a good director. Uneven. Louise Brooks was very fond of him, said wonderful things about *Beggars of Life* which is supposed to be his best picture. I've never seen it. Is it good?

JG: It has an opening where Wellman tells lots of story in a purely visual way, very quickly, very economically.
PB: He was a good storyteller. I liked some of his pictures. I never really got into his pictures the way I did with some of the others.

JG: How about Henry Hathaway?
PB: No, I never liked him. He didn't like me personally and I didn't much like him. I met him a couple times and I just didn't like him. I don't like his pictures.

JG: Gregory La Cava?
PB: *My Man Godfrey* is as good as it gets in that kind of comedy. That's the best one, he made a few others but that seemed to me to be the best of them. *Private Worlds* is his, that's a nice picture.

JG: *The Half-Naked Truth.*
PB: That's also quite good. I haven't seen all of his pictures. Of course, he died long before I could have met him.

JG: Lumet.
PB: I think it closes the book nicely, brings it back to New York. After all, Dwan was shooting in New York during the silents.

JG: And Walsh was from the Upper West Side of Manhattan.
PB: That's right. So that kind of brings it back to New York, which is where I'm coming back to. I'm moving back to New York. I grew up here. 15 West 67th Street for years, then my parents moved to 90th and Riverside Drive. I went to Collegiate.

JG: And the RKO-Colonial Theatre.
PB: And the Loew's Lincoln. Both of them are gone long ago. Loew's Lincoln preceded Lincoln Center.

JG: There's a wonderful story about your mother forcing you to go to a play. You just wanted to go to the movies.
PB: Yeah, she did, she forced me to do that. We had a big huge argument about it. That was a major thing.

JG: You wrote about maintaining a big file on all the movies you saw. When I was a kid I used to tape record credits off of pictures playing on TV, make notes, put them on index cards.
PB: See, I didn't have television. My parents didn't get television until I had already moved out of the house.

JG: You were doing all that from seeing the movies in theatres?
PB: Either from the movies or down at the public library. I still have all those files.

JG: When I was in school in Philadelphia I took a lead from you and wrote program notes for the cinematheque in exchange for free admission.
PB: *(laughter)* So it worked. Yeah, I had done that at the New Yorker Theatre.

JG: Where was that?
PB: Between 88th and 89th on Broadway.

JG: That was a big influence on you.
PB: Huge. It was a nine-hundred-seat theatre. I saw Dan Talbot yesterday. He's still a friend.

JG: Andrew Sarris and Eugene Archer.
PB: We used to hang around at the New Yorker in this little office in which Jonas Mekas came in one day and wrote on the wall, "All the good movies are made in Hollywood." Everybody thought I had written it. It was really Jonas.

JG: Really? Mr. Experimental Cinema?
PB: Yeah, I guess he'd written it as a tongue-in-cheek thing. At that point we were showing a lot of good old Hollywood pictures. As I say in the book, I don't think one should call them old movies, I think that there's good movies and there's not good movies, and there's movies you've seen and there's movies you haven't seen. If it's a good movie and you haven't seen it, it's new.

JG: I taught American Film Comedy one semester at School of Visual Arts and the very first thing I put up was *The Awful Truth*. As soon as the Columbia logo came up in black-and-white, I got groans from the film students.
PB: I know.

JG: Until they saw the movie, of course. There's an attitude people have about vintage films. Knowledge of classic American cinema is dismissed as film trivia.
PB: I know. It just isn't taken seriously and that's an American tragedy. We don't take seriously the stuff that we're best at. Jazz is the same thing. It took the French to discover that too. To say it was good. The kids just don't know what they're missing. People who haven't seen these movies don't know what they're missing. It's like an extraordinary treasure that's right under their noses and they're just too ignorant to know it's there. And they better get wise to it because it's really a tragedy, lost to people. It's like having never read a novel.

JG: Which is another problem.
PB: That's another thing that seems to be happening. Nobody reads anymore.

JG: Do you have a personal favorite among your films?
PB: *They All Laughed.* That's probably for very personal reasons but it is a personal question so that's my personal answer! *(laughter)* That's the picture I like best. I think people who know me would say that picture is kind of the way I am. It's more like me than any other picture I've made. I don't really dislike any of them except the ones that aren't the way they're supposed to be.

Interview with Peter Bogdanovich

Gerald Peary / 2002

Previously unpublished. Reprinted by permission of the author.

I met Peter Bogdanovich when I interviewed him in his hotel suite at the Montreal World Film Festival in 1993, where he was showing what would prove to be River Phoenix's final completed work, *The Thing Called Love*. I liked that movie, and I told Bogdanovich how much I admire *Daisy Miller* and *Saint Jack* and especially *Texasville*, a worthy sequel to *The Last Picture Show*. We immediately connected, not just about his films but because of our shared love of John Ford and other Hollywood classic-era directors.

A few years later, I was making a feature documentary, *For the Love of Movies: The Story of American Film Criticism*. Bogdanovich seemed to remember our brief Montreal meeting, and agreed to be interviewed on camera at his Manhattan Upper West Side brownstone. Well, the interview came at a raw time for Boganovich, with a recent divorce in the mix. But he was a trouper, sublimely gracious, and he spoke at length for my movie.

The only problem: Bogdanovich's honesty kept him from being in the actual documentary. He kept insisting that he was not a critic, never really a critic, just a feature writer. The Q&A, though an excellent discussion, languished on tape. It's only, a decade later and with a book of Bogdanovich interviews, that Bogdanovich's on-camera words from 2002 have been plucked (happily) from the audio track.
—*Gerald Peary*

Gerald Peary: You would know: what did the critics say originally about *Citizen Kane*?

Peter Bogdanovich: *Citizen Kane* opened to rave reviews, with the exception of the *New York Times*. Bosley Crowther said it was a sensational movie, but he thought that the center of it was hollow. He criticized the character of Kane as being somebody without a soul. But he was the only one. The reviews were awfully good. Some of them were great.

It wasn't reviewed in the Hearst papers. The Hearst blacklist definitely hurt the movie, because a lot of theatres didn't play it for fear of reprisals. Orson suggested that they put up tents across the country and show it: "The film you're not allowed to see in your theatre!" He thought they would have cleaned up, but RKO didn't go along with it.

Having been a box-office disappointment and a critics' delight, the picture basically disappeared. It started to be talked about in the late 1950s, early 1960s, but it was sort of underground and French-inspired. Twenty years after *Citizen Kane*, Orson Welles was a kind of legend in Europe. But in America, he was largely forgotten. *Touch of Evil*, which had been his last released film, was reviewed as a second-rate thriller, "B" picture. At the same time, it was opening in Paris and getting front-page attention. Truffaut wrote a front-page piece for the most influential French weekly.

We had a theatre called the New Yorker, which showed revivals of unusual or forgotten American films. Dan Talbot's theatre was very influential in the early 1960s and [into the] 1970s. We booked [Orson Welles's] *Othello*, which hadn't been seen in New York in ten years. I wrote a program note about it, which was very laudatory. In fact, I called it the best Shakespeare film ever made, which at that time was absolute heresy. I mean, the best Shakespeare film was *Hamlet* by [Laurence] Olivier or *Richard III* by Olivier or *Henry V* by Olivier. By no means was it *Othello* by Orson Welles! *Othello* was not highly thought of in the States. The *New York Times* had panned it. It had won the Grand Prize at Cannes, but in those days the Cannes Film Festival meant virtually nothing in the United States.

Anyway, I wrote this program note. Richard Griffith, who was curator of the Museum of Modern Art, called me a few months later and said that they were planning a retrospective on Welles, the first in his own country. He asked if I would organize the show and write the monograph. I asked Richard why he didn't do it himself. Well, he had to admit that he wasn't a big fan of Welles. But there were many people in Europe who believed that he was a great director, and, here, a few members at the Museum of Modern Art thought that he was worthy of a retrospective. Since I was a big admirer of Welles, and he had read my program note on *Othello*, he thought I would be the right person. Of course, I agreed to do it. They paid me a pittance.

I worked for a few months to organize as full a retrospective as we could. We published a small monograph along with it called *The Cinema of Orson Welles*, which sold for fifty cents. I did not have any contact with Welles at that time. I wrote the monograph, got an address for Welles, sent it off to him in May of 1961, never heard anything for seven years. Until one day Orson called me out of the blue when I was living in California, and he said, "Hello, this is Orson Welles. I can't tell you how long I've wanted to meet you." And I said, "You just took my line. Why would you want to meet me?" He said, "Because you've written the truest words ever published about me . . . in English." There was a slight pause, and then, "in English." I liked that! He said, "Can you meet with me tomorrow at the Beverly Hills Hotel?" I went over and met him, and that was the beginning of a long friendship. That was in 1968. It lasted until his death in 1985.

GP: Long before you wrote about films, or made films, you were in theatre. Is that right?
PB: Well, I always thought I was going to be an actor and a director. I was acting in plays when I was twelve, and directing in high school and acting in high school, and then professionally when I was fifteen. But around the time when I was turning fifteen, I started writing movie reviews and theatre reviews for my high school newspaper. I had a column in there for [almost] four years. I don't know why I started doing these columns, which were eight a school year. I guess I had to open my mouth about something. I had this movie index and card file of all the films I had seen since 1952. This was now 1954, so I had a few hundred cards on file.

The first thing I ever reviewed was a play that Ben Gazzara did off-Broadway called *End as a Man*, by Calder Willingham. The last thing I reviewed for the newspaper was a movie version of *End as a Man* called *The Strange One*, directed by Jack Garfein in 1957. When I got out of high school, somebody told me, "You know, you can see movies for free if you write about them." I could've been getting in the movies for nothing. I never knew that. Now, eighteen and broke, I thought, "Well, if I can save money getting in the movies for nothing . . ." I sent all my high school reviews to a new magazine called *Ivy*, which was run for all the Ivy League colleges. They said, "Okay, you can have a column in our new magazine." So then I put my name on screening lists all over New York, and pretty soon was getting free books, free theatre tickets, and free movie screening invitations, which was all very pleasant. I did in fact write for *Ivy* magazine for about two or three years. That got me to meet all the critics and so on. I blossomed from there to writing for *Film Culture*, and then the *Village Voice* and *Cahiers du Cinema*, and so on.

GP: Bosley Crowther—what did you think of his writing? And did you know him personally?
PB: Bosley Crowther was the main critic for the *New York Times*, the most influential critic. I didn't get along with him [aesthetically]. I didn't know him personally. I met him a few times. One time, when I was a brash nineteen, I did the unthinkable. We all were riding down in an elevator [after a film screening], and I turned to Crowther (crowded elevator) and said, "So what did you think of it?" He kind of flushed and looked down and said, "Interesting, interesting." I think he was amused by my moxie. You didn't ask old Bosley what he thought. But anyway, I didn't have that much respect for him. Eugene Archer was the fourth-string critic of the *New York Times*, and he and I became friends. I hung out with him quite a bit. And Andrew Sarris, who was the kind of underground critic; he was with the *Village Voice*. And Herman G. Weinberg, who wrote the subtitles for any foreign film that ever came through New York, whether it was Egyptian, French, Italian, or Persian. I knew Archer Winsten of the *Post*, and, I mean, I knew them all—Howard Thompson of the *Times*. I really got interested in the French view of films based on what Eugene Archer and Andrew Sarris were telling me. And Jonas Mekas, who was the editor of *Film Culture*. That was the kind of people I was hanging around with, at the same time trying to pursue my interest in directing theatre, and ultimately film.

I think the first time I met Andrew Sarris was probably—I don't remember exactly, but I would guess it was at the New Yorker [Theatre], where I was hanging out. He and Eugene Archer came there all the time to see the movies we were showing in the early 1960s.

GP: When did you start noticing who directed films?
PB: I had noticed directors early on because of my parents—my father was a kind of a deep-dish European intellectual. He was a good deal older than my mother. He was a painter, and he knew everything there was to know about painting, and everything there was to know about classical music. He knew a lot about a lot of things. And so he had grown up watching movies in the 1920s in Europe. He knew about directors. He would talk about Pudovkin or Eisenstein. But the American directors that often came up were Frank Capra, John Ford. I think Ford was probably the first director I remember hearing about from my parents.

"John Ford, John Ford, John Ford. He was a good director." They thought highly of him based on *The Grapes of Wrath*, based on *How Green Was My Valley*.

I think the first director I became emotionally aware of was Welles, when I saw *Citizen Kane* when I was sixteen or seventeen. Because I was an actor, I sort of could identify with that. There he was in the movie and, oh yes, he also must've stepped behind the camera. It sort of began to put a face on the idea of a director. My favorite film at the age of ten was *The Ghost Goes West*. My father would talk about Rene Clair. My parents liked Hitchcock—some of Hitchcock. Some of Hitchcock they didn't like. But that's how I first became in touch with directors. That got taken to the next step with Archer and Sarris, who went into it more deeply and were really talking from the "politique des auteurs"—the whole idea of a director's personality guiding a movie, whether it was the Hollywood system or an independent film.

GP: When you saw *Citizen Kane* at sixteen, had you read criticism of the film?
PB: No, I hadn't read anything much about it. I had heard my parents, and they said, "Oh yes, it's a great film." This was when there was a revival of it in New York. It was one of the first revivals of it—about 1955. I could look it up for you in my card file, because I kept track of every movie I saw for almost twenty years, from 1952 to 1970. *The Lady from Shanghai* was revived shortly thereafter, and I was blown away by that, and then I saw *The Magnificent Ambersons* on a very small, very bad television. My parents talked about it, "Oh yes, that's one of the great films, *The Magnificent Ambersons*." They had just been new to the United States when it came out, and they loved it.

GP: Had you read James Agee's film criticism?
PB: I read *Agee on Film*—I was very interested in that—and I was very taken with Agee and was very impressed, particularly with his piece about comedy—on the Golden Age of comedy. I totally agreed with him about Chaplin at that time, and Keaton and Harold Lloyd. My parents loved those three, and Laurel and Hardy.

I knew Dwight Macdonald and got friendly with him. We constantly disagreed. We agreed about some of the older films. We liked *Potemkin*, I remember. We agreed on that one. But there were many films that he hated that I liked, or that I liked and he hated. So we used to have a kind of a sparring relationship. Sarris and Archer and I agreed a lot.

GP: So when you switched to being a film critic...
PB: Well, you see, there's a misconception about me, which is that I was a critic, and then a filmmaker and director. And the truth is I was [far more an] actor. The chronology went like this: actor, actor, actor, director, critic, actor, director. So I just went back to how I started. Don't forget, I made my first name where somebody heard of me....

I directed in the theatre and got some good reviews and had a little bit of a small reputation in New York—very small. The critic stuff came in the middle of it. I never thought of myself really so much as a critic as I did as a feature writer. The first time nationally I was heard of was as a feature writer for *Esquire*, not as a critic. I wrote feature articles about Humphrey Bogart, Jerry Lewis, Jimmy Stewart. These were major pieces. It was because of those *Esquire* pieces that Roger Corman, when I met him in a movie theatre in Los Angeles, said, "I've read your stuff in *Esquire*. Would you like to write a script for me?" That's how I broke into the movies as a writer, because I'd been read in *Esquire*.

The fact is, I'd been writing scripts since I was sixteen. I wrote my first script for a short film when I was, well, eighteen. So it was all mixed up. If something was written about my first film, *Targets*, the media line about me was, "He's the first American critic to become a filmmaker." Wasn't exactly accurate to my money, but it became the standard bio on me—kind of left out a bit. The fact that I studied acting for four years when I was a teenager was kind of left out.

GP: When your moment came directing *Targets*, did you look to the French as a way to shoot?
PB: I didn't think about the French as an inspiration. I mean, I liked what Godard and Truffaut and all those cats were doing, and I was impressed with it. But I didn't think about that.

GP: Why have so few American critics become directors?
PB: I don't know why. As I said, I wasn't really a film critic. I had been trained to be in show business as an actor/director, and the critic part writing about movies was a kind of an adjunct, a kind of an interesting thing that I got involved in. But it wasn't where I was headed, you see. There isn't much example of it here. There's Rod Lurie, I think, directed from being a critic. Paul Schrader was a critic. Susan Sontag. But I don't think there's a tradition for it.

GP: Have you ever talked to a Hollywood director who did not feel adversarial in relationship with critics?

PB: No, as a matter of fact, there is an adversarial relationship between most people and critics. I remember one time when I was at Jennifer Jones's house for a party, and I had done a couple of pictures or *a* picture by then at least, and was there because of her stepson. I turned to her at one point and said, "You don't really like me, do you, Jennifer?" She looked at me and said, "Well, you're a critic." And I said, "Well, I'm not exactly." But I never forgot that: "How can I like you? You're a critic."

Being a director, being a critic—it isn't really the same thing [here]. In France, things like that can happen, but then, it's a much more intellectual community. There's more of that in Europe. I mean, let's look at Shaw. Bernard Shaw was a music critic and a writer. Graham Greene could be a [film] critic and a novelist. It just doesn't happen that much in movies in America.

GP: Have you become disappointed with the abilities of American critics?

PB: Well, I tell you something. I'm pushing thirty films of some kind or another that I've worked on. It's awfully difficult for critics to know, to understand how a film achieves what it achieves, and to know who's really responsible for each element. The thing I liked about the politique des auteurs was that it opened up a world beyond the camera. But it's a very special way of looking at films, and it's rather subtle, and you really have to see an awful lot of films to get it. It has to do with personality, yes, and how you can say that *Exodus* and *Anatomy of a Murder* are from the same personality. To see the same signature behind *Citizen Kane* and *Othello* is not as difficult as it is to see the same signature behind *Ruggles of Red Gap* and *The Awful Truth*, even though they're both [Leo McCarey] comedies. I had the advantage also of interviewing a lot of these people, so I could say, "Well, that's just like McCarey. That's his sense of humor. He's like that in person." Or John Ford, who had a certain kind of sense of humor, so that when I see a Ford movie I sort of feel I can tell, "Ford threw that line in." And [I] sort of laugh, thinking of Ford throwing that line in. I must say that's the part that interests me the most. To try to feel the personality of the filmmaker through the images, through the dialogue.

I got interested so much that I was curious to see if I could tell the difference between a Bugs Bunny cartoon directed by Chuck Jones and a Bugs Bunny cartoon directed by Friz Freleng. And I could. Sometimes it's hard to analyze, but there it was, even in a cartoon. [I] could tell the difference between a George Cukor movie and a Frank Borzage movie. I remember having an argument with Dwight Macdonald. He said, "Oh, that picture, *Born Yesterday*. It was directed by Michael Curtiz. He's terrible." And I said, "No, it wasn't directed by Curtiz. It was Cukor." And Macdonald said, "Oh, well, same thing." And I thought, "Now Dwight, Jesus. I mean, the same thing? Michael Curtiz and George Cukor?" It's like saying Garbo and Gary Cooper were the same person, which is what Lubitsch used to say as a joke. "You know, Garbo and Gary Cooper are really the same person." "Why do you say that, Ernst?" "Have you ever seen them together?" he'd say.

When I once asked Howard Hawks about it, he summed it up in the way that gave me the title of my book [*Who the Devil Made It*]. I said, "Which directors over the years, Howard, have you liked the most?" And he said, "I like anybody that made you know who the devil was making the picture. Because the director's a storyteller and he ought to have his own way of telling it." I still go for that.

We tend to take in America one film at a time, one novel at a time, one painting at a time. Well, you know, a man who's made fifty films, or thirty films, or twenty-five films, or ten films for that matter, has a body of work. Yes, certain films might be formally less interesting than others, or even formally less accomplished than others. But they were part of a whole kind of oeuvre, a whole kind of opus. And I think it was worth seeing within that opus. I can't argue that there are Ford films that aren't better than others. With every director, I would say there are always films that you prefer to see. I don't run to see *Red Line 7000* by Howard Hawks. But there are some French people who would say it's one of his best pictures. I don't agree. Howard didn't agree. He said, "Oh, I just screwed that one up." But I won't say it's a piece of shit. I won't say it's a no-good movie. On the other hand, *To Have and Have Not*—I don't know a prose film that could be much better than that.

GP: Do you feel that critics are looking at your films as one body of work?
PB: No, they're not. That whole idea of looking at a body of work doesn't really carry weight anymore. There was the standard Bogdanovich review, which was, "Who's he paying an homage to in this picture?" So, *The Last Picture Show* was my homage to Orson, *Targets* was my homage to Hitchcock, and *Daisy Miller* was my homage to Cukor, and so on. It was all a lot of crap. All of it. None of them were homages to anything. I was trying to make a good movie, and there were things that were inspired by, or influenced by, or stolen from, but they weren't homages.

Don't forget, when I started making pictures, virtually all the directors

I most admired were still alive, and I knew them. And I felt a kind of chagrin that I was working and they were not, that they were nearing the end of their careers and I was starting mine. I felt that I owed them something. They were generous to me, and I felt, "Be generous back." I was trying to tell a story with my own set of rules, my own ideas, influenced by a great many artists, not the least of them my father, who was not a filmmaker, but a painter. I think I was influenced most by people like Renoir, Hawks, Welles, Hitchcock. I was concerned if critics would enjoy it or get it, but I was mostly thinking about the audience.

GP: I've been disappointed in some of the criticism of your films. Too few critics got *Daisy Miller* and *Texasville*, for example.
PB: Well, I was often struck, before I started to make films, by how certain films were missed—how a point was missed, how they were not understood. A film like *The Man Who Shot Liberty Valance* by John Ford, for example. It felt to me like it was absolutely in keeping with where Ford had been going for the last ten, twenty years. The picture was dismissed as a somewhat senile odor, and of course that was ridiculous to me.

GP: In your film, *Directed by John Ford*, is Ford being so nasty to you because he hates film critics? Or is he your friend, and putting on a performance?
PB: Where he is surly with me and testy, he's putting on a very good performance. It wasn't hard for him to be that. He was crusty, surly, didn't want to talk about intellectual things, didn't want to be thought of as an intellectual, or an artist, or a poet, or any of that stuff. He knew what he was. But that was part of staying alive in an anti-intellectual country. With Ford, he had an intellectual side, which he hid, and a poetic side, which he hid. He could be very funny, though. Underneath all that, he could be very charming.

GP: Was he secretly complimented that certain critics knew everything about his movies?
PB: I think he liked if you knew his pictures. I mean, the first time I met him I gave him something that I had written about him, and he liked it. He said, "Thanks for the kind words," You know, that kind of stuff.

GP: Thinking of both your films and Ford's: Do you think critics today are biased against a classical way of filmmaking and telling screen stories?
PB: I think there's a kind of a fashionable attempt to go with what's

hip and modern, and so on. But I don't know what is hip and modern anymore. I don't know if there's any kind of movement among critics these days. It seems all hit-and-miss. The auteur theory, or the politique des auteurs, worked its way into the mainstream in a sort of generalized, largely incoherent way. The well-known directors seem to have an auteur kind of audience, like Marty Scorsese or Spielberg. I don't know. I feel that there's a tremendous lack of film culture in the United States—that very few people seem to know the older films. I find that from looking at the new films you could tell that [directors] haven't seen the older films. So there's a kind of a wit that's missing. A lot of American films have become a bit witless.

GP: Are there critics now whom you read with interest?
PB: I read Anthony Lane in the *New Yorker*. I think he's funny. He liked some movie of mine, so that's nice. And David Denby. I think the *New Yorker*'s really good. Sarris still writes a good piece. I don't know. I don't read as much film criticism as I used to.

GP: Every critic I know has a primal memory of going early to the movies. I heard somewhere about you going to see *Dumbo*, and freaking out.
PB: My earliest memory of moviegoing, but I don't know that it's a memory or just a story told in the family. They took me to see *Dumbo* when I was about three, and I evidently was very upset about it, and started screaming in the middle of the show, and had to be taken out of the theatre. I've often wondered if it was some kind of infantine precognition of facing the disaster of the movie business. Who knows? That's what happened.

Peter Bogdanovich's Year of the Cat

Alex Simon / 2002

From *Venice Magazine*, April 2002. Reprinted by permission of the author.

Peter Bogdanovich is a Hollywood survivor. Few veterans of the business have reached such high highs and hit such low lows as the man who was born to a Serbian father and a Viennese Jewish mother, July 30, 1939, in Kingston, New York. Raised in New York City, Bogdanovich was a precocious child, showing an early affinity for performing and a love of the arts, particularly film. He studied with acting guru Stella Adler in his teens and was acting on stage, as well as directing theater, by his early twenties. Bogdanovich was primarily an actor in his early years, and not a critic, as many people believed due to erroneous reporting and word-of-mouth.

Deciding that making films was where his true passion lay, Bogdanovich came west in the mid-sixties, where he quickly forged friendships with some of Hollywood's most revered veterans: Orson Welles, John Ford, and Howard Hawks, among others. Bogdanovich sat with many of these men for in-depth interviews, many of which are compiled in his much-beloved book, *Who the Devil Made It* (which was followed by a compendium of his actor interviews, *Who the Hell's In It*, in 2004). He was able to cut his filmmaking teeth working for B-movie legend Roger Corman on such classic trash as *The Wild Angels* (1967), which led to his directing debut, the thriller *Targets* (1968), about a mad sniper and an aging horror film star (Boris Karloff, in one of his last, and greatest, turns) whose synchronous paths eventually cross. A low-budget gem, the film brought Bogdanovich to the attention of producers Bert Schneider and Bob Rafelson, whose BBS Films was the DreamWorks of the late sixties/early seventies. They asked Bogdanovich what he wanted to do next, and the young director told them of this little-known novel about small town Texas in the 1950s. . . .

The Last Picture Show (1971) is widely regarded as one of the seminal films of the seventies, if not the century. A bittersweet coming-of-age film, *Picture Show* garnered eight Oscar nominations, winning two, for Supporting Actor (Ben Johnson) and Actress (Cloris Leachman), and helped launch a new generation of stars: Jeff Bridges, Cybill Shepherd, Timothy Bottoms, Randy Quaid, Ellen Burstyn, and, especially, Bogdanovich himself, who garnered almost as much press for his affair with Shepherd and the dissolution of his marriage to writer/producer Polly Platt during the film's production, as he did for the film itself. Bogdanovich had truly arrived. He and Shepherd moved into a palatial estate in Bel-Air. He was an occasional guest host on *The Tonight Show*, and contributor to such high-profile magazines as *Esquire* and *Playboy*. Two more cinematic triumphs followed: the zany comedy *What's Up, Doc?* (1972) and the charming *Paper Moon* (1973). He formed a production company with pals and fellow wunderkinds Francis Coppola and William Friedkin, called the Directors Company. It seemed the sky was the limit.

In the mid-seventies, Bogdanovich's fortunes started to shift slightly, starting with a string of box office and critical flops: the period piece *Daisy Miller* (1974), the musical *At Long Last Love* (1975), and the comedic look at the early days of moviemaking, *Nickelodeon* (1976). By 1978, his relationship with Shepherd was over, but he did score a modest critical success with the fine *Saint Jack*, a low-key gem starring Ben Gazzara as a Vietnam-era American pimp in Singapore.

In 1980 Bogdanovich began his descent into personal and professional hell. While shooting his most personal film, the delightful *They All Laughed*, he fell in love with actress Dorothy Stratten, 1980's Playboy Playmate of the Year. Two weeks after the film wrapped, Stratten's estranged husband murdered the young starlet, and then himself, events later dramatized in Bob Fosse's final film, *Star 80* (1984). It was a horrific end to not only a young woman's life, but a budding talent that both critics and her co-stars agreed would have developed into something special. Bogdanovich retreated from moviemaking and the public eye for the next four years, writing the controversial book *The Killing of the Unicorn*, detailing his love for Stratten and the still-reverberating effect her death had on him, and all those who knew her. By the time he did *Mask*, a critical and box office success in 1985, Bogdanovich was bankrupt, having spent his fortune trying to distribute *They All Laughed* on his own. He also unsuccessfully sued Universal Pictures for tampering with *Mask*'s final cut.

The next decade and a half saw a string of attempted come-backs by the once red-hot director, but nothing seemed to take hold, in spite of some solid television work, and a poorly received sequel to *Picture Show* entitled *Texasville* (1990), which was hacked to pieces by its studio, removing nearly twenty-five minutes of key footage. Bogdanovich's restored cut is available on Pioneer laserdisc.

In spite of these myriad setbacks, Bogdanovich stayed in the ring and kept swinging. He's scored a knock-out punch with his latest effort, *The Cat's Meow*, a fascinating piece of historical conjecture, detailing what might have happened on newspaper magnate William Randolph Hearst's yacht in November 1924, when a disparate group that included Charlie Chaplin, Marion Davies, Louella Parsons, and movie mogul Thomas Ince went for a relaxing getaway to Catalina, only to have one of the passengers mysteriously wind up dead. . . . The film is part Hitchcock, part drawing room comedy, and a pure joy to behold. Fine work across the board from Kirsten Dunst (in her first adult role) as Davies, Edward Herrmann as Hearst, Eddie Izzard as Chaplin, and Cary Elwes as Ince. The Lions Gate release hits theaters on April 10.

Peter Bogdanovich sat down recently to reflect on his remarkable life, openly discussing all its triumphs, tragedies, and quirks of fate.

Q: When I heard you were making this film, I was thrilled. I've wanted to see this story filmed since reading *Hollywood Babylon* as a kid.
A: Well, I read about it in *Hollywood Babylon*, as well, but the person who first told me about it was Orson Welles, about thirty years ago, when I interviewed him for a book we did (*This Is Orson Welles*). The story didn't make it into the book, but there is a reference to it, which Orson referred to as "a notorious incident." At the time we did the book, we still couldn't get into it, if you know what I mean. But thirty years later, the script came to me, and I said, "My God, it's that story Orson told me!"

Q: Even though the story is based on conjecture, since no one really knows what happened on Hearst's yacht that night, the events in the film, as they're portrayed, are pretty much the way most people believe things went down, right? I mean, I don't think anyone who knows the story today believes that Thomas Ince died of "gastrointestinal distress."
A: No, no. And I don't think they did then, either. The famous quote from D. W. Griffith was "Anytime anyone mentions Tom Ince around Hearst, he turns white. There's somethin' funny there." (laughs) But (the story) feels right. The death haunted everyone who was on that ship.

Q: Well, why else would someone like Louella Parsons have had the

career, and the amount of power, that she had? It all started right after Ince died.
A: That's certainly a strong argument. She was a real pain in the neck to a lot of people.

Q: I'm glad to see that Thomas Ince is being brought back into the public consciousness because, aside from Ince Boulevard in Culver City, he's largely a forgotten figure, and he was a real pioneer filmmaker.
A: Well, he wasn't a poet like Griffith was, but he was a real pioneer in terms of how films are made, particularly the Western, and he was the first person to really come up with the process of doing a lot of pictures at once, which we bring up in the film. He was very ahead of time with the assembly line idea of making pictures.

Q: Ince's death was almost symbolic, wasn't it, of a shift in how movies were made and studios were run?
A: Very true. Coincidentally that year, 1924, was the year (director) Ernst Lubitsch came to Hollywood, which really changed movies forever. He brought Europe to Hollywood in a way that hadn't happened yet. I asked Jean Renoir once what he thought of Lubitsch. Renoir said "Lubitsch? He invented the modern Hollywood." Of course, this was during the sixties, and the Hollywood of today is nothing like the Hollywood of that period. So what he really meant was films done from about 1925 to 1960.

Q: You assembled an incredible cast for this, starting with Edward Herrmann, who's a brilliant choice for Hearst.
A: We got lucky. He wasn't the first choice initially, and then he wasn't available. We were very close to shooting and we didn't have a Hearst yet. The actor we had cast backed out at the last minute, saying he was exhausted. Finally, it was suggested "What about Ed Herrmann?" who I always thought would be great in the part. So it was fortuitous, really. A lot of luck.

Q: There is a Movie God, isn't there?
A: Yes, and sometimes He's against you! (laughs) But sometimes the Gods are on your side. John Ford said to me once, "Most of the good things in pictures happen by accident." I was shocked by that, at that point having only made one picture. But now I believe it to be very true. Luck is either on your side, or it's not. (laughs)

Q: It was terrific to see Kirsten Dunst playing an adult. She gave the part a lot of depth. The other portrayals of Marion Davies I've seen have been pretty cartoonish.
A: She was wonderful, wasn't she? She worked really hard at it, and always wanted to do a twenties story. She has a wonderful period face, looks great in those clothes, and has great instincts.

Q: Eddie Izzard, who plays Charlie Chaplin, was terrific also. I wasn't that familiar with him, prior to this film.
A: Well, Eddie's a very famous British comedian. He's not a standup in the traditional sense. He's more like Richard Pryor was: he acts the comedy. He got two Emmys for the HBO special he did a couple years ago. Again, luck. My manager was handling him for a while and suggested that I see his act. So I went and saw his act, and he was hilarious. And while I was watching him being hilarious, acting this comedy, it suddenly hit me that he'd be perfect for Chaplin, because that was the toughest part to cast. He doesn't look like Charlie, but the idea of an English comedian playing an English comedian wasn't too much of a stretch. It turned out that he loved Chaplin, and also loved the idea that Chaplin wasn't funny in this. He wanted to play a dramatic role.

Q: From everything I've heard, in real life Chaplin was as serious as a heart attack.
A: Yeah, he was pretty serious. I met him once, late in his life, when he came out for the Oscars in '72. He was having problems with his memory at the time, but was still madly in love with his wife, Oona. He was a little frail, and not particularly funny. You know how I met him? He was given a special Academy Award that year, and my film, *The Last Picture Show*, was nominated for several awards. Coincidentally, the producer of *The Last Picture Show*, Bert Schneider, had made a deal with the owner of the Chaplin film library to bring all of Charlie's old movies out again. Bert knew that I knew a lot about old pictures and asked if I would cut together a bunch of clips for the tribute before the award was given to Chaplin. He asked me what I needed, and I gave him a list of the pictures and an editor to work with. The compilation of clips I put together was thirteen and a half minutes long, with the final four minutes being from *The Kid* (1921). I get a call from Bert later: "The Academy said it's too long. We can't run it. What do you want to do?" I said, "Bert, it's Charlie Chaplin!" Bert agreed and called the Academy back, saying, "We won't cut

it. It's Charlie Chaplin, for God's sake!" The Academy said, "We won't run a thirteen-and-a-half-minute film clip on a live broadcast!" Bert said, "Okay, then Charlie won't come to the ceremony!" They ran it. (laughs)

Q: Yeah, I'd say that was a deal-breaker.
A: (both laugh) It was marvelous. Everyone was crying at the end of it.

Q: Your book, *Who the Devil Made It*, is a terrific collection of the interviews you've done with classic filmmakers, from people like silent film pioneer Allan Dwan (who helmed the 1922 version of *Robin Hood*, with Douglas Fairbanks), to Sidney Lumet (*Serpico*, 1973), who got his start in live TV.
A: Thank you. I'm actually working on a sequel, called *Who the Hell's In It*, which is a collection of pieces on actors. There's profiles of John Wayne, Cary Grant, Jimmy Stewart, Marlene Deitrich. . . . It's a different kind of book than the first one. It's not all Q&A like the first book, although there is some. The first chapter is about Lillian Gish, and the second is about Bogart, who I never met. It's got some of the magazine articles that I've written over the years. There's a brief chapter on Marilyn Monroe also, who I never really met, although I saw her once in an acting class of Lee Strasberg's that I audited, in New York.

Q: Let's talk about your background. You grew up in New York. Your father was a Serb, and your mother a Viennese Jew.
A: Mom was Jewish and dad was Serbian-Greek Orthodox, although we had no religious training at all. My parents were turned off by orthodox religions.

Q: For your early youth, you were essentially an only child.
A: Yeah, my younger sister was born when I was thirteen.

Q: It sounds like it was your dad who really introduced you to the movies.
A: They took me to see regular pictures like *Dumbo* (1941), which was the first picture I ever saw, and I had to be taken out of the theater, screaming! (laughs) But my first really exciting experience at any kind of theater was at the opera, at the old Metropolitan Opera House. It was *Don Giovanni*. I remember him going to Hell at the end. It scared the shit out of me! (laughs) Then I started going with my dad to the Museum of Modern Art, where we saw silent movies, which is where I first saw Chaplin,

Buster Keaton, Laurel and Hardy. I loved silent movies, actually, and it's a good thing that I did, because it's the foundation of movies. I think we've kind of lost contact with that.

Q: Was there one film you saw during that period that did it for you, where you said, "This is what I have to do"?
A: Well, I always loved the movies, but originally thought I was going to be an actor. When I was ten years old, my three favorite movies were *Red River* (1948), *She Wore a Yellow Ribbon* (1949), and *The Ghost Goes West* (1936), which was written by Robert E. Sherwood, produced by Alexander Korda, directed by Rene Clair, and starred Robert Donat. I must've seen that picture six or seven times. I just loved it, my favorite of the three. In fact, I've been planning a ghost picture. I've been planning one for twenty years. Mine's called *Wait for Me*. I'm sure it all goes back to *The Ghost Goes West*.

Q: Stella Adler was your primary acting teacher. Tell us about her.
A: She was a great woman, larger than life, very theatrical, very funny. She was extraordinarily influential on me, and a number of other people. Marlon Brando said that she taught him everything he knows. She influenced acting in movies to such a degree that she changed acting, as did Brando. She was just an extraordinary woman. I learned so much about the art of the theater and art in general. Stella didn't think that art of any kind should be small. She thought it should be bigger than the kitchen sink, and should speak to important subjects.

Q: Was Orson Welles sort of a second father to you?
A: It's funny, several people have commented that I've had several different fathers in my life. Orson filled in an awful lot of things that my father wasn't equipped to do. My father was equipped to do a lot of things, but emotionally . . . he'd had a tough life. Unfortunately, I didn't get to spend as much time with my father as I'd have liked. He died when I was quite young, while I was shooting *Picture Show*, in fact. Orson was more like an older brother, in many ways. He was a great authority figure, but he was still very boyish. It's funny, Orson always wanted a son, but had all these daughters instead. He always said, "I don't know what to do with women." (laughs)

Q: The first thing you directed was in New York on the stage, right?
A: Yeah, in 1959. I was twenty. My first claim to fame was introducing

Carroll O'Connor in the production. From there, he got an agent, went to Hollywood, and the rest is history. He gave me credit for that, once. When he won his first Golden Globe, for *All in the Family*, I was nominated for *Picture Show*. I was sitting down by the winner's podium and he said "There's a young director who's nominated here tonight who gave me my start in New York. He's an arrogant son of a bitch, but I thank him." (laughs)

Q: When you realized you wanted to direct films instead of plays, you came to Hollywood. It was then that you met all these amazing directors of yesteryear, whom you interviewed. Since you didn't go to college, was this your film school, so to speak?
A: Absolutely. You put it in a nutshell. It was like the greatest university, or master's class that one could get. I was able to put myself through this with all these pioneers who were still alive then. Independent film wasn't really around at that point and the only thing going on in New York was the underground movement, with Andy Warhol and that crowd. That wasn't my thing. One of the main reasons I came out to Hollywood was to meet and learn from these old masters. How do you get to know about this medium unless you ask the people who've done it? And they were all here: Jack Ford, Howard Hawks, King Vidor. There's a lot of people I talked to who I didn't officially interview. But I was able to actually sit and interview eighteen of these directors.

Q: Stylistically, the two directors who've influenced you the most are John Ford and Howard Hawks.
A: I guess that's true, although you'd also have to include Orson Welles, not stylistically, but in other ways.

Q: If I were someone off the street, with just a layman's knowledge of movies, and I asked you to tell me the difference between the films of Hawks and Ford, what would you tell me?
A: I asked Orson that question once, and he gave me the best answer. He said, "At their best, Hawks is great prose, but Ford is poetry." I think he was right. That's accurate. Although Ford made more pictures that don't work today, than Hawks did. Ford's films had a sentimentality that Hawks's didn't.

Q: What's your favorite Ford picture?
A: It varies. I love *The Quiet Man* (1952), *The Searchers* (1956), *The Man*

Who Shot Liberty Valance (1962). Also *My Darling Clementine* (1946), *They Were Expendable* (1945). These were all great pictures.

Q: What about your favorite Hawks film?
A: *To Have and Have Not* (1944), *Rio Bravo* (1959), *The Big Sleep* (1946), *Bringing Up Baby* (1938), *Twentieth Century* (1934).

Q: It's amazing that one man made all those movies, all from different genres.
A: I know. He was remarkable.

Q: I think *Scarface* (1932) still holds up really well. It was one of the first films cut for action, wasn't it? The editing still feels very contemporary.
A: Yeah, it's just superb on every level, except for that horrible postscript that was slapped on the end of it, with these newspaper men standing around, pontificating about what a horrible thing we'd just witnessed. And what really irks me about *Red River*, which is one of my favorites, is that you can't see the right version anymore. The version they have on video, which is listed as the "Director's Cut," is not! I've tried to call the people who own the rights and tell them, "Not only is this not the 'Director's Cut,' it's the cut that Howard disowned!"

Q: How are the two cuts different?
A: There's the narrated version, and the text version, where there's this big book where the pages keep turning. That was the preview version which Hawks threw out, and rightfully so. It's too slow. Then he had the version that Walter Brennan narrated. That's the version that Howard liked, but you can't see it anymore. Maybe they can't find the other cut, which would be tragic.

Q: Let's talk about your time with Roger Corman.
A: Previous to my work on *The Wild Angels*, Roger had asked me to write a script for him, a war script, something that he could shoot in Poland, where he had a great location scouted out. "Sort of like *Bridge on the River Kwai* and *Lawrence of Arabia*, but cheap!" (laughs) And that was the beginning of a script called *The Criminals*, which never got made, but was a pretty good script. Then I got the call from Roger to work as his assistant on *The Wild Angels*, which was then called *All the Fallen Angels*. That was an incredible experience. Twenty-two weeks I worked on that. I directed second unit and cut my own footage. I also rewrote the entire script,

but didn't get credit. To this day, I don't think even Peter Fonda knows I wrote that picture. (laughs) I learned a lot. Roger throws you in the water and says, "Swim!"

Q: All of this led to a terrific film, called *Targets*.
A: Thank you, and unfortunately, it's still relevant. We based it on Charles Whitman's shooting spree at University of Texas in 1966. My first wife (Polly Platt) and I collaborated on the story. I wrote the first draft of the script, then Samuel Fuller (*The Steel Helmet*, 1951; *Shock Corridor*, 1963) asked to read it, and during about two hours of conversation, he rewrote the entire script! Sammy wouldn't take credit for his work. He said "No credit, kid! If you give me credit, they'll think I did everything!" And he practically did! He was a great guy. Boris Karloff owed Roger two days work on a picture, so that's how Karloff became involved, and we interwove the parallel stories of this aging horror film star and this homicidal maniac until their paths eventually crossed.

Q: Was your character in the film, Sammy, named after Samuel Fuller?
A: Right, "Sammy Michaels," Michael being Sam's middle name. I owe a lot to Sammy. The film got some good reviews and some attention, and that's really what got me *Picture Show*.

Q: What was Mr. Karloff like?
A: Oh, what a wonderful man he was. He was just sweet and dear, and very funny, very acerbic. He was seventy-nine when we shot that, and very ill at the time. But he never complained. He was a real trooper, especially when we shot the drive-in stuff. We only had him for one day during that sequence!

Q: Let's talk about *Picture Show*.
A: Sal Mineo gave me the book originally, and had always wanted to play the part of Sonny (played in the film by Timothy Bottoms). By then, he was too old, but he thought I'd like it, and I did. I didn't really know how to make it initially, until I realized the only way to make it was just to make it! (laughs) To shoot the book, which is basically what we did: we just shot the book. The script followed Larry McMurtry's original construction which was basically one football season to the next in this small town.

Q: How were you able to make the film relevant to yourself since, here you were, a New Yorker, making a picture about kids in small town Texas during the early fifties?

A: I think the teenage experience is similar everywhere, which is why people who saw the picture and grew up in places like New York, or Europe, or Australia, all related to it very deeply. That's why it has universality. It did for me, even though Texas for me was a foreign country. I approached it like a foreign country, learning about the music, watching the people, how they dressed, how they interacted. I never even knew who the hell Hank Williams was before that picture! (laughs)

Q: Do you feel that *Picture Show* on one hand was a terrific experience because it made your career, but on the other hand, that it's also become your cross to bear?

A: No, I don't. I mean, unlike Orson, who did feel that way about *Citizen Kane*, I don't feel that way because I have made other pictures that did business and that people liked, whereas with Orson, it was the only one that people had ever heard of. He made great films that no one's ever heard of. When people approach me, they don't just mention *Picture Show*, there are other films they've liked, but that wasn't the case with Orson. In fact, he said to me once—we were talking about Greta Garbo, and he loved Garbo—I said, "Isn't it a pity with all the movies she made, she did only two really great ones." Orson says, "Well, you only need one." (laughs) So I thought, if you only need one, at least I got the one out of the way early on.

Q: *What's Up, Doc?* is another terrific film. It's been said by critics and film scholars that *Picture Show* was your John Ford homage and *Doc* was your Howard Hawks homage.

A: (groans) Oh God, they always say that shit. I think all that started because I had to open my big mouth, and I said something to the effect that *The Last Picture Show* was inspired by *The Magnificent Ambersons* (Orson Welles, 1942) because they're both about the end of an era. From there on it went because there were some obvious John Fordian moments with a couple of the long shots and shots of the sky. All of my reviews in the seventies and eighties were predicated on a basic piece of misinformation, which is that I began as a critic. So all the reviews were "Well, he was a critic, so this is his 'X' movie and this is his 'Y' movie," which is bullshit! I was never a critic. I was an actor!

Q: They were trying to make you into the American Francois Truffaut.

A: Right, exactly. I had written about film, but I was a popularizer more than anything. I wrote features and interviewed people who interested me. But to say that I consciously thought this picture was an homage to someone was ridiculous! They even said that *Paper Moon* was my homage to Shirley Temple! Give me a break! (laughs) Did you ever see Shirley Temple light up a Lucky Strike or swear? It was anti-Shirley Temple! So it was completely wrong and it went on for years. With *What's Up, Doc?* we had a similar set-up to Hawks's *Bringing Up Baby*, which was "daffy dame meets stuffy professor," plus one joke, where she rips his jacket, but that's it. The challenge on that picture was "How do you do a picture with Barbara Streisand?" Well, you make a screwball comedy. She actually wanted to do a drama because she'd just done a comedy (*The Owl and the Pussycat*, 1970), but I'd just done a drama, so I wanted to do a comedy. (laughs) In the end, I won. It was really a picture that was almost made on a dare. I had more fun on that picture than anything I've ever done.

Q: *Paper Moon* recreates a time and place better than any film I've ever seen.
A: We worked really hard to get that period-feel right. We shot all over Kansas and a few weeks in Missouri. I think it's the best work Ryan O'Neal's done. That wonderful laugh he came up with, that cackle, was just wonderful. Paramount owned the property originally and had John Huston lined up to direct with Paul Newman and his daughter to star. Then they wanted me to direct, but I didn't particularly want to do it with Paul. I wanted to do it with Ryan, so that's what happened.

Q: Around this time, you, William Friedkin, and Francis Coppola formed the Directors Company, which seemed like a great idea. What happened?
A: I thought it was a great idea and made two pictures for the company (*Paper Moon* and *Daisy Miller*). Francis made one (*The Conversation*, 1973), and Billy never did a picture for the company, then decided he didn't want to make any pictures for the company. He wanted to make more money. The money we could make was limited to a certain amount, which I thought was perfectly good, but Friedkin felt he wanted more money, and more money for the budget. Our deal was, we could make any picture we wanted, as long as it was $3 million or under, which was a lot of money in those days. We could also produce a movie for someone else if it wasn't more than $1.5 million. We didn't even have to show them a script! It was a great deal, and I wish I could get one like it again. That kind of freedom is worth gold, I think. It was a shame.

Q: What did you think of Peter Biskind's book *Easy Riders, Raging Bulls*, the notorious account of this period in Hollywood?
A: I dipped into about three pages of it in a book shop and got nauseous. (Biskind) just didn't get it at all. He'd interviewed me a couple times and quoted people who either weren't around or didn't know what they were talking about. It was just awful. A bad book from a very good writer.

Q: *Nickelodeon* was an interesting film.
A: Well, I'm not completely happy with the way that picture turned out. Both *Nickelodeon* and *At Long Last Love* were sort of pet projects of mine and neither came out the way I wanted, which is the reason I stopped making pictures for three years. I mean, they were okay, but they just didn't turn out right. *Nickelodeon* was meant to be in black and white and I wanted John Ritter and Cybill and Jeff Bridges and . . . I just had a smaller picture in mind. Both Burt Reynolds and Ryan (O'Neal) were good in it, and Jane Hitchcock was good, but she didn't have any threat about her. So I quit making pictures for a while, because I felt both films had been compromised. Somehow, I'd had all this success, then suddenly made these pictures that I felt were compromised. So I went back to basics and made my next two pictures exactly the way I wanted, but for less money. People thought I couldn't get a job during that period, which is absolute nonsense.

Q: What did you do during that period?
A: I went around the world with Cybill twice, and turned down a lot of pictures. I didn't want to work again until I figured out how I could work with integrity. So after that, I did *Saint Jack*, which turned out well and was an amazing experience, and then *They All Laughed*, which is my own favorite, but became a tragedy when Dorothy (Stratten) was murdered. That's something that we've never gotten over, but we've all had to move on from. I say "we" meaning the people who were close to her.

Q: What was it like shooting *Saint Jack* on location in Singapore?
A: Well, it was . . . fascinating. (laughs) One of the most life-altering experiences I've ever been through. It was comparable in my life to the upheaval of my personal life during *Picture Show*. My relationship with Cybill technically ended with that. I was gone for six months and Ben Gazzara was there for four months. We only shot twelve weeks, but the rest of the time was spent doing a lot of research and preparation. We had a bare bones script but no real characters and no women at all. It was

a story about a pimp and his hookers, and we had no women characters! So, to be candid, I didn't know that much about hookers and the writer, Paul Theroux, wasn't much help, so Benny and I and all of us got pretty involved in the scene there. It was pretty extraordinary, what we learned, about all of these women and how they came to be there, and basically much of what's in the film was based on what we learned from these real hookers. Singapore is sort of the melting pot of Asia, like New York is for the U.S. All those locations you saw were real, most of which are gone now, and most of the cast were non-professionals.

Q: *They All Laughed* is one of my favorite of your films.
A: It certainly is mine. It was a labor of love. Everyone in it was either in love, falling in love, falling out of love, or having problems with love. In that film, like in *Saint Jack*, we inferred a lot, instead of spelling it all out, which some people took as meaning it had nothing to say. Unfortunately, tragically, Dorothy Stratten was murdered two weeks after we wrapped, so nobody from that moment on could ever see her or the movie as we intended it. It was intended to be bittersweet. The sweet was supposed to be Dorothy and John Ritter. The bitter was supposed to be Audrey Hepburn and Ben Gazzara. But after Dorothy's death, it was all bitter.

Q: Tell us about Audrey Hepburn.
A: She was so magical. She broke your heart. Audrey was everything anybody thought she was: she had grace under pressure; she was a complete professional without one egoesque moment in her life; she cared about people; she had a great sense of humor; she was quietly sexy in a very ladylike way; she was very girlish, still at age fifty. It was her last starring picture, which I knew it would be, strangely enough. She just wasn't that into (acting) anymore. I think she preferred bringing up her children. . . . I always felt that picture would never really work until everyone in the picture was dead, and then it would sort of become neutral again. With Dorothy and Audrey now gone, I think it's taken on a little distance. A lot of audiences, like in Seattle and Beverly Hills, really liked it and got it, but I never should have tried to distribute the picture myself.

Q: Why did you buy the rights to the film and then try to distribute it yourself after Dorothy's death?
A: Because I was out of my mind. It was a disaster. I was an idiot. I was so paranoid after Dorothy's murder, I wanted to protect the picture at all

costs and was afraid they would fuck up the distribution. I wanted to pull away from the studio that was handling it, and I did, by buying the rights to the picture for $350,000 cash, which at the time was a lot of money, plus the guarantees that wound up costing me $5 million! The point is, it was a mistake brought on by paranoia and grief, and not dealing with the grief, and just trying to write a book about it, thinking that would be enough, but it wasn't. In writing the book, I thought I was venting all my anger, which I was, but in the end, the only person I ended up hurting was myself. I lost my financial freedom as a result. Nevertheless, I learned a few things, one of which is you cannot, in any event, self-distribute. The only person who ever got away with it was (John) Cassavetes, who very successfully distributed *A Woman Under the Influence* (1974), but then lost it all over *Killing of a Chinese Bookie* (1976). You just can't fight these people. By 1985, I was bankrupt. The only reason I got through '83 is because I did *Mask*, which I had to do because I was broke.

Q: There was a four-year gap between *They All Laughed* and *Mask*.
A: Yeah. I was consumed with distributing *They All Laughed* and writing *Killing of the Unicorn*. I turned down a lot of offers during that time. I just couldn't do anything. My agent (would say), "Forget it, don't even ask him. He's writing a book," which, of course, got me into even more trouble.

Q: It sounds like you did *Mask* for the money, initially.
A: Initially, yes. The script, which was originally one hunred pages that dealt with Rocky Dennis's life, needed a lot of work. So I sat through nine drafts of that picture working with this writer, working on the construction and the dialogue. Then we shot the picture and I rewrote most of the biker dialogue on the set with Cher and Sam Elliott. I got into it, aside from the money, because it reminded me of how Dorothy was very taken with *The Elephant Man*. She bought a book that was a serious study of John Merrick, the Elephant Man, and had seen the play on Broadway. I remember her buying it at Doubleday one night and the photographs were rather graphic. I couldn't look at them, but she was riveted. I figured out later that she identified with him. Here was this gorgeous creature that everyone would stop and stare at, from adults, to kids, to dogs. Just gawk at her. Dogs especially would just go to her like she was a goddamn milkmaid! And she never understood why she had this extraordinary affect. She just radiated this extraordinary beauty and goodness, which the camera never captured. She was too complicated for the camera. Her

face changed every few seconds. It was quite amazing. A lot of people who knew her said that. So what made me decide to do *Mask*, really, was thinking back to Dorothy's complete lack of ease when people looked at her. She said, "I feel like I have ice cream on my shirt, or something." There was this connection with Dorothy feeling like an outsider because of her beauty, and Rocky Dennis's feeling like an outsider because people found him hard to look at. The two are not dissimilar.

Q: Making it must've been a cathartic experience for you.
A: Yeah, it was, although what you saw up on the screen was only 90 percent of what we did. We ran afoul of the studio head, who had other interests in mind, and ours was not one of them. They cut about eight minutes of key scenes, and changed the music on the soundtrack. The character of Rocky loved Bruce Springsteen. His whole room was the Beatles and Bruce Springsteen posters, for God's sake! They didn't want to make a deal to use Bruce's music, so they replaced it with Bob Seger, without my approval. There was a deal to be made, too. Bruce wanted his music to be a part of this film. We had an understanding that if it wasn't going to be Springsteen, it would be the Beatles! But they made a deal with Seger behind my back. And I like Bob Seger's music very much, so it had nothing to do with the quality of his work, but it just wasn't right for the picture. So, I filed a lawsuit which, again, I shouldn't have done. That was a mess. It hurt the picture and it hurt me.

Q: After seeing your original cuts of *Mask* and *Texasville*, both of which were tampered with by their studios, it's amazing how different, and how much better, your cuts are. They're completely different films than what were released.
A: Yeah, they cut twenty-five minutes out of *Texasville*, which was supposed to be a bittersweet picture like *Picture Show* was. They wound up cutting most of the bitter and keeping in the sweet, which completely threw it off balance. And the thing is, when the schmucks in the executive suite do this to your picture, you as the director are the one who gets blamed, not the studio people who ruined it! I did another film called *Illegally Yours* (1988), with Rob Lowe, that I had high hopes for, but it was recut completely by Dino De Laurentiis. It's not a good picture, and that's why. I hope we can do DVDs of the original cuts of *Mask* and *Texasville*, which actually was available on Pioneer laserdisc, but is now out of print. We'll see . . . *(Author's note: PB's cut of* Mask *is now available on DVD, as is his black and white cut of* Nickelodeon.*)*

Q: Obviously with twenty-five minutes added, *Texasville* is a completely different picture, but it amazed me how different *Mask* was with just an extra eight minutes and Springsteen on the soundtrack, instead of Seger.
A: Yes, it all counts. It all matters. If you tamper with something like that and remove a part of it, the whole structure comes tumbling down, like a house of cards. The people who run the studios don't realize this because they're not filmmakers. But this is nothing new. You can go back to the silent days and filmmakers were treated the same way, like Erich von Stroheim, whose eight-hour epic masterpiece *Greed* (1925) was cut down to two hours and twenty minutes by its studio. Think that was a different movie? (laughs) The point is, they know what they're getting into going into it. To green light a picture that's built a certain way, and then tear it apart once it's been completed in that way, does this make sense?

Q: You've probably had more high highs and low lows than anyone I've interviewed in the film business. How do you keep hope alive and keep your chin up during those bad times?
A: I don't know. (long pause) I don't know. . . . My mother and father, I suppose, set a fairly good foundation for me, so I haven't sunk into the earth yet. (laughs) I think they had kind of a sense of art and culture and civilization that they instilled in me that helped give me some strength. Then, of course, there's my family, and in the case of Dorothy, Dorothy's family as well. So I was never alone in these things. Some sense of the past, I suppose, also helps.

Q: Do you think it's just a matter of knowing who you are?
A: That doesn't hurt. A lot of people, especially recently, have experienced tragedy on a huge scale. I think you learn to live with it, as opposed to getting over it. As far as movies are concerned, they pale in comparison to a real life tragedy.

Q: You've been acting a lot again, most notably in Henry Jaglom's new film *Festival in Cannes* and in *The Sopranos*, in a recurring role as Dr. Elliot Kupferberg.
A: I love doing that! It's been a tremendous thing for me to be able to do that, and I'm forever grateful to David Chase for allowing me that opportunity, because a lot of other people would've given their eye teeth to be in that show, and he just offered it to me. The other thing I'm very happy about that show is that it's clarified in a lot of people's minds that

I started out as an actor and have always been aligned to that side of the camera, as opposed to having people think I was a critic. (laughs)

Q: What advice would you have for a first-time director?
A: Well, one of the main things is knowing what you want in terms of the scene, so you don't make your actors do it seventeen different ways. At the same time, you want to leave yourself open to the possibility that there might be better ways of doing it. Respect Lady Luck, because she'll be there sometimes. Also, I would read as much as you can about filmmakers. My book *Who the Devil Made It* was written just for that purpose. I recommend it not because I wrote it, but because it offers a wealth of knowledge from some of the greatest filmmakers of all time. And that's where you have to go for knowledge, back to the source.

Peter Bogdanovich

Stephen Lemons / 2002

Published April 19, 2002. This article first appeared in Salon.com, at http://www.Salon.com. An online version remains in the Salon archives. Reprinted with permission.

Q: Do you think your old friend Orson Welles would have liked the film [*The Cat's Meow*]?

A: I hope so. I certainly felt his spirit around when we made it, watching. I don't know about guiding me, but I think he was on our side. He was the one who told me the story in the first place. He told it to me over thirty years ago as an example of how different Hearst was from Charles Foster Kane. The general misunderstanding about *Citizen Kane* is that it was supposed to be about Hearst, but it wasn't.

Charles Foster Kane was a composite character based on three or four press lords including a famous one in Chicago named McCormick, who built the Chicago Opera House for his girlfriend, who was a singer. That whole aspect of Kane had nothing to do with Hearst. And Orson didn't play it like Hearst. Hearst was a kind of pear-shaped fellow who had a high voice and whose hair fell down over his forehead. He looked a lot like Edward Herrmann, but not as handsome.

Q: How did Mr. Welles come to tell you the story?

A: I was interviewing him for the book we did, *This Is Orson Welles*, but we didn't use it in the book because at the time, it seemed a bit incendiary. Interestingly enough, he heard the story from a member of Hearst's inner circle—Marion Davies' nephew Charles Lederer, the screenwriter. I talked to Charlie Lederer a few years later and he confirmed it. Charlie had known it since he was twelve. That's about how old he was when it happened. He confirmed this as fact, that there was this "accident" during the cruise.

Q: How ironic that after Welles told you that story so long ago, you wound up directing this picture.
A: Yes, it was ironic. The script arrived on my desk thirty years later and neither the writer nor the producer had any idea that I knew anything about it. . . . I don't know if I would have read it with as much interest if Orson hadn't told me. I often don't read scripts that are sent to me, I have someone read them for me. This one I read on my own. I saw these characters in it and I thought, "My God, it's that story." So I owe it to Orson. If it hadn't been for him, I might not have done it.

Q: Your Hearst seems rather likable in some ways.
A: Actually, he's pretty ruthless. But he's human. It's the humanity, I think, that makes you understand him. When you understand someone, it's hard to hate them. If you get to know anybody, I suppose, you discover that people are good and bad and all the shades in between. Nobody's all one thing.

Q: Do you think people have changed much since that era, or do you think we're all pretty much still the same?
A: Human nature stays the same, but maybe certain aspects of it get exacerbated. I think we're in a more cynical era than ever before, and I think that the audience for movies, for example, has been somewhat debased and brutalized by the enormous amount of violence and slaughter on the screen. You sort of say, "Well, thirty people just got killed, so what's next?" Having been, I'm afraid, part of a murder, when Dorothy Stratten was murdered, I can tell you that one murder reverberates for the rest of the life of the people who were close to that person. That's one of the things about this picture, it's about a murder that changes everything. One murder. Not three, not ten—one.

Q: So we've been "desensitized," as they say.
A: Yes, a little. On the other hand, you take any individual out of that audience and have them exposed to the murder of someone they care about, they won't be desensitized. We're only desensitized to the spectacle of it.

Q: Did Ms. Stratten's death change the way you look at violence?
A: Yes, it did. I never particularly liked violence in movies, but I didn't

have the same reaction to it that I do now. I think it's all handled by people who don't know what it's really like. It's just people making movies, and saying, "OK, well, this guy gets killed, and then we go over here and this guy gets killed," and I'm thinking, *each death counts*.

Q: Is there any solution to that problem, or is it something we just have to accept?
A: I think it's everybody's personal responsibility. Filmmakers have a responsibility to the audience and to the work, and I wish they felt that responsibility more, especially to what's true in life. The tragic events of September [9/11] brought knowledge of premeditated murder to an awful lot of people who didn't know about it.

I watched those people on TV afterwards, and it broke my heart. I knew where they were coming from. And I knew they were in for a life of it. They talk about closure and getting past it—Christ, it doesn't ever happen that way. These poor people on television a week later talking about it, thinking that they're dealing with it. You know, it's a truism for people who've been through this that the fifth year is the worst. It happened to me. For some reason after five years, it's like it's just happened again. It's also something you don't recover from, you learn to live with. You don't get past it, you learn to move on with it as part of your life.

You have to think of it in this context; the murder in *The Cat's Meow* affects everyone there for all their lives. I don't know that Marion would have stayed with Hearst had it not been for the murder. I think she felt guilty that she was kind of the cause of it.

Q: Then it's established that Chaplin and Davies actually were fooling around?
A: Well, nobody was under the bed. But that gossip item that's referred to in the film linking Chaplin and Davies actually appeared in the *Daily News* that weekend. I have a copy of it. Chaplin was a notorious philanderer. And Marion evidently had some affairs with other people. We presume it happened.

Q: Of all the characters in the film, who do you identify with?
A: That's an interesting question. Really, I can identify with all the men. I've been down and out like Ince. I've been obsessed with a woman like Hearst. I've been lookin' to get laid like Chaplin. So, I understand where they're coming from. And I understand, as I said, what a murder does.

My sympathy, if you want to ask that, is with Marion, which you can see in the picture to a degree.

It's her tragedy, I think. It's a woman's story—she's trapped between powerful men. In 1924, women had only been able to vote for the second time. I made a reference to that in the film, because it's fairly shocking to remember that. It was November of 1924 and the election had just happened. Nineteen-twenty was the first year women were allowed to vote. It's about a woman who seems to have everything, but doesn't quite. "I have me," she says. But she's not really right.

Q: If you could go back in time, which decade would you want to go back to?
A: If I had a time machine? I'd pick the thirties. I'd want to be a filmmaker under contract at Paramount as Lubitsch was head of the studio.

Q: So you might've been one of Mr. Welles's colleagues?
A: I would've met him, yeah. I looked it up one time and I told Orson, "You know the day you started shooting *Citizen Kane* I was one year old?" And he said, "Aw, shut up!"

Q: You think about him often, don't you?
A: He was a very dear friend for most of our association, and yes, his spirit ranges over everything. He was quite extraordinary.

Q: You speak of Mr. Welles's spirit. I'm curious, what do you think happens to us after we die?
A: Kind of a personal question. I don't think the spirit dies. I think the spirit is imperishable, that it remains, and is around or not, depending on different things. I don't know about murderers, though. I don't know where they go. I keep feeling that the murderers who blew up the World Trade Center are doomed to haunt that area for the rest of their lives.

Peter Bogdanovich

Peter Tonguette / 2005

From *Orson Welles Remembered: Interviews with His Actors, Editors, Cinematographers and Magicians* © 2007 Peter Prescott Tonguette by permission of McFarland & Company, Inc., Box 611, Jefferson, NC 28640. www.mcfarlandpub.com

Peter Bogdanovich: I don't think there's anything original about it, but when I first saw *Citizen Kane*—like everybody else, particularly people who would ultimately make films—I was blown away by it. It's sort of a cliché, but it's true. It was amazing to me. It was the first time that I was aware that somebody directed a movie. I don't know why—probably because Orson [Welles] was in it. That was probably the obvious reason. "Oh, he's in this and he also directed it." So you could sort of picture him behind the camera. Whereas people like Ford, whom I knew about by that point, you had sort of a vague idea of what they were like and what they looked like. You didn't really picture it. But with Orson, there he was and you thought, "Well, this is the guy who is behind the camera too."

My parents never talked much about *Kane*, but had remembered *Ambersons* as a film they had particularly liked when they came to America. They saw it in the first three years of their being in America. It seemed to them a great piece of Americana. The first time I saw it was on a very dim, lousy TV in the middle of the night, somewhere in New York. Even then, it was extraordinary. You could hardly see it because the dark stuff was unviewable. The television would tend to make dark scenes invisible. Nevertheless, it impressed the hell out of me even then, even under those circumstances. Everything I saw that Orson directed had an equal impact on me. I sort of sucked it in and it became part of my life.

I had written a program note about *Othello* for the New Yorker Theatre in which I'd said that it was the best Shakespeare film ever made. Now this was a very controversial opinion in 1960, hardly the general consensus. In fact, it was just the opposite. So it attracted the attention of Richard Griffith, the curator of the Museum of Modern Art, who called me out of the blue and said he wanted to know if I'd like to curate or put together the first Orson Welles retrospective in the United States at the Museum of Modern Art, and write the accompanying monograph. I was flabbergasted and said that I would, but why wasn't he doing it himself since he often wrote the monographs for the retrospectives? He said that he wasn't a particularly big fan of Welles, but many of the members of the museum were and his colleagues in Europe were. He thought that a retrospective was justified, but he didn't have the passion to write it. Since he read my program note on *Othello*, he thought that I did.

So I organized it and put it together. I think I got paid fifty or a hundred dollars for the whole job, which took a while. We pulled everything we could that existed. We found *Mr. Arkadin*. Orson at that moment was shooting *The Trial* in Europe, so I had no contact with him at all. The monograph was published.[1] The series went on in the spring and summer. It was quite extensive and it was very popular. I was out of the city for most of it, directing summer theatre. Two copies of the monograph were sent to Orson at some address in Europe. I never heard a word about it until seven years later.

It was sometime in August or September—if not later—of '68. I get a phone call. I'm living in Los Angeles by now. I have a daughter and am married and so on—first wife. And the phone rings and a familiar voice asks for me. I said, "Speaking," thinking, "Could it be?" He said, "This is Orson Welles." I said, "Oh, hello." He said, "I can't tell how long I've wanted to meet you." I said, "That's my line. Why?" He said, "Because you have written the truest words ever published about me . . . in English." I was bowled over by that statement. He was rather brief. He always hated talking on the phone. He said, "I'm staying at the Beverly Hills Hotel. Can you meet me tomorrow at the Polo Lounge around three o'clock?" I said, "I'll be there."

I drove over the hill to Beverly Hills in a Chevy station wagon that I put in the wrong gear because I was so apprehensive and nervous. The car overheated and I arrived with steam coming out of the hood. He was waiting for me in a large black caftan or something—he was wearing something loose. But he was very warm and we spent a couple or three hours together. He was so disarming, as Orson could be—enormously disarming—that I felt that I could say anything to him. I even had the nerve to tell him that there was one film of his that I didn't particularly like, which was *The Trial*. He said, "I don't *either*!" Which turned out to be a lie, but nevertheless it made me feel like, "Wow, I can say anything to this man."

Peter Tonguette: I suppose that Welles knew you were an actor before becoming a director.[2] Is that why he thought to cast you in *The Other Side of the Wind*?

PB: He knew that, but by the time he started shooting *The Other Side of the Wind*, which was in the fall of '70, we'd spent quite a lot of time together in Rome when I was there preparing a [Sergio] Leone picture that I didn't make, and Orson was cutting. So we spent quite a bit of time in Rome. We spent time in Guaymas, Mexico. I was doing the book with him. He'd agreed that we would do an interview book together.

Actually in Guaymas, when we were there, we had a long talk about directors, certain directors being considered over the hill and not bankable anymore. He was very upset about that. I remember we had a very late night conversation about that and the next day he said he hadn't slept for thinking about that. He said that there was a movie that he'd been thinking about making for years. It was about an older movie director and a young filmmaker *[the roles of Jake Hannaford and Brooks Otterlake, eventually played by John Huston and Bogdanovich, respectively]*. It was originally going to be a young bullfighter and an older bullfighter, but he'd decided to make it about two directors. He said that he must make that film now. Well, this was in early '69. I said, "Do you have a script?" He said, "I've written four scripts"—or something—"I know this by heart. I know how to do this." He was talking about it a lot.

But I didn't know he was starting to shoot what turned out to be *The Other Side of the Wind* until he called me. I think it was in October of '70. He was in L.A. We'd been talking and he didn't like the script of *[The Last] Picture Show*. He didn't like the whole subject matter. He thought it was grim and thought it was a dirty movie. He referred to it as "that dirty movie." But he called me up and said, "What are you doing next Thursday?"—or whatever day it was. I said, "Well, I'm leaving for Texas that day." "Oh, really, what time?" I said, "Well, I don't know, two o'clock in the afternoon or something." "Good. Can you meet me at eleven at the airport? You know where the planes fly low over the street?" I said, "Yeah." "Well, there's a fence there and we're going to be shooting there." I said, "Shooting? What are you shooting?" He said, "I'm shooting a dirty picture." I said, "What?" He said, "Well, you're shooting a dirty movie, so I'm going to be shooting a dirty movie." "Oh, okay. What do you want me to do?" "I want you to be in it." "Oh, okay." "I want you to do your Jerry Lewis impression and you're going to play a cinephile named Charles Higgam"—which was an inside joke—"and I want you to do it like Jerry Lewis." Orson loved it when I did impressions. "Let me hear Jimmy Stewart, let me hear Jerry Lewis, let me hear Howard Hawks." He was very keen on the impressions. He'd laugh and the room would shake.

So that's how I started in the movie. It was me showing up and asking questions like *[in a Jerry Lewis-esque voice]*, "Mr. Hannaford, do you believe that the cinema is a phallus?" Stupid things like that. Well, Orson thought that was hilarious. *[Laughs.]* We shot for a couple of hours and then I got on the plane and flew to Texas to make *Picture Show*. I was there until December and he kept shooting. Then when I came back in '71, we did shoot some more of me playing that character—not that much, but enough.

Although it wasn't the role he was first cast in, Bogdanovich always felt that the character of Brooks Otterlake was, as he told me, "sort of based on me because it was a young director who'd had a couple of hits, very successful pictures, and who also did impressions and was friendly to Huston's character. They cast Rich [Little] because Rich did his impressions and he had a similar complexion to me, so I assumed he was sort of doing me in a way. And Polly Platt, my first wife who I was divorced from by now and she was the mother of my kids, had been involved in the picture briefly and had visited him in Carefree or in Beverly Hills. She said, 'Well, he's doing you, you know.'"

Bogdanovich and Welles were talking on the phone after Little left the picture when Bogdanovich made a suggestion:

PB: I said, "Well, why don't I play it?" There was a long pause. He said, "Well, that never occurred to me." *[Laughs.]* I said, "Orson, the guy does impressions, he's had three hits, he's friendly with the director. I mean, how could it not have occurred to you?" He said, "No, no, it didn't occur to me because you're in the picture. You're playing that other role." I said, "Well, that's not a big part. Get somebody else to fill in those lines." He said, "My God, you're right. Of course you could do it. Of course we could get somebody else."[3] I could hear him cottoning to the idea in a big way. He said, "Would you come down?" I said, "Sure." "Oh my God, you've just saved my life." He was very, very happy about the idea. Whether he'd had the idea anyway and was waiting for me to have it, I don't know.

Welles asked Bogdanovich to bring two suitcases of his clothes to the shoot in Carefree, Arizona.

PB: When I got there, I had these two suitcases full of stuff and I said, "Do you want to see the clothes?" He said, "No, sit down, let's talk." And we talked for an hour, just talking about things, laughing and having a good time. I said, "Don't you want to shoot?" He said, "Yes, but I want you to be comfortable." I said, "Well, I'm comfortable." He said, "Well, let's just talk." So we talked for another forty minutes or so. Finally I said, "Well, Orson, aren't you shooting?" He said, "I want you to be *very* comfortable and relaxed." I said, "Well, I am. Do you want to see the clothes?" He said, "Yes, let's look at the clothes."

So he looks through them and in about five minutes picks out pants, shirt, sweater. I said, "Geez, Orson, it's weird—these are my clothes, but I've never worn them in this combination." He said, "Well, there you see. Now you know how a successful young film director dresses!" Those were the clothes I wore: cotton turtleneck, a wool sweater, and a pair of slacks.

I think we shot with John Huston for about ten days. It's hard for me to remember the exact sequence of events. I should have kept a journal, but I didn't. I was there for a while, for a couple of weeks, and he was shooting John for some of it. Then John left and I shot some of it with Orson. I think that was the only time I was in Carefree. He shot at my house later quite a bit and I worked in that stuff too. But the most intense stuff was a period of about ten days.

When Bogdanovich discussed how he'd sometimes "play scenes to Orson off camera," I was reminded of what Keith Baxter told me about the shooting of the coronation scene in Chimes at Midnight. *Baxter said that Welles was in costume when Baxter delivered his lines: ". . . I was always looking at him dressed as Falstaff."*

PB: In a way, it made it easier. There was the last scene that we did that was supposed to be taking place in a drive-in. I don't remember where he shot it. I think it was at my place, outside. I was playing it to him. It was very much the end of the relationship between Hannaford and Otterlake. He wanted me to think about him and to play it like we were talking about our relationship. At one point, he's being very cold to me and dismissive and I say something like, "Our revels now are ended?" That was a tricky line and he had me say it many times. [Hannaford's] line was, "You bet your sweet cheeks," and he drives off. It was the end of the relationship, so he said, "Play it to me."

He did everything in little pieces, little short takes, a lot of it, and I kept saying, "Can't we do a long take, like from *Ambersons*? A long scene, play the whole scene out?" He said, "Well, I haven't got actors. It's very difficult to do it because I haven't got all the actors at one time." I said, "I know, but it'd be fun if you could." One day, he said, "All right, you're going to get what you want. We're going to do this in one, with you and John." I said, "Really?" He shot this two or three page scene in one shot, putting the camera in the middle and I think we walked around. The camera stayed in one place, but the staging was elaborate. It involved Huston exiting at one point and me kind of trying out sitting in his throne-like chair—it was clear what was going on, that I was thinking about being him.

It was all sorts of stuff that I didn't think existed in my relationship with Orson at all, but I guess it did as far as Orson was concerned. I didn't feel that kind of thing with Orson. It would be absurd to be competitive with him. But I think he basically fictionalized our relationship and a lot of other relationships that he'd known, and used stuff of me and so on to make it closer to some sort of reality.

I never read the script at the time. I just learned the scene.

PT: Even when you were cast as Otterlake?
PB: I didn't really read it all the way through because it wasn't necessary. Maybe I skimmed it. But it was a long script. He told me what I needed to know. A lot of the lines he'd make up just before you shot it.

We would get together often socially. He lived in my house for three years off-and-on, so of course we saw each other socially. We had dinner or breakfast or lunch or we'd just hang out. When we were both in New York, we'd go to dinner. We did a lot of socialization in Paris when we were alone together there.

PT: How did it develop that he moved into your house?
PB: I asked him if he wanted a place to stay and he said, "Yes."

PT: What was that experience like?
PB: It was kind of marvelous. I miss him. It went on for a couple of years off-and-on. He'd come in, he'd leave, he'd come back. Oja *[Kodar, Welles's companion]* was there at times, with him. He sort of took over the house. *[Laughs.]* He had a room and a bathroom that were his, but he liked the room that was outside his room which had a big long table that he liked to sit at. He also liked to sit at the dining room table, which was all the way across the house. He didn't use my office, but he did like that

dining room table quite a bit. It was big. It could seat twelve, so he used to spread out his papers and work there.

I asked Bogdanovich about his memories of Kodar.

PB: I never saw Orson with anybody the way he was with Oja. He was very unbuttoned with her and very much smitten by her. It was easy for her to get her way with him. He would give in easily with her. She sort of knew how to handle him. Being Slavic, we both spoke Serbo-Croatian. She spoke it and I spoke it and she would speak it in front of him. Serbo-Croatian, and generally people from that part of the world, are sexually kind of candid, which Orson wasn't. It was funny because she would tease him. He would really get embarrassed. He'd be amused, but slightly scandalized by her. She could get away with things that nobody else could. He'd shake his head and say, "These Balkan people!"

PT: Did you ever meet his third wife, Paola Mori?
PB: I met Paola once at the AFI tribute. He was very formal with her—very nice, but he was formal. She was quite formal. She was very warm to me and very nice, as was Beatrice, but there was a certain formality.

Bogdanovich wanted Welles to direct a film for the Directors Company, which he founded with Francis Ford Coppola and William Friedkin.[4]

PB: There was one based on a Joseph Conrad novel, *Victory*, and I think he wanted to call it *Surinam*. He wrote a script on it and we were going to do it, but then we found out that somebody else owned the rights to the book. He thought it was public domain and it wasn't. That fell apart. He did get some money from Paramount on that, through the Directors Company, but it never happened.

There were a number of things we talked about, but I don't know if we actually tried to get money on anything besides *Surinam*. We got money on that. That was really the last money he ever got from a studio, but then the Directors Company fell apart. We had plans to have Orson do pictures.

I remember a project I really wanted very much to do with him was one about Alexandre Dumas. It's a wonderful idea. It was based on the relationship between the father and the son, the father aging and being the writer of *The Three Musketeers* and all those great novels, and the son writing *Camille* and having a big hit with that. And the irony of the fact that the son asked the father to stop having an affair with a young actress/dancer because it was ruining the son's reputation. He loved the irony of that. He was going to play Dumas, the father, and I was going to play the son.

Welles recommended that Bogdanovich read the work of writer Robert Graves.

PB: He said, "You should read Robert Graves." "What should I read?" "*The White Goddess* and *The Greek Myths*." I remember getting them and giving them to Cybill [Shepherd] and telling her to read them and fill me in. *[Laughs.]* She did zip right through them. Looking back on it, I don't know how she did it.

In *The Other Side of the Wind*, I've seen some scenes where some of the things that Huston's character talks about—somebody says, "You know what the old man says . . ."—are definitely taken from Graves. Definitively. They're Robert Graves kinds of things about the mother goddess and things like that.

PT: In your new introduction to *This Is Orson Welles*, you write that you feel Graves had an influence on Welles's work.[5]
PB: I think it was very strong, starting in '48 with *Macbeth*. That's when *The White Goddess* came out.

Welles and Bogdanovich's relationship "faded," Bogdanovich told me, towards the end of the 1970s.

PB: It was compounded by two things. One is that he was going to be in *Nickelodeon* (1976) and play the Brian Keith part. We couldn't work out the deal with the studio. They didn't want to pay him what he wanted. Then Ryan [O'Neal] and Burt [Reynolds] both put up some money for Orson. He found out about it and wouldn't take it.

I think he was a little bit afraid of doing it on a certain level because it would have meant my directing him. I think he was having trouble with remembering lines and I didn't think he wanted to go through it. So I think he created an atmosphere where he'd have to get out of it, but it sort of screwed things up for me. Then he gave me some bad advice on *Nickelodeon*, which was good advice but bad advice, if you know what I mean. It was good artistically, bad from a business point of view. He suggested that I don't do it unless I do it in black-and-white, which he was right about, but it sort of fucked up things.[6]

We had gotten the rights to *Saint Jack* (1979) for him, but it was Cybill who really owned them because she got them in a lawsuit against *Playboy*. Part of a settlement was that she would get those rights—it was the reason she settled, to do it for Orson. He said he wanted Jack Nicholson, we got Jack for him, and then he decided he didn't want Jack Nicholson, which was very embarrassing. Then he wanted Dean Martin, and Cybill and [Hugh] Hefner, who also had a piece of the action, didn't want to do it with Dean Martin and started not wanting to do it with Orson because he wouldn't let himself be pinned down as to when he would do it or how he was going to do it. We had this terrible thing when we had to tell Jack that now he didn't want him to do it.

Eventually, Bogdanovich directed Saint Jack.

PB: I had to make the picture and that didn't exactly sit too well with Orson. He was pretty pissed off. So the relationship faded, but we still saw each other a few more times and we still talked on the phone. It was not the same.

It was strained. He invited me to a few things that I went to, but we never quite regained it. Although the last couple of phone conversations, as I wrote *[in* This Is Orson Welles*]*, were almost back to normal.

Notes

1. *The Cinema of Orson Welles* was published by the Museum of Modern Art in 1961. It was Bogdanovich's first book.

2. Bogdanovich began his show business career as an actor on the stage.

3. The role of Charles Higgam was recast with an actor named Howard Grossman.

4. Andrew J. Yule, *Picture Shows:The Life and Films of Peter Bogdanovich* (New York: Limelight Editions, 1992), 64; Welles and Bogdanovich, *This Is Orson Welles*, revised edition (New York: Da Capo Press, 1998), 441.

5. Welles and Bogdanovich, xxxii

6. Bogdanovich ended up having to make the movie in color.

Additional Resources

Books

Harris, Thomas J. *Bogdanovich's Picture Shows*. Metuchen, NJ: Scarecrow Press, 1990.
McCluskey, Paul, ed. *Conversations with Peter Bogdanovich*. New York: Harcourt Brace Jovanovich, 1974.
Yule, Andrew. *Picture Shows: The Life and Films of Peter Bogdanovich*. New York: Limelight Editions, 1992.

Articles and Interviews

Dawson, Jan. "The Continental Divide." *Sight and Sound*, Winter 1973/4.
Diehl, Digby. "Q&A: Peter Bogdanovich." *Los Angeles Times*, April 2, 1972.
Easton, Nina J. "The Next Picture Show: Peter Bogdanovich and the Cast of His 1971 Classic Reunite in Texas for a Sequel's Sake." *Los Angeles Times*, October 15, 1989.
Ebert, Roger. "A New Take on Hearst Saga." *Chicago Sun-Times*, April 24, 2002.
Friend, Tad. "The Moviegoer." *New Yorker*, April 8, 2002.
Gordinier, Jeff. "The Past Picture Shows." *Entertainment Weekly*, May 3, 2002.
James, Clive. "Hit Men." *New Yorker*, July 7, 1997.
Longino, Bob. "Peter Bogdanovich Back with *The Cat's Meow*." Cox News Service, April 26, 2002.
Mann, Roderick. "Bogdanovich: A Book for Stratten." *Los Angeles Times*, April 20, 1982.
McGilligan, Patrick. "Peter Bogdanovich and Cybill Survive." *Boston Globe*, April 25, 1974.
McGilligan, Patrick. "At Long Last, Bogdanovich." *Boston Globe*, March 30, 1975.
Quinn, Sally. "The Heartbreak Kids: The Lives, Loves and Hard Times of Peter Bogdanovich and Cybill Shepherd." *Washington Post*, December 20, 1976.

Saroyan, Strawberry. "A Way with Women." *Los Angeles Times*, February 29, 2004.

Stone, Judy. "All Because of Boris Karloff." *New York Times*, September 15, 1968.

Taylor, Clarke. "Bogdanovich Presents NYC." *Los Angeles Times*, August 3, 1980.

Thomson, David. "Older, Sadder, Maybe Wiser." *New York Times*, April 7, 2002.

Tonguette, Peter. "Let Us Sing of the Days That Are Gone . . . Peter Bogdanovich: A Cinema of Silent Exchanges." *Senses of Cinema*, July 2004.

Warga, Wayne. "Bogdanovich: Love, Comedy and Tragedy." *Los Angeles Times*, December 13, 1981.

White, Armond. "Directed by Peter Bogdanovich." *Film Comment*, March–April 1993.

Yabroff, Jennie. "*Soprano* Shrink Bogdanovich Nostalgic for Studio System." *San Francisco Chronicle*, October 31, 2004.

Index

Ackland, Joss, 65
Adler, Stella, 4, 24, 42, 53, 142, 148
Agee, James, 136
Agee on Film (Agee), 136
Aldrich, Robert, 12
All in the Family, 149
Allan Dwan: The Last Pioneer (Bogdanovich), 108
Allen, Woody, 114, 125
American Graffiti (Lucas), 98
Anatomy of a Murder (Preminger), 122, 138
Andrews, Dana, 29
Antonioni, Michelangelo, 19
Apple Tree, The (Galsworthy), 24, 27-28
Archer, Eugene, 4-5, 130, 135, 136
At Long Last Love (Bogdanovich), x, xii, 41, 69, 78, 80, 84, 86, 89-90, 92, 103-4, 105, 114-15, 126, 143, 154
Awful Truth, The (McCarey), 110, 111, 130, 138

Bach, J. S., 23
Battleship Potemkin (Eisenstein), 136
Baxter, Keith, 168
Bay of Angels (Demy), 6
Beatty, Warren, 66-67
Beggars of Life (Wellman), 128
Benton, Robert, 26, 60

Bergman, Ingmar, 4, 19
Bertolucci, Bernardo, 19
Bewes, Rodney, 65
Big Knife, The (Odets), viii, 4, 24, 42, 53
Big Red One, The (Fuller), 42, 80-81, 119
Big Sleep, The (Hawks), 150
Birth of a Nation, The (Griffith), ix, 23
Biskind, Peter, 154
Black Cat, The (Ulmer), 121
Blonde Venus (von Sternberg), 111
Blue Moon (Gallagher), 123
Boetticher, Budd, viii, 3
Bogart, Humphrey, 4, 32, 137, 147
Bogdanovich, Peter: childhood, 37-38, 42, 45, 109, 129, 135-36, 142, 147-48, 158, 164; cinematography, 12-13, 19-21, 36, 45-46, 47, 51, 75, 86-87, 93, 95-96, 102, 104, 125, 168-69; film editing, 7, 30-31, 47, 71-72, 87-88, 96, 124-25; location shooting, 44, 48, 57-58, 63-65, 76, 86-88, 154-55; music in films, 22, 55, 69-70, 96; working with actors, 47-48, 59-60, 89, 94-95, 112
Bogdanovich's Picture Shows (Harris), viii, 99
Bombshell (Fleming), 112

Bonnie and Clyde (Penn), 26
Born Yesterday (Cukor), 139
Borzage, Frank, 38, 138
Bottoms, Timothy, xii, 19, 48, 49, 58-59, 78-79, 84, 143, 151
Brando, Marlon, 148
Brennan, Eileen, 35, 50, 55-56
Brennan, Walter, 3, 150
Bridge on the River Kwai, The (Lean), 6, 24, 54, 150
Bridges, Jeff, 49, 79, 84, 143, 154
Bringing Up Baby (Hawks), 17, 26, 76, 111, 150, 153
Brooks, Louise, 128
Brown, Barry, 32, 116
Brown, Harry Joe, 118
Brown, Johnny Mack, 12
Burstyn, Ellen, 50, 84, 143

Cagney, James, 89, 95
Cahiers du Cinema, 4, 42, 108, 135
Calley, John, 25, 56, 57
Camille (Dumas), 170
Camino Real (Williams), 24
Canby, Vincent, 102
Cannibals and Christians (Mailer), 13
Capra, Frank, 111, 118, 135
Carey, Harry, Jr., 99, 126
Carradine, Robert, 119
Carson, Johnny, 61
Carter, Jimmy, 61
Cassavetes, John, 19, 50, 66, 89, 114, 122, 156
Cat on a Hot Tin Roof (Williams), 123
Cat's Meow, The (Bogdanovich), 144-46, 160-61, 162
Chabrol, Claude, 18
Chakiris, George, 54

Chaplin, Charlie, 16, 38, 61, 136, 144, 146-47, 162
Chase, David, 158
Cher, 95, 100, 101, 156
Cheyenne Autumn (Ford), 78
Chimes at Midnight (Welles), 168
Christie, Agatha, 4
Cimarron (Ruggles), 45
Cimino, Michael, 114
Cinema of Orson Welles, The (Bogdanovich), 134
Citizen Kane (Welles), ix, xi, 22, 132-33, 136, 138, 152, 160, 163, 164
Clair, Rene, 136, 148
Clift, Montgomery, 32
Cohn, Harry, 86
Collegiate School, 42, 129
Colman, Ronald, 118
Colorado Territory (Walsh), 127-28
Conversation, The (Coppola), 114, 118, 153
Conway, Jack, 112
Cooper, Gary, 139
Coppola, Francis Ford, 98, 114, 117, 118, 143, 153, 170
Corman, Gene, 81, 119
Corman, Roger, ix, 6, 7-8, 9, 10, 21, 23, 24-25, 42, 53-55, 63, 93, 127, 137, 142, 150-51
Criminal Code, The (Hawks), 17, 121
Crist, Judith, 115
Crowd, The (Vidor), 118
Crowther, Bosley, 132-33, 135
Cukor, George, vii, ix, 43, 108, 111, 113, 138, 139
Curtiz, Michael, 139

Daisy Miller (Bogdanovich), ix, x, xii, 27, 28-37, 38-40, 41,

44–46, 80, 84, 92, 102, 104, 105, 115–16, 117–18, 132, 139, 140, 143, 153
Daisy Miller (James), 27–30, 33, 34–35, 36–37, 38, 39, 44–45, 46–47
Davies, Marion, 144, 146, 160, 162–63
Dean, Jimmy, 50, 73
Death on the Sixth Day (Farrell), 16
De Laurentiis, Dino, 126, 157
Deli, The (Gallagher), 123
Denby, David, 141
Dennis, Rocky, 156–57
De Palma, Brian, 98
Destry Rides Again (Marshall), 112
De Toth, André, 3
Die Bergkatze (Lubitsch), 62
Die Puppe (Lubitsch), 62
Dietrich, Marlene, 147
Dinesen, Isak, 42
Dinner at Eight (Cukor), 112
Directed by John Ford (Bogdanovich), vii, 23, 27, 70–71, 122, 140
Director's Event, The (Sherman and Rubin), viii, 3
Donat, Robert, 148
Dos Passos, John, 56
Drums Along the Mohawk (Ford), 85
Duck, You Sucker! (Leone), 123
Dumas, Alexandre, 170–71
Dumbo (Disney), 141, 147
Dunne, Irene, 109–10
Dunst, Kirsten, 144, 146
Dwan, Allan, ix, 12, 16, 85, 108, 109, 121, 126, 128, 129, 147

Easy Rider (Hopper), 25, 75
Easy Riders, Raging Bulls (Biskind), 154

Edel, Leon, 29
Eisenstein, Sergei, 135
El Dorado (Hawks), 78
Elliott, Denholm, 65, 68–69
Elliott, Sam, 156
Elwes, Cary, 144
End as a Man (Willingham), 122, 134
Esquire, 3, 4, 6, 24, 42, 53–54, 109, 117, 137, 143
Estes, Larry, x, xi, xii
Everson, William K., 107
Everyone Says I Love You (Allen), 114
Exodus (Preminger), 138

Fairbanks, Douglas, 147
Father of the Bride (Minnelli), 18, 21
Fellini, Federico, 4, 19
Festival in Cannes (Jaglom), 158
Film Culture, 114, 135
Films in Review, 107
Five Easy Pieces (Rafelson), 114
Fonda, Henry, 23, 60
Fonda, Peter, 6, 7, 54, 151
For a Few Dollars More (Leone), 123
Ford, Barbara, 122
Ford, John, vii, ix, xiii, 3, 4, 12, 13, 15, 18, 20, 22–23, 47, 50, 58, 59, 60, 69, 78, 84, 85, 86, 87, 92, 96, 98–99, 111, 118, 120–21, 122, 124, 125–26, 132, 135–36, 138, 139, 140, 142, 145, 149–50, 152, 164
Fort Apache (Ford), 5
For the Love of Movies: The Story of American Film Criticism (Peary), 132
Freleng, Friz, 138

Friedkin, William, 117, 118, 143, 153, 170
Fritz Lang in America (Bogdanovich), 109
Fuller, Samuel, viii, 10, 14, 80–81, 119, 151

Gallagher, John, ix
Galsworthy, John, 27
Garbo, Greta, 83, 139, 152
Garnett, Tay, 118, 121–22
Gazzara, Ben, xi, 50–51, 63, 65, 66, 67, 68–69, 84, 122–23, 127, 134, 143, 154, 155
Gentleman Jim (Walsh), 127
Getaway, The (Peckinpah), 56–57
Ghost Goes West, The (Clair), 136, 148
Gish, Lillian, 147
Godard, Jean-Luc, 18–19, 137
Godfather, The (Coppola), x, 98
Gogol, Nikolai, 42
Golden Fleece, The (Graves), 105
Good, the Bad and the Ugly, The (Leone), 123
Gow, Gordon, ix, x, xi
Grant, Cary, 3, 9, 11, 17, 23, 66–67, 110, 111, 147
Grapes of Wrath, The (Ford), 136
Graves, Robert, 105, 171
Great Railway Bazaar, The (Theroux), 64
Greed (von Stroheim), 158
Greek Myths, The (Graves), 171
Greene, Graham, 138
Green Mansions (Hudson), 27
Griffith, D. W., ix, xi, 12, 16, 23, 85, 144, 145
Griffith, Richard, 133, 164–65
Guber, Peter, 120
Gulager, Clu, 50, 73

Hackman, Gene, 63
Half-Naked Truth, The (La Cava), 129
Hamill, Mark, 81
Hamill, Pete, 37
Hamlet (Olivier), 133
Harlow, Jean, 112
Harris, Thomas J., viii, xi
Hatful of Rain, A (Gazzo), 123
Hathaway, Henry, 128
Hawks, Howard, vii, ix, 3, 4, 5, 12, 13, 15, 16, 17, 18, 22, 26, 47, 76, 78, 84, 92, 96, 99, 108, 111, 112, 113, 121, 124, 125, 139, 142, 149, 150, 152, 153, 167
Hearst, William Randolph, 133, 144, 145, 160, 161, 162
Heaven Can Wait (Beatty), 66–67
Hefner, Hugh, 172
Hell's Angels (Hughes), 112
Henry, Buck, 26, 60, 76
Henry V (Olivier), 133
Hepburn, Audrey, xi, 90, 155
Hepburn, Katharine, 17
Herrmann, Edward, 144, 145, 160
High Sierra (Walsh), 7, 15, 127–28
Hillerman, John, 79–80
Hitchcock, Alfred, vii, ix, xi, 3, 4, 13, 15, 22, 23, 38, 39, 84, 92, 93, 98, 99, 108, 111, 112, 136, 139, 140
Hitchcock, Jane, 154
Hollywood Babylon (Anger), 144
Holt, Tim, 35
Horse Eats Hat (Welles and Denby), 56
How Green Was My Valley (Ford), 136
Huston, John, 82, 153, 166, 168, 169, 171

Illegally Yours (Bogdanovich), 126, 157
Ince, Thomas, 144, 145
In Cold Blood (Brooks), 11
Iron Horse, The (Ford), 85
It's a Wonderful Life (Capra), 119
Ivy, 53, 134
Izzard, Eddie, 144, 146

James, Henry, 27, 29–30, 33, 37, 39, 45, 46, 115
Jaws (Spielberg), 83
John Ford (Bogdanovich), vii
Johnny Got His Gun (Trumbo), 49
Johnson, Ben, 50, 66, 79, 84, 125–26, 143
Jones, Chuck, 76, 138
Jones, Jennifer, 138

Kanin, Garson, 110
Karloff, Boris, 8, 9–10, 11, 13, 14, 15, 17, 21, 49, 73, 121, 142, 151
Kazan, Elia, 38
Keaton, Buster, 18, 38, 61, 76, 136, 148
Keith, Brian, 171
Kennedy, Robert F., 10
Kid, The (Chaplin), 146
Killing of a Chinese Bookie, The (Cassavetes), 156
Killing of the Unicorn: Dorothy Stratten 1960–1980, The (Bogdanovich), 143, 156
Kingston, Mark, 65
Kodar, Oja, 113, 169–70
Korda, Alexander, 148
Kovacs, Laszlo, 75, 102
Kurosawa, Akira, 4

La Cava, Gregory, 128–29

Lady from Shanghai, The (Welles), 9, 136
Lambert, Gavin, 28
L'Amour, Louis, 124
Land of the Pharaohs (Hawks), 5
Lane, Anthony, 141
Lang, Fritz, 38, 83, 92, 98, 109
La Ronde (Ophuls), 103
Lasky, Jesse, 28
Last Picture Show, The (Bogdanovich), viii, ix, x, xi, xii, 17, 18, 19–20, 21, 22–23, 25, 27, 28, 41, 43, 44, 48–50, 51, 55–56, 58–59, 70, 71–74, 75, 84, 92, 94, 99, 106, 114, 119–21, 124, 125–26, 132, 139, 142–43, 146, 148, 149, 151–52, 154, 157, 166
Last Picture Show, The (McMurtry), 16, 49, 151
Laura (Preminger), 29
Laurel and Hardy, 110, 136, 148
Lawrence of Arabia (Lean), 6, 24, 54, 150
Leachman, Cloris, 19, 48, 50, 70, 79, 84, 94, 143
Lederer, Charles, 160
Leigh, Janet, 11
Lemons, Stephen, xiii
Lenny (Fosse), 75
Leone, Sergio, 123–24, 166
Lewis, Jerry, 3, 4, 136, 166–67
Lewis, Joseph H., 3
Light Your Torches and Pull Up Your Tights (Garnett), 122
Little, Rich, 167
Lloyd, Harold, 136
Lolita (Nabokov), 28
Lombard, Carole, 25–26
Looters, The (Reese), 16
Lost and Found on a South Sea Island (Walsh), 116

Lowe, Rob, 93–94, 157
Lubitsch, Ernst, 38, 42, 61–62, 83, 139, 145, 163
Lucas, George, 98
Lumet, Sidney, 129, 147
Lurie, Rod, 137

Macbeth (Welles), 171
Macdonald, Dwight, 136, 139
MacDonald, Jeanette, 83
Madame Dubarry (Lubitsch), 62
Magnificent Ambersons, The (Welles), 35, 136, 152
Mailer, Norman, 13
Mann, Anthony, 111, 112
Man's Favorite Sport? (Hawks), 78
Man Who Knew Too Much, The (Hitchcock), 13
Man Who Loved Women, The (Truffaut), 61
Man Who Shot Liberty Valance, The (Ford), 22, 140, 149–50
Marshall, Frank, 113
Martin, Dean, 172
Mask (Bogdanovich), x, 93–94, 95, 98, 99–100, 105, 120, 122, 126, 143, 156–57, 158
Mason, James, 66–67
Mastroianni, Marcello, 28
McCarey, Leo, 109–10, 111, 119, 120, 126, 138
McCarthy, Todd, 114
McCrea, Joel, 128
McGilligan, Patrick, xii
McMurtry, Larry, 16, 20, 49, 151
McQueen, Steve, 41, 56–57
Mean Streets (Scorsese), 98
Mekas, Jonas, 130
Mengers, Sue, 42, 56, 57
Merrick, John, 156

Merry Widow, The (Lubitsch), 83
Mills, John, 28
Mineo, Sal, 151
Minnelli, Vincente, 21
Mister Roberts (Ford and LeRoy), 60
Mogambo (Ford), 20
Monroe, Marilyn, 147
Morfogen, George, 67
Mori, Paola, 170
Mr. Arkadin (Welles), 165
Mr. Smith Goes to Washington (Capra), 112
Murray, James, 118
My Darling Clementine (Ford), 150
Myers, Stephen, x–xi, xii
My Fair Lady (Cukor), 43
My Man Godfrey (La Cava), 128

Natalka Poltavka (Ulmer), 114
Natwick, Mildred, 33–34, 117
Negri, Pola, 62
Newman, David, 26, 60
Newman, Paul, 153
New York, 13, 27
New York, New York (Scorsese), 114
Nicholson, Jack, 172
Nickelodeon (Bogdanovich), x, xii, 41, 42, 84, 85, 86, 92, 105, 126–27, 143, 154, 157, 171
North by Northwest (Hitchcock), 11

O'Connor, Carroll, 149
Odets, Clifford, 4
O'Kelly, Tim, 49, 73, 76
O'Neal, Ryan, x, xii, 17, 26, 45, 51–52, 77, 84, 127, 153, 154, 171
O'Neal, Tatum, 42, 51–53, 57, 77, 84
Once in a Lifetime (Kaufman and Hart), 5, 24, 53

Only Angels Have Wings (Hawks), 86–87, 111, 113
Opening Night (Cassavetes), 50, 66, 67, 122
Ophuls, Max, 103
Othello (Welles), 30, 133, 138, 164, 165
Other Side of the Wind, The (Welles), xii, 81–82, 113, 166–69, 171
Owl and the Pussycat, The (Ross), 153

Paper Moon (Bogdanovich), x, 27, 32, 44, 51–53, 75, 77–78, 80, 83, 84, 92, 105, 116, 118, 120, 143, 153
Parsons, Louella, 144–45
Peary, Gerald, ix, xi, xiii
Penn, Arthur, viii
Perkins, Anthony, 11
Phelan, Anna Hamilton, 95, 100, 101
Pickford, Mary, 62
Pieces of Time (Bogdanovich), 27, 84
Platt, Polly, xii, 54, 75–76, 143, 151, 167
Playboy, 64, 143
Polonsky, Abraham, viii, 3
Portrait of a Lady, The (Campion), 115
Portrait of a Lady, The (James), 30
Poseidon Adventure, The (Neame), x
Pound, Ezra, 85
Preminger, Otto, 112
Price, Frank, 120
Private Worlds (La Cava), 128
Pryor, Richard, 146
Psycho (Hitchcock), 5, 11

Public Enemy, The (Wellman), 112
Pudovkin, V. I., 135

Quaid, Randy, 79, 84, 143
Quiet Man, The (Ford), vii, 20, 38, 118, 149

Rafelson, Bob, 19, 142
Raphael, Frederic, 29, 32, 33, 35, 117–18
Red Dust (Fleming), 112
Red-Headed Woman (Conway), 112
Red Line 7000 (Hawks), 139
Red River (Ford), ix, 5, 18, 47, 148, 150
Renoir, Jean, 43–44, 104, 121, 140, 145
Reynolds, Burt, 55, 154, 171
Richard III (Olivier), 133
Rio Bravo (Hawks), 5, 6, 150
Rio Lobo (Hawks), 78
Ritter, John, xi, 84, 90, 125, 127, 154, 155
Robin Hood (Dwan), 147
Rubin, Martin, viii, ix, x
Ruggles of Red Gap (McCarey), 110, 138
Ruth, Babe, 115

Sackler, Howard, 67
Saint Jack (Bogdanovich), xi, 63–66, 67–69, 71, 81, 84, 93, 104–5, 119, 122, 123, 127, 132, 143, 154–55
Saint Jack (Theroux), 63–64, 65, 172
Salvation Hunters, The (von Sternberg), 12
Sarris, Andrew, 4–5, 84, 92, 130, 135, 136, 141

Scarface (Hawks), 150
Schneider, Bert, 20, 25, 57, 74, 142, 146–47
Schrader, Paul, 137
Scorsese, Martin, 98, 114, 141
Scott, Randolph, 118
Searchers, The (Ford), vii, 69, 149
Seger, Bob, 157, 158
Sennett, Mack, 61
Serpico (Lumet), 147
Seven Days in New Crete (Graves), 105
Shakespeare, William, 30, 42, 83, 133, 164
Shaw, George Bernard, 138
Shepherd, Cybill, xii, 28, 41, 49–50, 62, 79, 84, 116, 117, 143, 154, 171, 172
Sherman, Eric, viii, ix, 3
Sherwood, Robert E., 148
She's Funny That Way (Bogdanovich), xiii
She Wore a Yellow Ribbon (Ford), ix, 5, 125, 148
Shock Corridor (Fuller), 151
Sidney, Sylvia, viii
Siegel, Don, 13
Silke, James, 109–10
Silver, Joel, 119
Sinatra, Nancy, 54
Sirk, Douglas, 35
Sling Blade (Thornton), 125
Sontag, Susan, 137
Sopranos, The, 158
Spaniard, The (Walsh), 116
Spielberg, Steven, 98, 141
Spikings, Barry, 127
Springsteen, Bruce, 100, 102, 103, 157, 158
Stagecoach (Ford), vii, 85

Star 80 (Fosse), 143
Steel Helmet, The (Fuller), 151
Steiger, Rod, 124
Stevens, George, 118
Stevens, Stella, 127
Stewart, Jimmy, 4, 13, 23, 29, 32, 111–12, 137, 147, 167
Stoltz, Eric, 94
Strange One, The (Garfein), 122–23, 134
Strangers on a Train (Hitchcock), 11
Strasberg, Lee, 147
Stratten, Dorothy, xi, xii–xiii, 84, 90–91, 119, 143, 154, 155–57, 158, 161–62
Streisand, Barbra, x, 17, 25, 26, 41, 56, 153
Sugarland Express, The (Spielberg), 98
Summer of '42 (Mulligan), 20
Sun Shines Bright, The (Ford), 20, 22
Surtees, Robert, 51, 75
Sylvia Scarlett (Cukor), 110, 111

Talbot, Dan, 4, 130, 133
Tarantino, Quentin, x
Targets (Bogdanovich), vii, ix, 3, 7, 8, 9–11, 12, 13–15, 16, 17, 18, 19, 21, 22, 25, 27, 42, 43, 49, 55, 63, 73, 76, 92, 121, 122, 123, 127, 137, 139, 142, 151
Tashlin, Frank, 5, 92
Taxi Driver (Scorsese), 114
Taylor, Elizabeth, 21, 28
Temple, Shirley, 153
Ten Little Indians (Christie), 4, 24
Terror, The (Corman), 8, 9
Texasville (Bogdanovich), xi, 99, 120, 132, 140, 143–44, 157, 158

Theroux, Paul, 64, 67, 155
They All Laughed (Bogdanovich), xi, xii, 84, 90–91, 93, 94, 95, 103, 105, 119, 131, 143, 154, 155, 156
They Were Expendable (Ford), 150
Thing Called Love, The (Bogdanovich), xi, 132
This Is Orson Welles (Bogdanovich and Welles), 144, 160, 171, 172
Thomas, Kevin, 109
Thompson, Howard, 135
Thornton, Billy Bob, 125
Three Musketeers, The (Dumas), 170
To Have and Have Not (Hawks), 139, 150
Tonight Show, The, 143
Touch of Evil (Welles), 133
Trade Winds (Garnett), 118
Trial, The (Welles), 165
Truffaut, Francois, 18, 61–62, 92, 133, 137, 152
Trumbo, Dalton, 49
Twain, Mark, 37
Twentieth Century (Hawks), 150

Ulmer, Edgar G., vii, 114, 121

Van Doren, Mamie, 8
Van Dyke, W. S. "Woody," 109
Ventura, Michael, xi, xii, xiii
Vertigo (Hitchcock), 29, 39
Victory (Conrad), 170
Vidal, Gore, 115
Vidor, King, 117, 118, 149
Village Voice, 135
Villiers, James, 65–66
Vincenzoni, Luciano, 123
von Sternberg, Josef, 12, 109, 111
von Stroheim, Erich, 38, 158

Voyage to the Planet of Prehistoric Women (Thomas), 8–9

Wagonmaster (Ford), 20
Wait for Me (Bogdanovich), x, 148
Walker, Robert, 11
Walsh, Raoul, 13, 15, 108, 116–17, 126, 127–28, 129
Warhol, Andy, 149
Wayne, John, 6, 23, 147
Weinberg, Herman G., 135
Welles, Orson, xii, xiii, 3, 4, 12, 20, 30, 32, 47, 56, 59, 73, 81–82, 87, 92, 98, 112, 113, 116, 133–34, 139, 142, 144, 148, 149, 152, 160, 161, 163, 164–72
Wellman, William, 128
What Ever Happened to Baby Jane? (Aldrich), 16
What Maisie Knew (James), 30
What Price Glory (Walsh), 116
What's Up, Doc? (Bogdanovich), x, xi, 17–18, 20–21, 25–26, 27, 28, 56, 57–58, 60–61, 75–77, 79–80, 83, 84, 92, 99, 105, 121, 127, 143, 152, 153
White Goddess, The (Graves), 171
White Gold (Howard), 107
White Heat (Walsh), 128
Whitman, Charles, 11, 151
Who the Devil Made It (Bogdanovich), vii, 107, 108–9, 121, 139, 142, 147, 159
Who the Hell's In It (Bogdanovich), viii, 110–11, 113–14, 142, 147
Wild Angels, The (Corman), 6–7, 24–25, 54–55, 142, 150–51
Wilder, Billy, 89
Wilder, Thornton, 56
Williams, Hank, 152

Wilson, Richard, 82
Winsten, Archer, 135
Wyler, William, 118

Yablans, Frank, 115–16, 119
Young, Roland, 110
Young Frankenstein (Brooks), 75
Young Mr. Lincoln (Ford), 85

Zacharek, Stephanie, viii

www.ingramcontent.com/pod-product-compliance
Lightning Source LLC
Chambersburg PA
CBHW021841220426
43663CB00005B/353